LIFE & AFTERLIFE

LIFE & AFTERLIFE

MICHAEL PRESCOTT

Life & Afterlife, by Michael Prescott
Copyright © 2023 by Douglas Borton
All rights reserved

ISBN: 9798871669884
Independently published

Images

Astral body leaving the body at death. Illustration in Andrew Jackson Davis, *Univercoelum*, 1849. Charles Walker Collection/Alamy Stock Photo. Image ID: MC6NB3. Standard license: magazines and books

Demon of the Southwest Wind. Author's rendering of an illustration in Georges Contenau, *Everyday Life in Babylon and Assyria*, p. 253

Ascent of the Blessed. Hieronymus Bosch: This work has been identified as being free of known restrictions under copyright law, including all related and neighboring rights. Source: Wikipedia

The Dawn of Day. C.K. Van Nortwick. Originally published in 1930. No copyright information available.

CONTENTS

INTRODUCTION 1

PART ONE: Separation 17

CHAPTER ONE: Separating from the Body 19
CHAPTER TWO: Separation in OBEs 37
CHAPTER THREE: Patterns and Exceptions 49
CHAPTER FOUR: Perception outside the Body 61
CHAPTER FIVE: Deathbed Visions 75
CHAPTER SIX: NDEs throughout History 87
CHAPTER SEVEN: How Is It Possible? 93
CHAPTER EIGHT: The Double 107

PART TWO: The Dark Side 113

CHAPTER NINE: Death by Violence or Suicide 115
CHAPTER ELEVEN: Lost Souls 135
CHAPTER TWELVE: Possession 147

PART THREE: Transition 161

CHAPTER THIRTEEN Beginning the Transition 163
CHAPTER FOURTEEN: Encounter 181
CHAPTER FIFTEEN: A Presence in the Light 199
CHAPTER SIXTEEN: Beings of Light 207
CHAPTER SEVENTEEN: The Life Review 219
CHAPTER EIGHTEEN: Mediumship 233

PART FOUR: Arrival 251

CHAPTER NINETEEN: Otherwhere 253
CHAPTER TWENTY: Life on the Other Side 265
CHAPTER TWENTY-ONE: Higher Planes 285
CHAPTER TWENTY-TWO: Reincarnation 293
AFTERWORD 309
POSTSCRIPT 311

BIBLIOGRAPHY 313
NOTES 323

Death is the entrance into the great light.

—Victor Hugo, *Les Miserables*

a note on the text

This book includes many quotations. In using them, I've followed certain rules.

Words I've added are in square brackets [ ]. Material in curved parentheses ( ) is found that way in the original.

All quoted *italics* are in the original.

British spelling and punctuation have been Americanized.

For the most part, smaller numerals are spelled out, while larger ones are not, regardless of their appearance in the original text. This practice, however, is not always followed consistently; I was guided by what I thought looked best.

Generally I provide page numbers for citations. Where I don't, the quoted material comes either from web sources or ebooks without embedded page numbers, or from books not presently available to me.

Citations in footnotes are abbreviated in standard fashion. The full title, author name(s), publisher, and publication date can be found in the Bibliography.

If I thank someone in a citation, it's because the person pointed me to that particular source.

M.P.

INTRODUCTION

VISIONS OF THE HEREAFTER, or insights into the deep nature of reality, crop up now and then in the last words of famous persons.

- Victor Hugo said, "I see black light."
- Film critic Roger Ebert, in a note to his wife shortly before his death, wrote, "This is all an elaborate hoax."
- Steve Jobs' final words, according to his sister, were "Oh wow. Oh wow. Oh wow."
- The poet Robert Browning wrote that his wife Elizabeth Barrett Browning died "smilingly, happily, and with a face like a girl's ... Her last word was ... 'Beautiful.'"
- Several days before his death, waking from sleep and gazing upward, Thomas Edison said, "It is very beautiful over there."

And here's one more anecdote to balance things out. Wild West lawmen Wyatt and Morgan Earp made a pact to report any vision of the next life if they had the chance. As it happened, Morgan passed first. Dying, he told his brother, "I can't see a damned thing!"

The skeptical minority

For thousands of years, most of humanity, across all cultures and continents, has believed in a higher spiritual reality—a belief grounded in such ubiquitous phenomena as apparitions, deathbed visions, near-death experiences, out-of-body experiences, past-life memories, and mediumship. Whole civilizations have been built on this foundation.

Militant skepticism of the paranormal is a comparatively recent development, one still limited to a small minority. That doesn't make it wrong, of course, but it does mean that skeptics face a greater burden of proof than they commonly realize. There's no inherent reason why the default position should be that paranormal experiences, widely attested throughout history, are an illusion. Only the dominant position of philosophical materialism in our intellectual life makes this position seem inescapable.

In my observation, highly intuitive people are far more likely to believe in paranormal talents and a higher spiritual dimension. On the other hand, determinedly left-brain thinkers, who have little place for intuition in their lives, typically dismiss such things as impossible. They've never experienced it, so how can it be real? And as for the afterlife, where is it? Let's see it through a telescope. Point to it on a map.

As with any innate talent, sensitivity to psychic impressions varies considerably from person to person. If we could graph its incidence in the general population, we would probably plot a bell curve. Most people are bunched in the middle, with some latent psi talent (the term *psi* encompasses telepathy, clairvoyance, precognition, and psychokinesis) that occasionally manifests in minor ways. A few people are clustered at the low end of the scale, with little or no psi ability. A few others are clustered on the high end. These are the prodigies, the ones who can demonstrate consistent results significantly above chance. They include the (legitimate) mediums and out-of-body travelers who, in some cultures, have served as shamans and sages.

It's similar to the way musical ability is distributed. A few people, like Mozart, are musical prodigies; a few others have "no ear for music." Most of us lie somewhere in the middle, with average musical talent. No amount of training will turn us into Mozarts, but with practice we should be able to plink out a tune on the piano.

An estimated 4% of the general population is afflicted with a condition called congenital amusia, or tone deafness. This means they are unable to discern differences in pitch; a high note is indistinguishable from a low one. Although some of them can still enjoy music on some level, many hear it only as ugly, meaningless noise.

Suppose a group of amusic individuals were to decide that, since they have never heard music, there is no such thing. The majority of people would beg to differ. But the amusic activists would insist that the rest of humanity is clearly lying or delusional. To make their case, they might form a nonprofit organization called, say, the Committee for the Scientific Investigation of Claims of Music (CSICOM). The organization might issue a peer-reviewed journal and publish books exposing "the myth of music." Their spokespersons would go on TV to insist there's no evidence for music, or at least none that can hold up to objective testing. They would ridicule anyone who claimed to be able to hear and appreciate music, and would be especially rough on professional musicians, who'd be dismissed as con artists of the worst kind. As a master stroke, they might offer a large, well-publicized cash prize to anyone who could produce music to their satisfaction. The prize money would never be paid out, because how do you produce music for people who are congenitally incapable of hearing it?

Admittedly, this analogy—like all analogies—can be pressed only so far. In real life, no one debates the reality of music, while the reality of the paranormal continues to be disputed, because psi phenomena are hard to nail down. A competent musician can produce music on demand, while even the most talented psychic will have his bad days, when he receives no impressions or wrong impressions. A musician can work while facing a hostile audience; many psychics find themselves blocked in such circumstances. Musical notes can be recorded and measured like any other sound waves; no one knows how to record or measure psychic impressions. Mainstream science is perfectly capable of explaining the mechanics of music, but has no explanation for psi.

Even so, a massive collection of case studies and experimental results has been built up over more than a century and a half of parapsychological investigations. Are all of these cases the product of deceit or illusion? Militant skeptics say yes. Their view is that people are inherently unreliable and just can't be trusted. *Other* people, that is. They themselves, and those who agree with them, are exemplars of impartiality, integrity, and clear thinking. It's the rest of the world that's the problem. This point of view would call into question the credibility of virtually all human testimony. It seems a bit extreme.

> Though I have no intention of addressing all skeptical arguments, which would take many books—Chris Carter's *Science and the Afterlife Experience* is a good place to start—I do want to briefly take up the most common objection to the afterlife offered by proponents of philosophical materialism: Everyone knows that consciousness is created by the brain, and therefore when the brain dies, consciousness cannot possibly continue. QED. To this I would reply that *not* everyone knows how consciousness is created; in fact, nobody does. The precise nature of consciousness and how it interacts with our nervous system is still sufficiently mysterious that it has been dubbed the "hard problem" of neuroscience.

A century ago, William James proposed what is today usually called the "transmission theory" of consciousness. His idea was that it's possible that consciousness originates and/or operates *outside* the brain and simply works *through* the brain in the manner of a signal interacting with a receiver. A modern analogy would be a television set. The pictures and sound you see on your TV do not originate inside the set; they originate as a signal delivered to the set and translated by the set's internal circuitry into the program you watch. You can turn off the TV, but the signal will continue uninterrupted. You can intentionally damage the TV, so that the picture and sound are distorted; but the signal itself is unimpaired. You can destroy the TV, run over it with a steamroller, so that it will never pick up the signal again. Still, the signal goes on.

Every argument that can be made for the brain as the originator of consciousness can be countered by a matching argument that the brain is only processing the signal of consciousness that arrives to it from some other source. This is, as I said, only an analogy; nobody is saying it's an actual electromagnetic signal. If it were, it would already be measured and known, and would be subject to interference. The so-called "signal" is only a metaphor for some mode of extracerebral, extrasensory awareness, not yet understood.

A sophisticated skeptic might object that this is not a scientific theory, because it cannot be falsified, even in principle. According to the philosopher of science Karl Popper, the hallmark of any truly scientific theory is that it can be tested and, if it fails the test, rejected. I think Popper is right, and the transmission theory is not a scientific theory. But there are other kinds of theories—for instance, philosophical theories. William James was a philosopher, and his transmission theory is essentially an epistemological theory. It is unfalsifiable, undisprovable, but so are many philosophical propositions.

The theory that the brain is the originator of consciousness and that consciousness cannot operate without a working brain *is*, however, a testable, potentially falsifiable or disprovable theory. It is scientific. Bully for it. The problem, though, is that if even a fraction of the evidence of parapsychology is true, then that particular scientific *theory* has already been falsified. As mentioned earlier, huge quantities of evidence point to the conclusion that consciousness can operate independently of the brain and can persist even when the brain is not functioning. Any piece of that evidence would be sufficient to disprove the contention that consciousness must always function in the brain itself. This is why people committed to materialism must try to discredit every lab test and case history suggestive of extracerebral consciousness. If even a smidgen of it is true, then their foundational principle is false.

Evaluating testimony

All experience is, by definition, subjective. When we talk about objective facts, what we mean are experiences that have been confirmed by repeated (or shared) observations on the part of different people. If one person calls the police department to report an elephant running loose on the highway, the police are likely to chalk it up to hallucination or a prank. If ten people call, the police may begin to take it seriously. If a hundred people call, it may be time to break out the elephant guns.

Eminent logician Richard Whately pronounced a principle of reasoning to the same effect:

> When many coincide in their testimony (where no previous concert can have taken place), the probability resulting from this concurrence does not rest on the supposed veracity of each considered separately, but on the improbability of such an agreement taking place by chance. For though in such a case

each of the witnesses should be considered as unworthy of credit, and even much more likely to speak falsehood than truth, still the chances would be infinite against their all agreeing in the same falsehood.[2]

Virtually all the evidence collected for life after death consists of subjective personal reports. The extent to which we take these reports seriously ought to depend on their number and quality, their mutual consistency, and an estimation of the possibility that the individuals in question either were consciously colluding or were subconsciously influenced by the same sources.

Arguing for the reality of what we would now call poltergeists, folklorist Andrew Lang wrote: "It is the extraordinary uniformity in the reports, from every age, country, and class of society, the uniformity in hallucination, that makes the mystery."[3] Remarking on Lang's point, poltergeist researcher Alan Murdie observes that

> widely separated writers confirmed a common pattern in disturbances many miles and many years apart. In doing so they had unwittingly acknowledged and enunciated a key principle enshrined in the law of evidence, as applied in court rooms in the English-speaking world. Known as the 'similar fact evidence principle,' it treats otherwise isolated reports or facts as probative if there are striking similarities between them ...
>
> Utilizing the similar fact principle, recurring patterns, facts or features are treated as probative, enabling the standard of 'beyond reasonable doubt.' The mere existence of similarity in itself is not enough; what is required is that the similarity must be striking and that no other explanation is feasible when viewed in terms of the totality of the evidence and testimony available. The rule has been used with some of the most serious offences on the statute book, including homicide and cases of multiple sexual offending.[4]

But isn't there one slam-dunk case that will conclusively settle the matter? Sadly, no—for the simple reason that it's impossible for a single, isolated experimental or observational result to be beyond all doubt. This is as true of mainstream science as it is of parapsychology. Any isolated result, in any field, is at least potentially open to challenge. In practice, most results in mainstream science are not challenged, because they fit in with previously accepted results and with the existing paradigm. But results considered unusual are often challenged. And this certainly includes any and all experimental or observational findings that support the reality of an afterlife or, more generally, of psi.

Here's a partial list of skeptical criticisms of parapsychology experiments that yielded positive results:

1. The experimenter was lying.
2. The experimenter was drunk.
3. The experimenter was insane.
4. The experimenter was hallucinating.
5. The experimenter was tricked by some specific (but unproven) ruse.
6. The experimenter was tricked by some unknown ruse that may be determined in the future.
7. The experimental protocol was flawed in some specific (but unproven) way.
8. The experimental protocol was flawed in some unknown way that may be determined in the future.
9. The equipment malfunctioned.
10. The photos (or videotape, etc.) were faked.
11. The witnesses were in cahoots with the experimenter.
12. The experimenter was in cahoots with the test subject.
13. The results were a meaningless fluke.

Some of these objections may sound too far-fetched to be made by even the most obdurate skeptic. But I've come across all of them. For instance, #2 ("the experimenter was drunk") has been stated or implied about psychologist Jule Eisenbud in his investigation of psychic Ted Serios. (Actually it was Serios who insisted on getting drunk in order to lower his inhibitions; Eisenbud and his colleagues drank no alcohol during the tests.)

How about #3, "the experimenter was insane"? This has been said (again) of Jule Eisenbud in connection with the same case. James Randi, in his popular book *Flim-Flam!*, concludes his discussion of the Serios matter this way: "Dr. Börje Löfgren ... had it right when he described parapsychology enthusiasts as 'decaying minds' with 'thinking defects and disturbed relations to reality' ... Dr. Eisenbud is not rowing with both oars in the water."[5]

Another experimenter branded insane by critics was W.J. Crawford, who over a period of years took numerous photos of rodlike "ectoplasm" extending from the body of medium Kathleen Goligher. *The Skeptic's Dictionary*, an online site, informs us:

"Goligher's story was told by William Jackson Crawford, a rather odd paranormal investigator—Houdini thought he was insane—with an underwear obsession."[6]

I guess I should add that one to the list. Objection #14: "The experimenter had an underwear obsession."

Objection #4, "the experimenter was hallucinating," crops up in skeptical critiques of physical mediumship (the kind of mediumship that ostensibly produces movements or manifestations of physical objects). Frank Podmore made this argument in connection with D.D. Home's séances, even though Home's physical phenomena were witnessed in good light by many people and were carefully observed by physicist William Crookes while a colleague looked on.

Objection #5, "the experimenter was tricked by some specific (but unproven) ruse," is found in abundance in C.E.M. Hansel's *ESP: A Scientific Evaluation*. Hansel comes up with all sorts of imaginative tricks by which test subjects at J.B. Rhine's parapsychology lab could have pulled the wool over the various investigators' eyes. But no evidence is ever offered that such tricks were in fact carried out.

Then there's objection #7: "The experimental protocol was flawed in some unknown way that may be determined in the future." Here we have gone too far. Surely no skeptic, no matter how bold, could advance this empty verbiage as a serious argument. Right?

Wrong. This "argument" has actually been put forward by well-known skeptic Ray Hyman in a serious, technical paper on the autoganzfeld ESP experiments—experiments that Hyman himself co-designed and which embarrassed him when they proved successful. Hyman wrote:

> I cannot provide suitable candidates for what flaws, if any, might be present. Just the same, it is impossible in principle to say that any particular experiment or experimental series is completely free from possible flaws. An experimenter cannot control for every possibility—especially for potential flaws that have not yet been discovered.[7]

So, you see, any experimental result can be challenged, questioned, and doubted, even if the doubt consists of nothing more than the notion that an *unspecified* and *presently unknowable* error *might* have been made. Go ahead and refute that claim. To quote Criswell in *Plan Nine from Outer Space*: "Can you prove it *didn't* happen?"

Running the gamut

Although skeptical resistance to the evidence can be carried to absurd lengths, even those who are sympathetic to the paranormal recognize the inherent weakness of relying on just one or two cases. Eleanor Sidgwick, past president of the Society of Psychical Research, observed,

> Exactly at what point of improbability this failure of other [i.e., non-paranormal] explanations is to be regarded as established, cannot, I think, be defined—at any rate, I feel quite unable to define it. But I may perhaps say that, in my opinion, it is a point which can hardly be reached in the case of any narrative of a *single event* considered by itself: if we had only a *single* ghost-story to deal with, I can hardly conceive the kind or amount of evidence which would lead me to prefer the hypothesis of ghostly agency to all other possible explanations. The existence, therefore, of phantasms of the dead can only be established, if at all, by the accumulation of improbabilities in which we become involved by rejecting a large mass of apparently strong testimony to facts which, as recounted, would seem to admit of no other satisfactory explanation.[8]

If any single case can be disputed or dismissed, then how do we get anywhere? We have to look at the big picture, consider the totality of the evidence, and draw an inference to the best explanation that covers it all.

> Inference to the best explanation, also known as abduction, is a method of reasoning commonly used in daily life and in the sciences. The article "Abduction" in the online *Stanford Encyclopedia of Philosophy* explains it this way:
>
>> You happen to know that Tim and Harry have recently had a terrible row that ended their friendship. Now someone tells you that she just saw Tim and Harry jogging together. The best explanation for this that you can think

> of is that they made up. You conclude that they are friends again …
>
> [This conclusion does] not follow logically from the premises … [but it] would, if true, best explain the fact that they have just been seen jogging together …
>
> Abductive reasoning is not limited to everyday contexts. Quite the contrary: philosophers of science have argued that abduction is a cornerstone of scientific methodology … According to Timothy Williamson (2007), "[t]he abductive methodology is the best science provides" and Ernan McMullin (1992) even goes so far to call abduction "the inference that makes science."[9]

One of the more famous examples of drawing an inference to the best explanation is Darwin's theory of evolution by natural selection. Though the essentials of Darwinism are widely accepted today, Darwin himself acknowledged that there was no conclusive proof of his theory. A recent monograph points this out and draws an analogy with afterlife studies:

> Darwin responded to a botanist who requested of him a clear proof for natural selection (Candolle, 1862): "… natural selection … hardly admits of direct proof or evidence. It will be believed in only by those who think that it connects and partly explains several large classes of facts."
>
> In a similar vein, the most compelling and "best available evidence" for [postmortem] survival comes from the convergence of the diversified and robust body of evidence of the persistence after death of the memory and character that makes up our personal identity. This evidence derives from a wide variety of human experiences (e.g., apparitions, mediumship, near-death experiences, cases suggestive of reincarnation, etc.) that mutually reinforce each other because they point to the same conclusion: survival of *consciousness*.[10]

This is the approach I take. Instead of relying on cases of only one or two types, I prefer to consider a wide variety of cases that have cropped up in different lines of inquiry. The consistently overlapping features of these cases strike me as compelling evidence for the view that human personality survives death.

As acknowledged above, no single case can ever be beyond criticism. Moreover, not all the cases I cite are equally strong. A certain percentage of them probably can be dismissed as the products of imagination, cultural influences, or even conscious deceit. Because I lean toward investigations by serious researchers, I believe the percentage of bogus cases is small. But even serious researchers can be unreliable at times.

In their book *Mindsight*, Kenneth Ring and Sharon Cooper noted several cases of reported vision in blind patients during near-death experiences that turned out to be problematic. One such case had been fabricated out of whole cloth by the person who wrote it up![11] Ironically, despite their best efforts, Ring and Cooper themselves published a bogus case in *Mindsight*. Included at the last minute, it later turned out to be fake, obliging the publisher to insert an explanatory note into printed copies.

Then there are cases that, while not necessarily fraudulent, were never properly investigated and cannot be verified. Again, *Mindsight* provides an example: a case reported by NDE researcher Raymond Moody, which involved a seventy-year-old woman, blind since age eighteen, who "was able to describe in vivid detail what was happening around her as doctors resuscitated her after a heart attack." Unfortunately, when Kenneth Ring contacted Moody to get the details, Moody could remember only "that he had learned of it from listening to an audio cassette provided to him by an elderly physician—but he no longer had the tape and could not recall the physician's name."[12]

Some of the cases I've included in this book are no easier to verify; they are purely anecdotal and were never independently investigated. Most of the reports collected by Robert Crookall, for instance, were simply mailed to him by his readers.

I'll go further and admit that I myself have doubts about the validity of certain cases. Some, like the well-publicized NDE reported by Mellen-Thomas Benedict, seem a little too elaborate to be fully believable. In fact, entire schools of investigation are open to methodological criticisms. One example is past-life hypnotic regression, intelligently critiqued by D. Scott Rogo in *The Search for Yesterday*.

Nevertheless, I've included Benedict's NDE and excerpts from regression-therapy transcripts. Why? Because, as noted, my intention is to draw from a variety of lines of inquiry, rather than sticking with just one type of case.

In what follows, I use material obtained from near-death experiences, out-of-body experiences, deathbed visions, apparitions, past-life regressions, children's memories of past lives, trance mediumship, experiences of sudden spiritual enlightenment, shamanic vision quests, experiments with mind-altering drugs, folklore and religion, remote viewing and other ESP tests, and even cases of spirit obsession and possession.

The reliability of these different approaches varies considerably. But what matters to me is not nailing down the validity of every single case, but providing the broadest possible perspective. Even if a particular case that I cite can be debunked (always a possibility), it's merely one case among many similar ones, any of which could have been selected. As William James—himself an investigator of mediums—pointed out a century ago, in order to disprove the contention that all crows are black, it is necessary to find only a single white crow. That is, only one case needs to be indisputably proven in order to establish the truth of postmortem survival. (In practice, as discussed above, an isolated claim can usually be disputed. But James's point still stands. An *incontrovertible* claim would prove the case.)

The skeptic, conversely, is obliged to contend that *all* the cases, without exception, are flawed, and that *not one single case* can be taken at face value. Since there are tens of thousands of cases, the will to disbelieve required by such position is pretty strong.

But are there really that many cases? Yes, indeed. Robert McLuhan makes this point nicely when he describes his first visit to the London offices of the Society for Psychical Research:

> Looking around their archives I was astonished by how much scientific work had been done on all kinds of paranormal topics. Nothing had prepared me for this; there was no hint of it in the skeptics' books or anywhere else, for that matter. To date the SPR has produced around one hundred and twenty-five volumes of proceedings and journals going back the same number of years, densely packed with scholarly reports of investigations and experiments into ghosts, mediums, telepathy and suchlike, as well as surveys, reviews and debates, and all accompanied by a very lively correspondence. I also found publications by other research organizations, such as the American *Journal of Parapsychology* and *Journal of Scientific Exploration*. In marked contrast to the popular books often found in shops and libraries, paranormal claims in these documents are picked apart in forensic detail, with a detached and often skeptical spirit.[13]

The quantity of evidence for postmortem survival is so large that it cannot be presented in full in any single book, because the book's sheer length would be prohibitive. Case studies of mediumship in the *Journal of the Society for Psychical Research* number many thousands of pages; and that's only one journal, albeit arguably the leading one in the field. Worldwide, there are more than 2,500 documented cases of children who spontaneously remember a past life. Near-death experiences occur in roughly "'10% of people who come close to death, or who survive actual clinical death' ..., and in an even higher percentage when looking only at cardiac arrest survivors (12-18%).'"[14] Countless NDEs have been investigated, usually by medical doctors. Apparitions and hauntings have been reported all over the world since ancient times.

The unabridged 1886 edition of *Phantasms of the Living* runs 662 pages, and it consists solely of sightings of apparitions of the living or newly deceased, reported in England of that era. And that's just Volume One! (Volume Two is 764 pages.) A 2007 overview covering far more ground, *Irreducible Mind*, consists of 800 pages of small print, including 100 pages of references averaging eighteen references per page.

The problem in presenting the evidence is not finding cases to include but choosing which ones—the overwhelming majority—to exclude.

Selecting the cases

How did I choose *my* cases? In part, according to my personal predilections. Like anybody else who's spent time reading these studies, I have my favorites. You may notice that many of the cases cited here are pretty old, dating back to the early 20th century or even the 19th century. That's not because there are no recent cases; new cases are reported and investigated every day. I focus on older ones, first, because they are less likely to be contaminated by the modern popularization of ideas like the near-death experience, and second, because I enjoy reading older accounts and I would like them to be remembered.

Many of the researchers active in the early years of parapsychology were remarkably well-educated, articulate, and insightful. They included such noteworthy figures as psychological theorists William James, F.W.H. Myers, and Théodore Flournoy; classicists Arthur and Margaret Verrall and E.R. Dodds; philosopher and economist Henry Sidgwick and his wife Eleanor Sidgwick, a mathematician and prominent activist in women's education;

physicists William Crookes and Oliver Lodge (both knighted for their scientific achievements); evolutionary theorist Alfred Russell Wallace; novelist and medical doctor Arthur Conan Doyle; physiologist and Nobel laureate Charles Richet; and criminologist Cesare Lombroso. Not all of the work done by these people has stood the test of time; Lombroso's phrenology, highly respected at the time, stands discredited today, and Doyle's positive assessment of certain claims, notably some prank photographs of "fairies," is now seen as credulous. Nevertheless, all these individuals were widely respected scientists, scholars, or public figures, all were of well above-average intelligence, and most of them wrote very well.[15]

Frustratingly, a vast amount of work, much of it of high quality, is being overlooked by modern parapsychologists. Writers like Michael Tymn, Deborah Blum, and Stephen E. Braude have made efforts to raise awareness of this early work, but too many researchers and writers seem interested only in observations and experiments performed under current conditions.[16]

This would be understandable if the work in question was flawed, and some of it is; William Crookes' experiments with Florence Cook, for instance, are too sketchily reported to be of more than anecdotal interest today. But a good deal of the early work is both competently designed and adequately described. Yet while other sciences advance by building on the work of those who came before, parapsychology seems intent on continually reinventing the wheel. Part of the reason, I suspect, is the desire to convince skeptics by continually refining precautions against fraud. But at a certain point, this becomes an exercise in futility, since for the more dogmatic skeptics, no controls will ever be good enough. A more fruitful approach, especially considering parapsychology's constrained resources, might be to accept the best of the earlier work as a given, and move on.

Although I'm partial to older cases, I've included plenty of more recent ones, too, and anyone can find innumerable others in any well-stocked bookstore or at high-quality websites like *Psi Encyclopedia*. I would advise, however, against relying on Wikipedia for info on this or any other controversial topic; the site's anarchic approach to editing means that anyone can inject personal opinions into an entry. In fact, self-styled "guerrilla skeptics" have declared they're on a mission to debunk every psi-related Wikipedia listing, which they do by deleting all references favorable to psi, even if those citations are obviously relevant.

Admission of bias

Since I'm complaining about Wikipedia's biases, it's only fair to admit to biases of my own. I accept—at least provisionally—some claims that other people familiar with this material reject, such as memories of a "between-lives" state. I reject some claims that others accept, such as most cases of materialization mediumship. I don't think a psychic or medium is invalidated simply because he earns a living—even a very good living—at his trade. What's more, I accept the reality that many legitimate psychics and mediums are tricksterish personality types, who will sometimes cheat to supplement (or jumpstart) their actual talents, or just to keep people guessing. As we'll see later, Sicilian medium Eusapia Palladino was known to cheat and sometimes even boasted of it; despite all this, having carefully read Everard Feilding's fist-hand account, *Sittings with Eusapia Palladino,* I don't doubt that she did produce authentic and robust paranormal phenomena at times.

I also am not enamored of the super-psi or living-agent psi hypothesis, which attempts to explain all afterlife-related evidence by the unconscious operation of a roving form of ESP that can pluck long-buried memories from anyone's head, clairvoyantly seek out hidden documents, and construct a plausible imitation of a deceased individual's persona, all in real time as the séance progresses. To me, super-psi is merely an attempt to explain away the evidence for an afterlife in terms of telepathy and remote viewing. It's a refuge for parapsychologists who accept psi but are embarrassed by the idea of "spirits."

I'm probably too quick to dismiss some skeptical objections and too liable to lump all skeptics together, when in fact they—like any other group of people—run the gamut from the well-informed and honest to the not-so-well-informed and not-so-very-honest. Frankly, after years of dealing with skeptical objections on the paranormal blog I used to host, I'm sufficiently convinced of my position that I'm less willing to spend time debating the fundamentals. But this could be self-delusion on my part. There is, after all, nobody who's easier to fool than yourself, as the skeptics never tire of reminding us—though, again, they seem to exempt themselves from this general principle.

Whenever you draw an inference to the best explanation, there's an unavoidable element of subjectivity. The rules of inductive inference have never been worked out with the same rigor that applies to deductive reasoning. Probably they can't ever be; unlike a syllogism, which can be analyzed by pure logic, the real world is messy, ambiguous, and confusing, and it requires an application of common sense. But what seems sensible to one person may seem absurd to another. Super-psi seems silly to me, while postmortem survival may seem silly to others. Ultimately, we all have to use our own judgment, and we can't expect that we'll all reach the same conclusions.

What we can agree on, I hope, is that there is considerable overlap among the findings of the diverse lines of inquiry I sketched out above. This overlap is what's known as *consilience*, an established principle of modern thought. As defined by an online dictionary:

> In science and history, consilience refers to the principle that evidence from independent, unrelated sources can "converge" to strong conclusions. That is, when multiple sources of evidence are in agreement, the conclusion can be very strong even when none of the individual sources of evidence are very strong on their own. Most established scientific knowledge is supported by a convergence of evidence: if not, the evidence is comparatively weak, and there will not likely be a strong scientific consensus. The principle is based on the unity of knowledge; measuring the same result by several different methods should lead to the same answer.[17]

Or, to repeat a statement already quoted: "the most compelling and 'best available evidence' for survival comes from the convergence of the diversified and robust body of evidence [derived] from a wide variety of human experiences ... that mutually reinforce each other."

And with that, let's begin.

PART ONE: *Separation*

If it were possible for the soul to die back into earth life I should die from sheer yearning to reach you to tell you that all we imagined is not half wonderful enough for the truth.

—channeled message ostensibly originating with F.W.H. Myers[1]

"Astral body leaving the body at death."
(from Andrew Jackson Davis, *Univercoelum*, 1849)

CHAPTER ONE:
Separating from the Body

IF YOUR DEATH IS PEACEFUL, your first subjective impression of the dying process may involve separating from the physical body. People who've undergone near-death experiences (NDEs) sometimes report that they found themselves hovering over their apparently lifeless physical form. In most cases, this happened after a momentary blackout, but occasionally they were aware of the gradual disconnection of their new spiritual body while it was taking place.

One such case was first published in 1897, long predating the popularization of NDEs in the 1970s. It was recounted by spirit medium John Brown (no relation to the famed abolitionist) in his memoir. Sometime around 1850 Brown was thought to have died.

> In a moment my entire nervous system gave one shake and all was still; all was quiet. I heard the doctors say, "that is the last; he will not move again; he is dead." Yes, I heard all, but I did not see with my eyes.
>
> At this time it seemed to me, that I was moving slowly through a warm atmosphere; and in the distance I began to perceive a lighter or whiter spot in the darkness. As this light gradually increased in size, it came nearer to me, till finally it filled the room, and all outside. It was not like the light of our sun—it was more white, more still. It appeared to carry with it a life principle.
>
> At this moment I found myself lying horizontally above my body and about two feet from it. With no effort on my part I moved off from over my body and stood upon my feet, about five feet from it. I knew that I had left my body. I could see it on the bed, and I saw Mr. Woodward, a near neighbor of mine to-day, let go my head that he had been holding, and straighten my body on the bed. I stood right there. I heard all that was said. I heard Dr. Dickey say to one he met on the stairs: "You are too late; he is dead." "Is that so?" replied the man. I could see and hear everything as well as I ever did in my life. I stood near the center of the room and did not move when others would pass where I stood. They seemed to go right through me and still not

interfere with me in the least. They, to me, were like men and women of wood.

Oh, how I wished to take hold of them and give them a shake and make them know that I was not dead, but I could not. I viewed with care, the dress I had on. I was dressed, not naked. During the time I had stood on the floor, my [spirit] guide stood with me a little to my right. He was constantly writing in a small book or diary, and while I was examining the clothes I had on, he pointed to the corner of the room, saying: "That is the dress, John, you will put on, but not yet; you shall not die yet!" ....

All at once I was raised by a power, unseen by me, and moved directly over my body. The neighbors and friends had all left except two of the doctors, who were consulting in an adjoining room, as to what they should name the disease of which I had died. Up to this time, I had been conscious of all that had been said and done. I then lowered down and seemed to soak back into the body which all had pronounced dead.

Then, for the first time, I went into a sleep, which was of short duration, for, in a minute or two, something caused a rush of air and froth to emanate from my breast. My eyes could see, and I was alive in the same body I now inhabit.[1]

This NDE shares features found in many other accounts: hovering in a horizontal position above one's physical body; an expanding white light; a frustrating inability to communicate with people in the room; a clear observation of what those people are saying and doing; perception of one's spirit body, which passes through physical bodies without obstruction; and a higher spiritual authority that orders one's return.

Seventy-four years later, a 68-year-old man who survived a heart attack provided a remarkably similar account to two physicians writing in the *Canadian Medical Association Journal*.

> The main thing that stands out is the clarity of my thoughts during the episode. They were almost exactly as I have written them and in retrospect it seems that they are fixed in my memory—more so than other things that have happened to me. It seemed at times that I was having a "dual" sensation—actually experiencing certain things yet at the same time "seeing" myself during these experiences ...
>
> [After losing consciousness in the intensive care ward, he found himself] looking at my own body from the waist up, face to face (as though through a mirror in which I appear to be in

the lower left corner). Almost immediately I saw myself leave my body, coming out through my head and shoulders (I did not see my lower limbs). The "body" leaving me was not exactly in vapor form, yet it seemed to expand very slightly once it was clear of me. It was somewhat transparent, for I could see my other "body" through it. Watching this I thought, "So this is what happens when you die" (although no thought of being dead presented itself to me).[2]

In a book originally published in 1945, Rev. Charles Drayton Thomas, who spent many years working with the medium Gladys Osborne Leonard, describes the early part of what we would now call an NDE:

> A long illness and sickroom experience may be difficult, disagreeable and possibly painful, but leaving the body finally is as easy as falling asleep. That is the testimony of the few who have almost died and then, after partially leaving the body, returned again; they found themselves still in the sickroom, or the operating-chamber, but standing clear away from their bodily form on which they look down with surprise. They felt a freedom and lightness previously undreamed of, a sense of mental freshness and well-being. They say that, if this is death, then all fear of it has forever left them. While preparing this chapter I listened to a broadcast talk in which a medical man described his experience in exactly that way.
>
> This doctor told of having been operated upon and making some progress until, a few nights later, he awoke with intense pain and called for help. It was a serious relapse and he shortly fell into a semi-conscious condition and suddenly found himself away from his body and gazing down upon it. He felt a surprising lightness and peace. It came to his mind that he was now dying. Yet he was able to notice the anxiety of the doctors who were watching his body on the bed. He felt no fear at all. Then, as he re-entered his body, he heard one doctor say to the other, "He was nearly gone that time." Gradually he recovered and, as he asserts, no fear of death has since troubled him; for he is certain that his ethereal body is the essential one, the one in which he will live when the physical finally dies.[3]

In the 1960s and '70s, British geologist Robert Crookall compiled hundreds of cases involving the out-of-body experience (OBE), including some that today would be classified as NDEs.

- From 1920: A correspondent's sister, on her deathbed, "passed into complete unconsciousness ... her feet and hands were like ice." But she revived and "said she had found herself slipping out of her material body through her feet, and she stood at the foot of the bed, looking back on her body ... She realized herself as being in the spirit and very luminous, like an electric light. She rejoiced to find herself in full possession of all mental and spiritual faculties and identity."
- From 1935: "To my surprise, I found myself looking at myself lying on the bed. The thought just flashed through my mind that I didn't think much of me—in fact, I didn't approve of me at all. Then I was hurried off at great speed. Have you ever looked through a long tunnel and seen the tiny speck of light at the far end? It seems an incredible distance off. Well, I found myself with others vaguely discernible hurrying along just such a tunnel or passage ... but was gradually forced back. Then there was a complete black-out ... The next thing I knew was that I was alive again—only just, and very sorry for myself."
- From 1941: "I had a very serious illness from which I almost died. One night I left my body and saw it quite clearly lying motionless on the bed. It all seemed perfectly natural."[4]

In 1975 Raymond Moody published his groundbreaking book *Life After Life*, which first brought the subject of NDEs to the attention of the general public. In fact, Moody was the one who coined the term "near-death experience." He provides various examples of NDEs involving separation from the body.

- A seventeen-year-old boy who nearly drowned: "I kept bobbing up and down, and all of a sudden, it felt as though I were away from my body, away from everybody, in space by myself. Although I was stable, staying at the same level, I saw my body in the water about three or four feet away, bobbling [sic] up and down. I viewed my body from the back and slightly to the right side. I still felt as though I had an entire body form, even while I was outside my body. I had an airy feeling that's almost indescribable. I felt like a feather."

- The survivor of a car crash: "Then, I was sort of floating about five feet above the street, about five yards away from the car, I'd say, and I heard the echo of the crash dying away. I saw people come running up and crowding around the car, and I saw my friend get out of the car, obviously in shock. I could see my own body in the wreckage among all those people, and could see them trying to get it out."
- A woman in the hospital: "I turned over, and as I did I quit breathing and my heart stopped beating. Just then, I heard the nurses shout, 'Code pink! Code pink!' As they were saying this, I could feel myself moving out of my body and sliding down between the mattress and the rail on the side of the bed—actually it seemed as if I went *through* the rail—on down to the floor. Then, I started rising up, slowly ... I drifted on up past the light fixture—I saw it from the side and very distinctly—and then I stopped, floating right below the ceiling, looking down. I felt almost as though I were a piece of paper that someone had blown up to the ceiling."
- Another hospital patient: "A solid gray mist gathered around me, and I left my body. I had a floating sensation as I felt myself get out of my body, and I looked back and I could see myself on the bed below and there was no fear."[5]

Moody notes that in a few cases the patients felt they had no body at all and were pure consciousness. "Far and away the majority of my subjects, however, reported that they did find themselves in another body upon release from physical one." They complained that their attempts to communicate with the people around them were fruitless and that they were invisible to others. They found themselves able to move through physical objects, including people. They were weightless, usually "floating" or "drifting," and they experienced a sense of timelessness.

"I have heard this new body described in many different terms," Moody writes, "but one may readily see that much the same idea is being formulated in each case. Words and phrases which have been used by various subjects include a mist, a cloud, smoke-like, a vapor, transparent, a cloud of colors, wispy, an energy pattern and others which express similar meanings."[6]

If people who are near death sometimes observe the formation of their astral body as it separates from the physical one, is it ever possible for an independent observer to observe the same thing? Yes.

Formation of the spirit body as seen by an observer

Hospital worker Joy Snell was frequently in attendance on the dying. In *The Ministry of Angels* (1918), she records various instances of seeing the soul leave the body.

- "Always, immediately after the physical life had ceased, I saw the spirit form take shape above the dead body, in appearance a glorified replica of it. However painful might have been the last hours, however protracted and wasting the illness, no trace of suffering or disease appeared upon the radiant spirit face. Striking, at times, was the contrast which it presented to the human features, pain-distorted and deep-furrowed by suffering."
- A dying girl was visited by two "spirit forms" recognizable as her deceased friends. They "remained by the bedside during the brief space that elapsed before the [patient's] spirit form took shape above the body in which the physical life had ceased. Then they rose and stood for a few moments one on each side of her."
- "Then again I witnessed what had now become a familiar spectacle to me—the formation of the spirit body above the discarded earthly body."[7]

During a hospital visit, 19th-century American medium Andrew Jackson Davis closely observed two patients dying within an hour of each other in beds set close together. He reported that the emanation of a spiritual form began in the area of the heart ("death started at the very center of vitality"). "There was, at first, a broad, ribbon-shaped current arising from the epigastrium. As it ascended, it separated, and expanded into a sort of fleecy steam-cloud, about three feet above the bosom." Gradually it proceeded upward to the head. At all times until the completion of the process, the vaporous form was attached to the physical body "by a strong psychical cord ... a sort of linea alba tube." In contrast to some other descriptions, the figure was vertically oriented as it was being formed.

This spiritual cloud, looking initially like an inverted pyramid, "manifested several remarkable innate movements. There were vertical motions, upward and downward; lateral motions, like an anchored balloon, from side to side; then rotatory or gyrating motions, like a spinning-top immediately before losing its momentum."

Once the cloud was fully formed, Davis says, the patient's spirit flowed through the cord "with lightning rapidity and vividness," rendering a full-sized, "perfect" replica of the patient's body, starting with the head and working downward.[8]

George Wehner was a successful opera composer and artist who also claimed clairvoyant abilities. In his 1929 memoir *A Curious Life*, he recorded his observation of the death of his mother: "A misty blue-white form, the counterpart of my mother's, but radiant, like a blue-white diamond's flame, was slowly rising from her body on the bed. This form lifted at an angle, the feet rising higher than the head, which remained attached to the physical head. The form now seemed to try to free itself, and after several tugs, the misty head separated from the body's head, and the freed form righted itself in the air exactly as a log rights itself after it has been dropped into deep water."[9]

NDE researcher Kenneth Ring quotes a 1943 account by the esoteric writer Charles Hampton that agrees in striking detail with the above:

> As the rest of the body becomes negative and dead, the heart and brain become more alive because all the forces of the body are now concentrated in the upper part of it. When a dying person says: "Everything is becoming clear; my mind is more lucid than it has ever been," we may know that the transition is taking place. The head becomes intensely brilliant; it is like a golden bowl. All this time the silver cord also becomes more alive; etheric matter flows over it like a rapidly moving fluorescent light, but imperceptibly extracting the life force more and more, somewhat as a suction. Where the silver cord joins the main nerve ganglia it consists of thousands of very fine threads. As the life forces flow back into the higher world, those threads begin to break ...
>
> Its appearance is that of a bluish-white mist.[10]

E. W. Oaten observed the death of his friend Daisy:

> I saw a faint, smokelike vapor rise from the body. It rose some few feet above the bed and stayed there ... It condensed and grew larger, supplied with a steady stream from the body, a stream of vapor some three inches in diameter ... Then gradually, definition began to come. It assumed the form of a roughly molded dummy of the human form ...
>
> An umbilical cord united it with the physical body. I could see the flow of energy (pulsating) in the umbilical cord.

Presently there was the exact duplicate of Daisy floating ... in the air. It was connected to the body by the silver cord through which her life slowly escaped. Then the form began to heave and rock, like a balloon tearing at its moorings. The silver cord began to stretch. It grew thinner and thinner at the middle until at last it snapped and the floating form assumed an upright attitude. It was the living duplicate of the sleeping form on the bed. She turned to me and smiled. She was thanking me for the hours I had spent in trying to help her ... Then ... she floated away."

Physician R.B. Hout describes the death of his aunt:

My attention was called ... to something immediately above the physical body, suspended in the atmosphere about two feet above the bed. At first I could distinguish nothing more than a vague outline of a hazy, foglike substance. There seemed to be only a mist held suspended, motionless. But, as I looked, very gradually there grew into my sight a denser, more solid, condensation of this inexplicable vapor. Then I was astonished to see definite outlines presenting themselves, and soon I saw this foglike substance was assuming a human form ...

Soon I knew that the body I was seeing resembled that of the physical body of my aunt ... The astral body hung suspended horizontally a few feet above the physical counterpart ... I continued to watch and ... the Spirit Body now seemed complete to my sight. I saw the features plainly. They were very similar to the physical face, except that a glow of peace and vigor was expressed instead of age and pain. The eyes were closed as though in tranquil sleep, and a luminosity seemed to radiate from the Spirit Body.

As I watched the suspended Spirit Body, my attention was called, again intuitively, to a silverlike substance that was streaming from the head of the physical body to the head of the spirit "double." Then I saw the connection-cord between the two bodies. As I watched, the thought, "The silver cord!" kept running through my mind. I knew, for the first time, the meaning of it. This "silver cord" was the connecting-link between the physical and the spirit bodies, even as the umbilical cord unites the child to its mother ...

The cord was attached to each of the bodies at the occipital protuberance immediately at the base of the skull. Just where it met the physical body it spread out, fanlike, and numerous little strands separated and attached separately to the skull base. But other than at the attachments, the cord was round, being perhaps about an inch in diameter. The color was a translucent luminous silver radiance. The cord seemed alive with vibrant energy. I could see the pulsations of light stream along the course of it, from the direction of the physical body to the spirit "double." With each pulsation the spirit body became more alive and denser, whereas the physical body became quieter and more nearly lifeless ...

By this time the features were very distinct. The life was all in the astral body ... The pulsations of the cord had stopped ... I looked at the various strands of the cord as they spread out, fanlike, at the base of the skull. Each strand snapped ... the final severance was at hand. A twin process of death and birth was about to ensue ... The last connecting strand of the silver cord snapped and the spirit body was free.

The spirit body, which had been supine before, now rose ... The closed eyes opened and a smile broke from the radiant features. She gave a smile of farewell, then vanished from my sight.[12]

The "silver cord"—a term originating in the Book of Ecclesiastes[13]—is often mentioned by OBErs and clairvoyants, less often by NDErs. Robert Crookall remarks,

Peter M. Urquhart ... saw his own "silver cord" during a temporary out-of-the-body experience. Again, when the Reverend Dr. Staver ... saw "a wisp of connection which remained for some little time" joining his newly dead father to the latter's newly released "double," he said, "It reminded me of the oft-mentioned 'silver cord.'"[14]

But the description can vary. James Carney, who had an OBE while on anesthesia, said, "When I looked down, although I could not see my body, I could see I was attached by a light grey rope."[15]

Seeing at a distance

Many clairvoyants in the immediate vicinity of the dying have seen the spirit double. But how about people who happen to be far away? Have any of them seen the double, even at a distance of miles?

The answer is an emphatic yes. Such cases are, in fact, astonishingly common—so much so that they've earned their own designation, "crisis apparitions."

Some people are confused by this term, misunderstanding it to mean that the person who perceives the spirit double is in a state of crisis. Actually, the crisis is on the part of the person who shows up in apparitional form—the crisis in question being his own death, which is occurring at that moment or has just recently occurred. The percipient, by contrast, is typically in a relaxed or drowsy state of mind, a condition known to facilitate psychic perception (see the discussion of the ganzfeld tests in Chapter 7).

Here's a fairly standard crisis apparition case from the 19th century, reported by Ellen M. Greany and included in the massive compilation *Phantasms of the Living*.

Mr. Marchant, of Linkfield Street, Redhill, formerly a large farmer, wrote to us in the summer of 1883:—

"About two o'clock on the morning of October 21st, 1881, while I was perfectly wide awake, and looking at a lamp burning on my washhand-stand [sic], a person, as I thought, came into my room by mistake, and stopped, looking into the looking-glass on the table. It soon occurred to me it represented Robinson Kelsey, by his dress and wearing his hair long behind. When I raised myself up in bed and called out, it instantly disappeared. The next day I mentioned to some of my friends how strange it was. So thoroughly convinced was I, that I searched the local papers that day (Saturday) and the following Tuesday, believing his death would be in one of them. On the following Wednesday, a man, who formerly was my drover, came and told me Robinson Kelsey was dead. Anxious to know at what time he died, I wrote to Mr. Wood, the family undertaker at Lingfield; he learnt from the brother-in-law of the deceased that he died at 2 a.m. He was my first cousin, and was apprenticed formerly to me as a miller; afterwards he lived with me as journeyman; altogether, eight years. I never saw anything approaching that before. I am 72 years old, and never feel nervous; I am not afraid of the dead or their spirits."

In answer to inquiries, Mr. Marchant replied:—

"Robinson Kelsey had met with an accident. His horse fell with him, and from that time he seemed at times unfit for business. He had a farm at Penshurst, in Kent. His friends persuaded him to leave it. He did, and went to live on his own property, called Batnors Hall, in the parish of Lingfield, Surrey. I had not been thinking about him, neither had I spoken to him for 20 years ... As the apparition passed between my bed and the lamp I had a full view of it; it was unmistakable. When it stopped looking in the glass I spoke to it, then it gently sank away downwards."[16]

In a written statement, three people confirmed that Marchant had spoken of the apparition the day after seeing it, well before he could have learned of Kelsey's death. One of the investigators interviewed Marchant and came away with the impression that he was "a very vigorous and sensible old man, with a precise mind."

Kelsey, you may have noticed, was recognizable in part "by his dress." Perhaps surprisingly, it is not unusual for the astral body to be clothed. Crookall cites an OBE account:

> I became fascinated with the different ways in which 'I' appeared—sometimes naked, sometimes dressed in my own "clothes" that I was not wearing in bed, sometimes as I was actually dressed, sometimes in "clothes" I did not own, sometimes in "spiritual" garments of great beauty. Sometimes I could create my own "garments" by will and concentration.[17]

Dr. A.S. Wiltse, who had an NDE in 1889, made this observation:

> I seemed to be translucent, of a bluish cast and perfectly naked. With a painful sense of embarrassment, I fled toward the partially opened door to escape the eyes of the two ladies whom I was facing, as well as others who I knew were about me, but upon reaching the door I found myself clothed, and satisfied upon that point, I turned and faced the company [who, as it turned out, could not see him anyway].[18]

As both quotations indicate, the apparel in

> question seems to be generated by the person's thoughts. It appears that the newly departed—or any deceased person who wants to be recognized by those he's attempting to contact—can, in effect, dress himself as needed. Even if he feels the need for clothing merely from a sense of modesty, the desired ensemble will appear.

In cases where the time of death can be precisely determined, the apparitional sighting sometimes matches it to a degree inexplicable in terms of pure chance.

"On Saturday evening, March 24, [1883], N.J.S., who had a headache, was sitting at home. He said to his wife that he was ... rather too warm; after making the remark he leaned back on the couch, and the next minute saw his friend, F.L., standing before him, dressed in his usual manner. N.J.S. noticed the details of his dress, that is, his hat with a black band, his overcoat unbuttoned, and a stick in his hand; he looked with a fixed regard at N.J.S., and then passed away ... At that moment an icy chill passed through [N.J.S.], and his hair bristled. He then turned to his wife and asked her the time; she said, 'Twelve minutes to nine.' He then said, 'The reason I ask you is that F.L. is dead. I have just seen him.'"

His wife Maria reported answering, "What nonsense, you don't even know that he is ill; I daresay when you go to town on Tuesday you will see him all right." Even so, she couldn't convince him that he hadn't seen the apparition. She "noticed at the time that he looked very much agitated and was very pale."

It will come as no surprise that F.L. was indeed dead. And he appears to have died at or very near to twelve minutes to nine. "N.J.S. afterwards ascertained that [F.L.'s brother] called on Saturday to see his brother, and on leaving him noticed the clock on the stairs was 8:35 PM. F.L.'s sister, on going to him at 9 p.m., found him dead from rupture of the aorta." These times are not exact, as the brother later reported that he came down about 8:40 and remained with his sister downstairs "for about half an hour." When he left, she immediately went upstairs and found her brother dead. But it seems clear enough that F.L. died sometime between 8:35 and 9:10 p.m.[19]

Distance is no impediment to the timely arrival of an apparition. On January 3, 1856, Joseph Collyer was killed aboard the steamship *Alice* when it collided with another steamer on the Mississippi. A flagstaff or spar fell on his head, nearly splitting his skull in two. On that same night his mother Anne, who resided a thousand miles away in Camden, New Jersey, retired early, feeling unwell. "Some time after, I felt uneasy and sat up in bed; I looked around the room, and to my utter amazement, saw Joseph standing at the door, looking at me with great earnestness, his head bandaged up, a dirty night-cap on, and a dirty white garment on, something like a surplice. He was much disfigured about the eyes and face. It made me quite uncomfortable the rest of the night ... On the 16th of January I received the news of his death." ...

Anne's sister wrote, "The apparition appeared to my mother at the foot of her bed. It stood there for some time gazing at her, and disappeared. The apparition was clothed in a long white garment, with its head bound in a white cloth. My mother was not a superstitious person, nor did she believe in Spiritualism. She was wide awake at the time. It was not a dream. She remarked to me when I saw her in the morning, 'I shall hear bad news from Joseph,' and related to me what she had seen."

Joseph's brother Robert, who described himself as "a materialist," wrote: "My father, who was a scientific man, calculated the difference of longitude between Camden, New Jersey, and New Orleans, and found that the mental impression was at the exact time of my brother's death ... Joseph, prior to his death, had retired for the night in his berth [and] was in his nightgown ... I do not attempt to account for the apparition having a bandage, as that could not have been put on for some time after death."[20]

I suggest that the bandage was as much of a mental representation as the rest of his apparel. It probably signified the fatal injury to Joseph's head.

An element of intent is obvious in such cases. The deceased person evidently seeks out a particular individual, though not always somebody who was close to him. Possibly the contactee is selected, in part, because he happens to possess the latent clairvoyant talent necessary to perceive the apparition.

Catherine, a patient hypnotically progressed to a purportedly between-lives state, told her therapist, Brian Weiss:

> In spiritual form you can always contact those that are in physical state if you choose to. But only if there is importance there ... if you have to tell them something that they must know ...
>
> Sometimes you can appear before that person ... and look the same way you did when you were here. Other times you just make a mental contact. Sometimes the messages are cryptic, but

most often the person knows what it pertains to. They understand. It's mind-to-mind contact.[21]

Though most crisis apparitions involve an apparently deliberate attempt to contact a specific person, occasionally the apparition is seen by someone who just happens to be around at the time. Such was the case of Mrs. de Fréville, described by the vicar of her church as "a somewhat eccentric lady, who was specially morbid on the subject of tombs." On the evening of May 8, 1885, a gardener, Alfred Bard, was walking through the churchyard when he "looked straight at the square stone vault in which the late Mr. de Fréville was at one time buried. I then saw Mrs. de Fréville leaning on the rails, dressed much as I had usually seen her, in a coal-scuttle bonnet, black jacket with deep crape, and black dress. She was looking full at me. Her face was very white, much whiter than usual. I knew her well, having at one time been in her employ. I at once supposed that she had come, as she sometimes did, to the mausoleum in her own park, in order to have it opened and go in."

He describes walking around the tomb while keeping his eye on her the whole time, until a slight stumble caused him to look down. "When I looked up she was gone. She could not possibly have got out of the churchyard, as in order to reach any of the exits she must have passed me. So I took for granted that she had quickly gone into the tomb. I went up to the door, which I expected to find open, but to my surprise it was shut and had not been opened, as there was no key in the lock ... I was then much startled and looked at the clock, which marked 9:20. When I got home I have thought it must have been my fancy, but I told my wife that I had seen Mrs. de Fréville." His wife Sarah seconded this part of the story, writing, "When Mr. Bard came home he said, 'I have seen Mrs. de Fréville tonight, leaning with her elbow on the palisade, looking at me. I turned again to look at her and she was gone. She had cloak and bonnet on.'"[22]

The next day he learned that the woman had been found dead at around two o'clock in the afternoon of May 8, a few hours before her apparition was seen. Her death was sudden and unexpected. Perhaps sightings of this sort account for the persistent idea that some ghosts hover around tombs.

Though the accounts I've cited are old, there are plenty of newer ones. One rather striking incident comes from 1989.

> I woke up crying at three o'clock in the morning after a very "real" dream in which (my ex-husband) Vincent was sitting on the end of my bed and telling me not to cry anymore and that it

was all over and that he was finally at peace. I got up, "on automatic," did some work I needed to do, two clients phoned me around eight o'clock and I freaked them out completely as I told them I would be taking some time out because my husband had just died.

The narrator goes on to say that she went to his apartment, discovered his body, and called the police. "The coroner's report was that Vin had indeed died around three o'clock a.m."[23]

Distant sightings from the viewpoint of the dying

Occasionally we read of a crisis apparition from a different perspective—the event as described by the dying person whose apparition was seen elsewhere. The following two cases are quite old, and despite the claims of documentation in the second case, neither can be counted as more than a family legend. Still, they're consistent with other, more recent reports, and they demonstrate the persistence of such accounts.

The first story dates all the way back to 1691; in its present form it was related by the Reverend T. Tilson. Mary Goffe of Rochester, New York, suffering from an illness, had been moved to her father's house, nine miles from her own.

> She grew impatiently desirous to see her two children, whom she had left at home, to the care of a nurse …
>
> Between one and two o'clock in the morning she fell into a trance. One widow Turner, who watched with her that night, says that her eyes were open and fixed, and her jaw fallen; she put her hand on her mouth and nostrils, but could perceive no breath; she thought her to be in a fit, and doubted whether she was alive or dead. The next day the dying woman told her mother that she had been at home with her children … "I was with them last night while I was asleep."
>
> The nurse at Rochester, widow Alexander by name, affirms and says she will take her oath of it … that a little before two o'clock that morning she saw the likeness of the said Mary Goffe come out of the next chamber (where the elder child lay in a bed by itself, the door being left open), and [it] stood by her bedside for about a quarter of an hour; the younger child was there lying by her; her eyes moved and her mouth went, but she said nothing.[24]

The second case is a family story dating to 1739, narrated (in a later era) by Mrs. Charles Fox.

> In 1739 Mrs. Birkbeck ... was taken ill and died at Cockermouth, while returning from a journey to Scotland, which she had undertaken alone—her husband and three children, aged seven, five, and four years respectively, remaining at Settle. The friends at whose house the death occurred made notes of every circumstance attending Mrs. Birkbeck's last hours ...
>
> One morning, between seven and eight o'clock, the relation to whom the care of the children at Settle had been entrusted, and who kept a minute journal of all that concerned them, went into their bedroom as usual, and found them all sitting up in their beds in great excitement and the like. "Mama has been there!" they cried, and the little one said, "She called 'Come, Esther!'" Nothing could make them doubt the fact, and it was carefully noted down, to entertain the mother on her return home. [The nurse and children had no knowledge of Mrs. Birkbeck's condition.] That same morning, as their mother lay on her dying bed at Cockermouth, she said, "I should be ready to go if I could but see my children." She then closed her eyes, to reopen them, as they thought, no more. But after ten minutes of perfect stillness she looked up brightly and said, "I am ready now; I have been with my children"; and then at once peacefully passed away. When the notes taken at the two places were compared, the day, hour, and minutes were the same.[25]

Separation reported by the deceased

Throughout history, people with clairvoyant powers have seen a spirit double separating from the body at the point of death. But how about the deceased persons themselves? Have any of them witnessed the final, irreversible separation and still managed to speak of it?

In *Stop Worrying: There Probably Is an Afterlife*, Greg Taylor tells us of Dr. Horace Ackley, a 19th-century physician bedridden with a severe illness. "All of a sudden, he felt himself gradually rising from his body, with the distinct feeling that he had been divided, though the parts retained a tenuous connecting link of some sort. As the organs within his physical body ceased functioning, the feeling of being divided came to an abrupt halt, and he found himself whole again. Except he now appeared to be in a position slightly above his lifeless physical body, looking down on it and on those who had been in the room with him."

He re-experienced the events of his life in what would now be called a "life review," a common feature of NDEs. Though frustrated by his inability to communicate with the living, he still concluded, "Death is not so bad a thing after all."[26]

Coming at the end of Taylor's chapter on NDEs, this story could be mistaken for yet another such case. It has many of the now-familiar hallmarks—rising upward, seeing his physical body, and finding himself unable to make contact with the people in the room. But Taylor notes one crucial difference: "Dr. Horace Ackley truly did die that day, never to return to this life. The report that you read above was an account of his death, allegedly given by him through a spirit medium—one Samuel Paist of Philadelphia. And what makes it truly remarkable is that it was written down by Paist in his book *A Narrative of the Experience of Horace Abraham Ackley, M.D.*, which was published in 1861—more than a century before the near-death experience had come to the attention of researchers and the general public."

Another example is found in *Leslie's Letters to His Mother*, a book produced by automatic writing and originally published in 1926. The departed Leslie Stringfellow describes the dying process in terms almost identical to Dr. Ackley's.

> When you die—as you call it—your spirit body is really born.
>
> It begins to rise from your natural body at your breast, just over the heart, and it forms like a luminous vapor while you are "dying" until the last moment, when your heart ceases to beat. Then you are standing on your old body with your feet upon its breast, and you open your eyes and see a crowd of relatives and friends waiting to greet you and accompany you to some of their homes. They tell you you are in the Spirit World but you cannot believe it.[27]

Consider also the famous reincarnation case of Shanti Deva. When she was four years old, Shanti, a native of Delhi, India, began talking about a past life lived in a town 80 miles away. Though her parents did their best to discourage her, she eventually convinced them to take her seriously by naming her husband in her previous life and the address of their home. The husband had indeed lost his young wife in childbirth shortly before Shanti was born. Alert to the possibility of fraud, the husband's family subjected Shanti to various tests, all of which she passed. Finally they accepted her story as true.

In contrast to many such cases, Shanti retained her reincarnation memories until her death in 1987 at age sixty-one. In *Past Lives*, Peter and Elizabeth Fenwick observe, "To the end of her life she maintained her conviction that she had lived before as Lugdi. She remained in touch with Lugdi's family and was an honored guest at family occasions."

The authors continue:

> Four years after Shanti's initial reunion with her [previous-life] family, in 1939, the whole case was re-examined by Mr. Sushil Bose. He interviewed Shanti, and for the first time asked her detailed questions not just about her previous life as Lugdi but about her death ... Shanti described how just before death she felt a profound darkness and then saw a dazzling light. She knew then that she had come out of her body in a vaporous form. She described seeing four men in saffron robes who had come for her, a beautiful garden and a river.[28]

Like the account attributed to Dr. Ackley, Shanti Deva's testimony predates the popularization of NDEs by decades. Also like the previous account, this one is purportedly not the story of a *near-death* experience, but of an *actual* death experience. Shanti said she was remembering the death of Lugdi, the personality she'd assumed in her previous incarnation.

After a review of the accumulated evidence, longtime NDE researcher Kenneth Ring concludes:

> Not only is there a high level of agreement across independent witnesses concerning the formation of a spirit double at death, but their descriptions accord, on the whole, very neatly with the accounts provided by near-death survivors themselves! That is, both the *external* perspective of the witness and the *direct* testimony of the individual close to death converge on what is occurring during the *initial* stages of death: There is a splitting-off process that takes place during which one's center of self-awareness is freed from the constraints of the physical body.[29]

Before we go on, it might be interesting to know if this process of bodily separation can occur outside the context of medical crisis. Can it be brought about voluntarily, on demand?

Indeed it can.

CHAPTER TWO:
Separation in OBEs

PEOPLE WHO PRACTICE SO-CALLED "astral projection" attest to their ability to separate from the body at will. One of the most influential writers in this area was William Buhlman, who wrote about his first out-of-body experience (OBE) in *Adventures Beyond the Body*:

> Instantly I was awake, fully conscious, lying in bed facing the wall. I could hear an unusual buzzing sound and felt somehow different. Extending my arm, I reached for the wall in front of me. I stared in amazement as my hand actually entered the wall; I could feel the vibrational energy of it as if I was touching its very molecular structure. Only then did the overwhelming reality hit me. *My God, I'm not my body ...*
>
> Determined to stand, I began to move effortlessly to the foot of my bed, my mind racing with the reality of it all. Standing, I quickly touched my arms and legs, checking to see if I was solid, and to my surprise I was completely solid, completely real ... Glancing down, I noticed a large lump in my bed. Amazed, I could see that it was the sleeping form of my physical body silently facing the wall.[1]

Here are excerpts from three of Buhlman's later experiences:

- I think of floating and feel myself lift up and out of my physical body. I feel light as a feather and float slowly upward. As I float away from my body I realize that the vibrations and buzzing have diminished to a slight humming sensation. Feeling more secure, I open my eyes and find myself staring at the ceiling two feet in front of me.
- Drifting off to sleep I awaken to the sensation of intense vibrations and buzzing throughout my body. I recognize that I'm ready to separate and immediately think about floating. The vibrations and sounds rapidly diminish as I separate and float up to the ceiling.
- At first I was startled by the intensity of the vibrations,

but slowly I calm myself and focus my full attention on the idea of floating away from my physical body. In seconds I float up and out of my body and hover several feet above. I notice that the buzzing noise and vibrations immediately subside after complete separation. The sound and vibrations are replaced by a serene feeling of calm. It feels as if I'm weightless and floating like a cloud.[2]

Sometime later, Buhlman was able to perceive two distinct spiritual bodies. In notes written immediately after an OBE, he reported: "For the first time it becomes clear: the 'feel' of the two nonphysical bodies are [sic] dramatically different. The energy-body I'm now in is much denser, almost physical when compared with the lightness of the second energy-body." Upon later reflection, he expanded on his first thoughts: "With that experience, I realized that the first (dense) nonphysical body is actually an energy duplicate of the physical, while the second possesses a finer vibratory rate, like pure energy, ready to respond to the slightest thought … Now I understood how limited the first energy-body really is."[3]

Elsewhere, Buhlman observes, "The spiritual form experienced by most people during an OBE is their astral or emotional body. This energy body is the seat of our personal desires and emotional needs, so it is only natural that sensual experiences would manifest themselves there."[4] He uses the terms "astral body" or "emotional body" to refer to the spirit form that is first to separate from the body. "Energy body" is his more general term for any nonphysical body.

"In discussions with astral projectors," says OBE researcher Samantha Treasure, "I have … heard the [first energy body] described as translucent, iridescent, or star-like."[5] She reports "strange features of light" observed by OBErs, quoting one of them: "the nighttime occurrence revealed the walls and furniture in a blue-purple light and I could see them and see through them at the same time."[6]

Richard Bach, author of *Jonathan Livingston Seagull*, experimented with OBEs with his wife Leslie. At one point, while the two of them were in an out-of-body state, he perceived her this way: "Oh, my! I thought. The Leslie I've been seeing with my eyes isn't the tiniest part of who she is! She's body within body, life within life, unfolding, unfolding … will I ever know all of her?"[7]

All these OBEs were voluntary, but other people, while not near death, have had spontaneous involuntary OBEs. Dr. Peter Fenwick tells of a three-year-old girl, Amie Greensted, who reported recurrent OBEs with some features of a classic NDE. "Amie," he writes, "has a rare medical condition called reflex anoxic seizure (reflex cardiac standstill), in which the heart slows and may actually stop for a short time. Amie is not literally 'near death,' because the condition isn't dangerous ... Nevertheless, for a short time (up to a minute) Amie is unconscious, not breathing, and has no heartbeat."

He quotes her mother:

> Amie tells me about when she "goes," as she calls it, and how she floats out to the ceiling and watches her body and us. She has told me exactly what is happening and what I did, said etc. whilst she was "gone" on many occasions ... She is one hundred per cent right in everything that has happened ...
>
> While out of body, Amie has said she perceives a warm bright light "like the sun." She goes back into her body "head first—it's not very nice."[8]

Longtime psychic researcher D. Scott Rogo quotes a woman who fainted in public:

> One moment I felt hot, and the next I was looking down at a figure lying face down on the floor. I seemed to be quite high up ... then I realized the body was mine. I saw my body being picked up, could distinguish clearly individual people and what they were doing, I saw the main lights go on, and then just as suddenly was back in the body again ...
>
> I was able to note people's actions and afterward I told them of their exact movements, which they confirmed.[9]

Dream or reality?

Can OBEs be distinguished from hallucinations or dreams? Samantha Treasure interviewed OBErs who also had lucid dreams, in which they were aware of being asleep and dreaming.

> When asked, my interlocutors said that they mainly distinguished the OBE from dreams by a distinctive set of "transition" or "trance" indicators, such as vibration or electric-like sensations, loud noises, and the realistic sense of separating or floating from the body ...
>
> On the other hand, in cases when there was no transition, there was a blackout period followed by suddenly finding themselves in a different location. This was in contrast to their

lucid dreams in which they were typically already in a dream, and realized it within that environment."[10]

Astral projector Thomas M. Johanson writes, "Though I have, like most people, had vivid dreams, the experiences I had of astral projection were unmistakable and totally unlike any dream experience. I found that with astral projection the consciousness is on a completely different level. One knows it actually happened."[11]

I've never had an unambiguous OBE, but I can report a couple of intriguing personal experiences. Some years ago I tried using a relaxation tape made with binaural Hemi-Sync® technology. The tape was very effective; I was aware of being more relaxed than I could ever remember. Suddenly I began to notice a strange vibrating, buzzing feeling throughout my body.

As we've seen, many people report that an OBE can start with a humming, buzzing, or vibrating sensation, so perhaps this was the prelude to an OBE. The same people say that if you are alarmed by the sensation, the OBE will stop. In my case, I was sufficiently unnerved that I slipped out of my state of relaxation. If an OBE was about to commence, I must have aborted it.

I listened to the same tape several times after that event, but I never became relaxed to the same degree. Subconsciously, I may have been wary of doing so.

On another occasion, I had what I like to think of as an OBE, though it may have been a vivid dream. After falling asleep on my living room sofa, I floated out of my body, then over to the stairs and up the staircase to the second floor where, for some reason, I detoured into the walk-in closet in my den. I don't recall if I opened the closet door or simply passed through it.

I clearly remember three things: first, my progress up the stairs was very exciting, because I wasn't actually touching the steps but was "treading water" in the air; second, I felt a continuous electric tingle all over my body; and third, a strange yellowish-golden light seemed to travel with me wherever I went, illuminating my immediate environment. This light intensified once I went into the confined space of the walk-in closet, at which point I came into contact with a spiritual presence who gave me some meaningful personal information. The tingling sensation increased during this communication, creating a euphoric, transcendent feeling, the equivalent of thinking "it suddenly all makes sense."

Usually I forget my dreams almost immediately, but I've never forgotten this one. Was it a dream, or was it an OBE? I don't know. But an actual OBE can have some of these features.

In 2010 I had a rare lucid dream. In the dream, I was at home when I suddenly realized that the foyer was completely different from anything in my actual residence. At this point, realization struck, and I said to myself, "This isn't real. It's a dream. I'm having a lucid dream!" I was pretty excited about it, and did my best to maintain my concentration so as to stay "in the moment" as long as possible. Somewhere I'd read that it helps to focus on one's own hand; I remember touching the wall of the foyer and feeling its solidity and texture while watching my hand closely.

Continuing the dream in my self-aware state, I went to the front door and opened it. What I found outside was not my actual street, but a wide expanse of blue water. The weather was bright and clear, and the color of the water was almost painfully lovely.

I set about exploring the rest of my house, walking through a series of spacious and beautifully appointed rooms. I knew I was seeing an idealized dream-picture of a place to live.

While I don't remember climbing stairs, apparently there was a second floor, because I looked out through a high window and saw blue water dotted with white sails in one direction, a large sparkling community swimming pool in another direction, and directly across from me, a meticulously tended greensward dividing the rear of my home from a row of tree-shaded townhouses. There were unidentifiable people on some of the decks and patios. I had the impression that this neighborhood was ideally situated between the beach and a forest.

Now and then I again reached out to touch a wall—one of which had very nice wood paneling—in order to ground myself in the environment. There was no sense of being disembodied, but the only part of my body that I clearly visualized was my right hand as it touched the walls.

The whole experience was highly enjoyable, and I did my best to prolong it, but eventually my thoughts started to wander, and to my regret I found myself slipping out of the lucid state. I don't remember anything afterward, though presumably I continued to dream in the normal way.

When I awoke, I recalled the dream in considerate detail. But at no time, either during the dream or afterward, did I ever imagine that it was a "real" experience. I knew it was a dream while I was experiencing it, and I knew it was a dream when I recalled it. In this respect, the experience was different from many NDEs and OBEs, which often are described as being "realer than real." It was also different from my (possible) OBE; at no time during that episode did I think I was dreaming. Moreover, the intense emotion I experienced in the OBE was not part of the lucid dream. The dream was fun, but not meaningful or life-changing.

My memory of the lucid dream is now largely gone; to reconstruct it, I've had to rely on a blog post I wrote at the time. Conversely, my dream-OBE remains quite vivid more than a decade later.

On the basis of my experience and the comments of Samantha Treasure's interviewees, I would say that OBEs are not lucid dreams. Even so, I don't rule out the possibility that some kind of dream (or dreamlike) state is involved, at least some of the time. Some purported OBEs just sound too far-out to be believed.

I'm particularly skeptical about the wilder reports made by astral projector Robert Monroe, who in 1971 published *Journeys out of the Body*, an influential account of his experiments.

The experiences that Monroe reports are often nightmarish and bizarre. Here's one:

> At times, in visiting Locale II [Monroe's term for another dimension], a very unusual event periodically occurs. It makes no difference where in Locale II, the event is the same.
>
> In the midst of normal activity, whatever it may be, there is a distant Signal, almost like heraldic trumpets. Everyone takes the Signal calmly, and with it, everyone stops speaking or whatever he may be doing. It is the Signal that He (or They) is coming through His Kingdom ...
>
> At the Signal, each living thing lies down—my impression is on their backs, bodies arched to expose the abdomen (not the genitals), with head turned to one side so that one does not see Him as He passes by. The purpose seems to be to form a living road over which He can travel. I have gleaned the idea that occasionally He will select someone from this living bridge, and that person is never seen or heard from again. The purpose of the abdominal exposure is an expression of faith and complete submissiveness, the abdomen being the most vulnerable part of the body or the area that can suffer damage most easily ...
>
> After His passing, everyone gets up again and resumes their activities.[12]

Many similar accounts from the same book could be cited; they do not inspire confidence in the reality of these explorations. On the other hand, some of Monroe's astral traveling apparently yielded verifiable information about distant events. Monroe was sufficiently intrigued by his experiments that he founded the Monroe Institute, devoted to studying OBEs. The institute is still in existence.

Perhaps Monroe was sometimes able to maintain a state partway between sleep and wakefulness, known technically as a hypnagogic state, allowing him to weave complicated narratives reflecting his mood or subconscious thoughts. Since he often approached his experiments with trepidation, it wouldn't be surprising if the resulting experiences were scary. Nor would it be surprising that his travels frequently took on a bizarre dreamlike quality. There's very little difference between dreaming and hypnagogic hallucination, except that hypnagogic hallucination can seem much more real.

Beyond lucid dreams and hypnagogic hallucinations, there's another issue that may be relevant here. It's the problem of analytic overlay.

Analytic overlay

I learned of analytic overlay from reading about experiments in remote viewing (or clairvoyance). Suppose a remote viewer focusing on a set of geographical coordinates receives a mental image of parallel lines. If he jumps to the conclusion that he's seeing a railroad track, when in fact he's seeing a highway, then his mistake will affect all of his other assumptions. For this reason, remote viewers are taught not to report their interpretations, but to stick to the most literal statement of what they see or sense. Later there will be time to evaluate it.

Here is a more complete explanation from a remote viewing organization. In this post, the acronym AOL is used for analytic overlay.

> AOL is the response of the [remote] viewer's analytic mind to the information being received by the subconscious intuitive mind ...
>
> The [remote] viewer takes the coordinate, the intuitive mind receives and draws an ideogram of the primary gestalt based on factors perceivable by the intuitive mind, but immediately the analytic mind jumps in and "tries to help." The analytic mind tells the viewer that the last time a similar set of perceptions was received it was a (fill in the blank) ... This may be correct, it may be semi-correct, or it may be incorrect ...
>
> Remote viewers must learn to describe their perceptions of the site and not try to turn those perceptions into "things." Perceptions are most often expressed by the viewer as adjectives—colors, kinesthetic sensations, smells, tastes, sounds,

the perceptions of our traditional five senses. "Things" or tangible objects are nouns. When perceiving red, hard, smooth, metallic, manmade, etc., the analytic mind endeavors to turn these disparate elements into a cogent picture—a car for instance. "Car" is the analytic mind's suggestion to the viewer that these various perceptions are likely describing a car. Car is an AOL.

While the viewer can perceive tangible objects in the later stages of remote viewing, in the early stages of remote viewing, nouns are often products of the analytic mind and are almost certainly AOL. Remote viewers must learn to focus on describing the received perceptions [versus] attempting to turn those adjectives into nouns. Nouns are likely AOL and should be declared as AOL. If these perceptions are correct they will return; this is known as the self-correcting nature of remote viewing.[13]

The same issue seems to apply to other forms of paranormal knowledge and experience, including mediumship, where fleeting mental impressions can be misclassified, leading to erroneous readings, and NDEs, which, as we'll see, are known for cultural and idiosyncratic discrepancies.

Naturally, the same caveats apply to OBEs. It's possible that the more far-fetched "things" reported by astral projectors like Robert Monroe are simply misinterpretations of perceptions—hasty rationalizations of confusing visual and auditory impressions.

However we look at it, the bottom line is that we should take many OBE accounts with a grain of salt. Some, however, have the advantage of having been confirmed by outsiders.

OBEs verified by an independent observer

In a minority of cases, the astrally projected form has been seen by someone else. Such cases inevitably remind us of crisis apparitions, except in these instances there is no crisis, only a desire to make contact. D. Scott Rogo's book *Leaving the Body* includes an account of some famous experiments carried out in 1881 by the astral projector S.H. Beard.

> "I determined with the whole force of my being [Beard wrote] that I would be present in spirit in the front bedroom of the second floor of a house ... in which slept two young ladies." These were Miss Verity (aged 25) and her eleven-year-old sister ...

The tests began one Sunday night in November. Beard seated himself in his room and concentrated his mind on the Verity home. The young woman knew nothing of the experiment. Beard concentrated with all his might and fell asleep with no conscious recollection of having accomplished his purpose. The following day he visited the Verity home and learned, for the first time, that he had been successful. The elder Miss Verity told him that his apparition had suddenly appeared in her room the previous night. She had screamed in shock, awakening her sister, who also saw the apparition ...

Beard conducted his next impromptu experiment on December 1 at 9:30 p.m. Once again he went to his room and tried to project to a house in London where the Veritys were visiting. "I endeavored so strongly to fix my mind upon the house in which resided Miss Verity and her two sisters," he wrote in his journal, "that I seemed to be actually in the house." ... Later that night, he gave himself the suggestion that he would once again appear to Miss Verity ... this time at midnight.

Beard found that he had been successful the next day when he visited the Veritys and learned that his apparition had been seen in the hallway of the upper floor of the house at 9:30. At 12:00 Miss Verity had seen the apparition once again. She was awake in bed when the apparition suddenly appeared, entered her room, walked up to her, stroked her hair, and then disappeared.[14]

Robert Crookall provides a similar example from a certain Mr. von Szalay, who reported, "On January 10, 1954 I made an attempt to astrally visit Mr. Bayless at his home. I did my usual breathing exercises, etc., and found myself in a room which was not known to me but I did not see Mr. Bayless. I saw a pair of glass doors, went through them thinking that he might be having dinner in the dining area. I entered the living room but lost consciousness and returned to my studio."

Mr. Bayless, the intended contactee, wrote,

"I can in part verify Mr. von Szalay's experience. At 6:15 p.m. at my home in West Los Angeles, eleven miles from his studio on McCradden Place and Hollywood Boulevard in Hollywood, I was tying my shoe laces while sitting on a studio couch. I saw something flicker in front of me and thinking it was my cat I paid little attention but again I saw something move in front of me. I looked to the end of the couch, saw that my cat was sitting there, and looked back and saw a fantastic, slipped [sic] rectangular shadow about the height of a man floating about one foot from the floor in front of me. I received the definite impression that it was an aware entity and as I looked it 'turned' and rushed at a great speed through two glass doors which were open, reached the living room and disappeared. I immediately glanced at the clock and saw that it was 6:15 p.m. I then drove to the studio of Mr. von Szalay, knocked at his door, and when he answered I said, 'Guess what happened to me'. He spontaneously replied, 'You saw me!'"[15]

Note the detail of the glass doors, said by Mr. Bayless to have been open. Both von Szalay and Bayless report that the apparition passed through this doorway—von Szalay on the way in, Bayless on the way out. If von Szalay was correct in saying that the room was "not known to me," then he would have had no normal way of knowing about the glass doors in the first place.

OBEs in the laboratory

Modern parapsychologists have attempted to prove the reality of OBEs with laboratory tests. The most famous experiment of this type was carried out by Charles Tart and involved a test subject he called Miss Z, who reported having spontaneous OBEs while asleep. While wired to an EEG monitor, the sleeping Miss Z had an OBE (recorded as a highly anomalous EEG reading); upon waking, she accurately reported a random five-digit number that had been hidden from her normal view. She could not have gotten out of bed without interrupting the EEG recording, and she almost certainly could not have seen the concealed number from bed.[16] The odds of her guessing the number by luck are fantastically low.[17]

Although the experiment with Miss Z unfortunately was not repeated, Tart notes that

> Stanley Krippner (1996) had a similar experience with a young man who reported occasional OBEs. He was tested for four nights in the laboratory with an art-print target in a box near the ceiling of the room. On the occasion when he reported having had an OBE, he gave a suggestively accurate description of the target, and had shown an unusual EEG pattern of slow waves (unlike Miss Z) about the time the reported OBE occurred.[18]

A different kind of laboratory experiment also yielded positive, albeit not conclusive, results. The online *Psi Encyclopedia*, a hugely useful resource maintained by the Society for Physical Research, reports that researchers Karlis Osis and Donna McCormick

> argued that if a person experiencing an OBE was present in some measurable way at a particular location, the detection of their presence should coincide with veridical perceptions obtained in the same area. To test this they carried out experiments with the psychic Alex Tanous. A viewing window was constructed in such a way that the target pictures contained within could be seen only by looking through it from a close distance; it was also surrounded by strain gauges that detected nearby vibrations. Consistent with their expectations, the experimenters found that the sensors showed more responses during the trials in which Tanous obtained correct information from the window as compared to those trials in which he did not seem to perceive veridical information.[19]

At a minimum, these laboratory results are signposts pointing the way to future research.

CHAPTER THREE:
Patterns and Exceptions

I DON'T WANT TO GIVE the impression that everything about the process of separation is neat and simple. Most of the cases we've looked at tend to reinforce each other. But there are exceptions.

Not all NDEs or OBEs involve the perception of a double. In some cases, the person reports no sense of having a body at all. One of them was Harold Jaffe's NDE during the Korean War, who recalled "that my 'being' at the rooftop had no form, no mouth—only consciousness, vivid, painless, unimpaired hearing and vision and thought."[1]

Another such person was Doreen Wood:

> I actually felt myself come away from my body. I twirled so fast up in the air, so free, no pain, weightless, then I felt myself go back in my body and thought, was that old body with her knees curled up, facing the wall, was that *me*? I didn't see any lights, just went just round and round, so fast, and so free. Now I am not so afraid of death. I know this body stays here and was so disappointed that I came back, and wondering, why.[2]

This account is reminiscent of Ernest Hemingway's NDE, which occurred when he was wounded in Italy in 1918. In a letter to his family, he wrote, "Dying is a very simple thing. I've looked at death and really I know." Some years later he described what happened to him:

> A big Austrian trench mortar bomb, of the type that used to be called ash cans, exploded in the darkness. I died then. I felt my soul or something coming right out of my body, like you'd pull a silk handkerchief out of a pocket by one corner. It flew around and then came back and went in again and I wasn't dead anymore.

A scene in his novel *A Farewell to Arms* re-creates this experience:

I ate the end of my piece of cheese and took a swallow of wine. Through the other noise I heard a cough, then came the chuh-chuh-chuh-chuh—then there was a flash, as when a blast-furnace door is swung open, and a roar that started white and went red and on and on in a rushing wind. I tried to breathe but my breath would not come and I felt myself rush bodily out of myself and out and out and out and all the time bodily in the wind. I went out swiftly, all of myself, and I knew I was dead and that it had all been a mistake to think you just died. Then I floated, and instead of going on I felt myself slide back. I breathed and I was back."[3]

There are many other examples.

- Social worker Avion Pailthorpe was surprised by "how clearly I felt myself to *be* myself without my body."
- Frances Barnshey said, "I couldn't see any kind of body belonging to me. I seemed to be mind and emotions only, but I felt more vital, more myself than I felt in my life at any time before or since."
- Ella Silver said, "I felt as if I didn't have a body, but was all mind."[4]

Without knowing the mechanics of this process, the inconsistency is hard to explain. Perhaps it's worth pointing out that no single feature of the classic near-death experience is found in every case. Nor do we expect absolute uniformity in any other human experience—certainly not in emotional experiences (everyone has a different story about how it feels to fall in love) and not even in experiences that may be analyzed in strictly medical terms (no two childbirths, heart attacks, cancer cases, or deaths are exactly the same).

Still, it would be nice if we could explain why some OBErs and NDErs perceive themselves in a recognizable body while others have no sense of a body at all. One possible answer is that the spirit body itself is only a "thought-form," an objectified mental image, much like the clothing that conveniently appears if the person wishes not to be naked. This line of reasoning leads us in the direction of my earlier book, *The Far Horizon*, which explores the rather tenuous line between objective and subjective reality. It even raises the question of the reality of our physical body, which may also be construed as a kind of thought-form. From there, we might consider the possibility that all of our experience, whether on Earth or beyond, consists of objectified mental imagery. At that point we've entered the realm of Immanuel Kant, the philosopher who posited a noumenal realm of pure reality and a phenomenal realm of reality as processed and interpreted by the mind.

In the present book, I'm trying not to go that far afield; accordingly, I treat the spirit body and related phenomena in terms of what might be called, philosophically, "naïve realism." When we come up against inconsistencies like the one I've just pointed out, the weakness of this approach is revealed. Its advantage, however, is simplicity. Instead of getting bogged down in Kantian metaphysics, we can treat the whole process as relatively straightforward. This is not necessarily true, but it's just easier to think of it that way.

Similarities and differences

There are other variations in the accounts I've presented. Sometimes the person is aware of the process of separation.

- I saw myself leave my body, coming out through my head and shoulders (McMillan & Brown)
- She had found herself slipping out of her material body (Crookall 1920)
- I could feel myself moving out of my body (Moody)
- A solid gray mist gathered around me, and I left my body (Moody)
- he felt himself gradually rising from his body, with the distinct feeling that he had been divided (Ackley)

At other times, a momentary blackout intervenes, and the person simply finds himself out of his body.

- He fell into a semi-conscious condition and suddenly found himself away from his body (Thomas)
- To my surprise, I found myself looking at myself lying on the bed (Crookall 1935)

In OBEs, the same two possibilities apply. Some OBEs begin with "the realistic sense of separating or floating from the body … On the other hand, in cases when there was no transition, there was a blackout period followed by suddenly finding themselves in a different location" (Treasure).

Usually, the spirit form emerges from the head of the physical body.

- a sort of fleecy steam-cloud, about three feet above the bosom ... proceeded upward to the head (Davis)
- after several tugs, the misty head separated from the body's head (Wehner)
- The head becomes intensely brilliant ... the silver cord also becomes more alive; etheric matter flows over it (Hampton)
- streaming from the head of the physical body (Hout)

There can be apparent exceptions, but these should be interpreted with caution. Consider Crookall's 1920 case of a woman who "found herself slipping out of her material body through her feet." Any first sight, this seems like a clear contradiction, but not if we look at Wehner's observation of his mother's death: "A misty blue-white form, the counterpart of my mother's, but radiant, like a blue-white diamond's flame, was slowly rising from her body on the bed. This form lifted at an angle, the feet rising higher than the head, which remained attached to the physical head. The form now seemed to try to free itself, and after several tugs, the misty head separated from the body's head."

In Wehner's account, the spirit initially emerged from the feet, but the final separation was accomplished via the head.

The connection between the spirit form and the physical body is typically described as either a single cord or a series of cords or threads. These are luminous and silvery.

- At all times until the completion of the process, the vaporous form was attached to the physical body "by a strong psychical cord ... a sort of linea alba tube" (Davis)
- the silver cord also becomes more alive; etheric matter flows over it like a rapidly moving fluorescent light, but imperceptibly extracting the life force more and more, somewhat as a suction. Where the silver cord joins the main nerve ganglia it consists of thousands of very fine threads. As the life forces flow back into the higher world, those threads begin to break (Hampton)
- An umbilical cord united [the spirit body] with the physical body ... The silver cord began to stretch ... until at last it snapped (Oaten)

- a silverlike substance that was streaming from the head of the physical body to the head of the spirit "double." Then I saw the connection-cord between the two bodies … Just where it met the physical body it spread out, fanlike, and numerous little strands separated and attached separately to the skull base. But other than at the attachments, the cord was round, being perhaps an inch in diameter. The color was a translucent luminous silver radiance. (Hout)
- saw his own "silver cord" (Urquhart)
- It reminded me of the oft-mentioned 'silver cord (Staver)
- I could see I was attached by a light grey rope. (Carney)
- with the distinct feeling that he had been divided, though the parts retained a tenuous connecting link of some sort (Ackley)

But not all accounts, either of OBEs or NDEs, include the silver cord. In general, this detail is reported more often in OBEs, possibly because the OBEr, concerned with returning to his physical body once the experience is over, naturally wants to make sure he is still "connected." The NDEr, on the other hand, typically has no interest in returning to the body and, in fact, finds the very idea distasteful or even repellent.

Regardless of individual variations, I think we can see an overall similarity among the various accounts. The spirit body, when it is perceived, is described as initially vaporous or semi-vaporous …

- The "body" leaving me was not exactly in vapor form, yet it seemed to expand very slightly once it was clear of me. It was somewhat transparent (McMillan & Brown)
- a solid gray mist gathered around me, and I left my body (Moody)
- Words and phrases which have been used by various subjects include a mist, a cloud, smoke-like, a vapor, transparent, a cloud of colors, wispy (Moody)
- I saw the spirit form take shape above the dead body, in appearance a glorified replica of it (Snell)
- As it ascended, it separated, and expanded into a sort of fleecy steam-cloud … This spiritual cloud [looked] initially like an inverted pyramid (Davis)
- A misty blue-white form (Wehner)
- Its appearance is that of a bluish-white mist. (Hampton)
- I saw a faint, smokelike vapor … a stream of vapor (Oaten)

- a vague outline of a hazy, foglike substance … a mist held suspended … very gradually there grew into my sight a denser, more solid, condensation of this inexplicable vapor … and soon I saw this foglike substance was assuming a human form (Hout)
- it forms like a luminous vapor (Stringfellow)
- she had come out of her body in a vaporous form (Shanti Deva)

… luminous and often bluish, bluish-white, or silver …

- I seemed to be translucent, of a bluish cast (Wiltse)
- being in the spirit and very luminous, like an electric light (Crookall 1920)
- the radiant spirit face (Snell)
- radiant, like a blue-white diamond's flame (Wehner)
- The head becomes intensely brilliant; it is like a golden bowl … [The etheric body's appearance] is that of a bluish-white mist (Hampton)
- The color [of the cord] was a translucent luminous silver radiance. The cord seemed alive with vibrant energy. I could see the pulsations of light stream along the course of it. (Hout)
- I have … heard the [first energy body in an OBE] described as translucent, iridescent, or star-like (Treasure)

… and weightless.

- I had an airy feeling that's almost indescribable. I felt like a feather (Moody)
- I was sort of floating about five feet above the street (Moody)
- I started rising up, slowly … I drifted on up … I stopped, floating right below the ceiling, looking down. I felt almost as though I were a piece of paper that someone had blown up to the ceiling (Moody)
- I had a floating sensation as I felt myself get out of my body (Moody)
- They were weightless, usually "floating" or "drifting" (Moody)
- the freed form righted itself in the air (Wehner)

- she floated away (Oaten)
- the spirit body, which had been supine before, now rose (Hout)
- I twirled so fast up in the air, so free, no pain, weightless (Wood)
- I felt my soul or something coming right out of my body ... It flew around and then came back (Hemingway)

The spirit body is also weightless in OBEs.

- I think of floating and feel myself lift up and out of my physical body. I feel light as a feather and float slowly upward (Buhlman)
- I separate and float up to the ceiling. (Buhlman)
- I float up and out of my body and hover several feet above (Buhlman)
- It feels as if I'm weightless and floating like a cloud (Buhlman)
- she floats out to the ceiling and watches her body (Amie)

The spirit body in both NDEs and OBEs passes through solid matter.

- others would pass where I stood. They seemed to go right through me and still not interfere with me in the least (Brown)
- I could feel myself moving out of my body and sliding down between the mattress and the rail on the side of the bed—actually it seemed as if I went *through* the rail—on down to the floor (Moody)
- Extending my arm, I reached for the wall in front of me. I stared in amazement as my hand actually entered the wall; I could feel the vibrational energy of it as if I was touching its very molecular structure (Buhlman)

Once in the spirit body, the person on the verge of death often hovers horizontally and looks down upon his or her physical body.

- I left my body and saw it quite clearly lying motionless (Crookall 1941)
- To my surprise, I found myself looking at myself lying on the bed (Crookall 1935)

- I was sort of floating about five feet above the street ... I could see my own body in the wreckage (Moody)
- I stopped, floating right below the ceiling, looking down (Moody)
- I looked back and I could see myself on the bed below (Moody)
- The astral body hung suspended horizontally a few feet above the physical counterpart (Hout)
- he now appeared to be in a position slightly above his lifeless physical body, looking down on it (Ackley)

This is equally true of those having OBEs.

- Glancing down, I noticed a large lump in my bed. Amazed, I could see that it was the sleeping form of my physical body silently facing the wall (Buhlman)
- In seconds I float up and out of my body and hover several feet above (Buhlman)
- she floats out to the ceiling and watches her body (Amie)
- I was looking down at a figure lying face down on the floor. I seemed to be quite high up ... then I realized the body was mine (Rogo)

Less often in either case, the spiritual body is oriented vertically.

- she stood at the foot of the bed, looking back on her body (Crookall 1920)
- I saw my body in the water about three or four feet away ... I viewed my body from the back and slightly to the right side (Moody)
- This spiritual cloud, looking initially like an inverted pyramid (Davis)

This inconsistency is resolved in some accounts in which the spirit body takes form horizontally, but once the silver cord—or the last of many small cords or strands of webbing—is broken, the body tilts or rights itself, or drops and then rises, in either case finally standing erect or hovering vertically.

- I found myself lying horizontally above my body and about two feet from it ... With no effort on my part I moved off

- from over my body and stood upon my feet (Brown)
- I could feel myself moving out of my body and sliding down ... to the floor. Then, I started rising up, slowly (Crookall)
- This form lifted at an angle, the feet rising higher than the head, which remained attached to the physical head. The form now seemed to try to free itself, and after several tugs, the misty head separated from the body's head, and the freed form righted itself in the air exactly as a log rights itself after it has been dropped into deep water (Wehner)
- The silver cord ... snapped and the floating form assumed an upright attitude (Oaten)
- The last connecting strand of the silver cord snapped and the spirit body was free. The spirit body, which had been supine before, now rose (Hout)
- Determined to stand, I began to move effortlessly to the foot of my bed ... Standing, I quickly touched my arms and legs, checking to see if I was solid, and to my surprise I was completely solid, completely real (Buhlman)

In most cases, the spiritual form, once fully developed, subjectively appears solid and lifelike, regardless of its ability to pass through physical obstacles. This is true in NDEs and OBEs.

- he found himself whole again (Ackley)
- Standing, I quickly touched my arms and legs, checking to see if I was solid, and to my surprise I was completely solid, completely real (Buhlman)
- The [first] energy-body ... is much denser, almost physical when compared with the lightness of the second energy-body ... the first (dense) nonphysical body is actually an energy duplicate of the physical (Buhlman)

Moreover, this lifelike form, whether connected with an OBE or NDE, can sometimes be perceived by one or more observers.

- always, immediately after the physical life had ceased, I saw the spirit form take shape above the dead body, in appearance a glorified replica of it (Snell)
- the patient's spirit flowed through the cord "with lightning rapidity and vividness," forming a full-sized, "perfect" replica of the patient's body (Davis)

- this foglike substance was assuming a human form ... Soon I knew that the body I was seeing resembled that of the physical body of my aunt ... I continued to watch and ... the Spirit Body now seemed complete to my sight. I saw the features plainly ... With each pulsation the spirit body became more alive and denser (Hout)
- The elder Miss Verity told him that his apparition had suddenly appeared in her room the previous night ... Her sister ... also saw the apparition ... At 12:00 Miss Verity had seen the apparition once again. [It] suddenly appeared, entered her room, walked up to her, stroked her hair, and then disappeared (Beard)
- As the apparition passed between my bed and the lamp I had a full view of it; it was unmistakable (Marchant)
- He ... saw his friend, F.L., standing before him ... his hat with a black band, his overcoat unbuttoned, and a stick in his hand (N.J.S.)
- saw Joseph standing at the door, looking at me with great earnestness, his head bandaged up, a dirty night-cap on, and a dirty white garment on (Collyer)
- I then saw Mrs. de Fréville leaning on the rails, dressed ... in a coal-scuttle bonnet, black jacket with deep crape, and black dress (Bard)
- Vincent was sitting on the end of my bed and telling me not to cry anymore and that it was all over and that he was finally at peace (1989)
- she saw the likeness of ... Mary Goffe come out of the next chamber [and stand] by her bedside for about a quarter of an hour (Tilson)
- found them all sitting up in their beds in great excitement and the like. "Mama has been there!" they cried (Fox)

Perhaps most important, the experience of being out of the body is generally perceived as natural, painless, even pleasant, and sometimes joyous.

- It all seemed perfectly natural (Crookall 1941)
- She rejoiced to find herself in full possession of all mental and spiritual faculties and identity (Crookall 1920)
- I had an airy feeling that's almost indescribable (Moody)
- there was no fear (Moody)
- no trace of suffering or disease appeared upon the radiant spirit face (Snell)

- When a dying person says: "Everything is becoming clear; my mind is more lucid than it has ever been," we may know that the transition is taking place (Hampton)
- I saw the features plainly. They were very similar to the physical face, except that a glow of peace and vigor was expressed instead of age and pain. The eyes were closed as though in tranquil sleep … The closed eyes opened and a smile broke from the radiant features. She gave a smile of farewell (Hout)
- Death is not so bad a thing after all (Ackley)
- She described seeing four men in saffron robes who had come for her, a beautiful garden and a river (Shanti Deva)
- a serene feeling of calm (Buhlman)
- I twirled so fast up in the air, so free, no pain, weightless … Now I am not so afraid of death. I … was so disappointed that I came back (Wood)
- Dying is a very simple thing (Hemingway)
- how clearly I felt myself to *be* myself without my body (Pailthorpe)
- I felt more vital, more myself than I felt in my life at any time before or since (Barnshey)

In *Light and Death*, physician Michael Sabom recounts the case of a woman named Marty, who had a pulmonary embolism and lost consciousness. Note that she experienced leaving the body via the head, as seems typical.

> I felt a tremendous vacuum pulling me up. The force was so strong that it was pulling me from my head and I could not pull back.
>
> I remember thinking, *Well this is great*, because up to this point I had been hooked up to monitors, ripping out IVs, and I was in a lot of pain. I couldn't even lift my head off the pillow I was so weak.
>
> But now I felt great—better than I had ever felt. There was no pain, and I remember thinking, *I'm going to go with this. This is wonderful.*
>
> Then all of a sudden something kicked in and told me that this was it: I was dying. I knew it, but it wasn't a sad experience, it was wonderful. I never thought how young I was, about my two children, or my husband. I just wanted to go with this wonderful, wonderful feeling.[5]

Overall, the pattern observed is reasonably consistent. In the following summary, Robert Crookall recapitulates what we already know about the spirit double and looks ahead to later phases of the experience:

> Contrary to what one would expect, no one described pain or fear as having been caused by leaving the body—everything seemed perfectly natural. The persons concerned, moreover, commonly realized that the "double" was the primary body for thought and feeling, while the physical body (with which we all normally, and not unnaturally, tend to identify ourselves) was merely a secondary, and a temporary, instrument via which earth-life is rendered possible. Consciousness, as it operated through the separated "double," was more extensive than in ordinary life (when it operates first through the "double" and then through the physical body with its sense organs): There were sometimes telepathy, clairvoyance, and foreknowledge. "Dead" friends were often seen.
>
> Many of the deponents expressed great reluctance to re-enter the body and so return to earth-life ... As the "double" did reassociate with the body, there was a "blackout" in consciousness similar to that which had occurred at the beginning of the experience, when they dissociated.[6]

Conclusion

A large number of objective and subjective reports, contemporary and historical, agree that a spiritual body leaves the physical body at or near the point of death, and sometimes on other occasions.

CHAPTER FOUR:
Perception outside the Body

IN SOME CASES the earliest stage of separation is characterized by confusion or bleariness, often explained as the continuing hold of the physical body on the spiritual one. An example is this communication from the 1930s, via the medium Gladys Osborne Leonard.

> You will understand that there must have been a short period of unconsciousness before the actual end. It was during that period ... that I knew they [i.e., departed loved ones] were with me. It was like a very wonderful dream. I was not fully awake to the strangeness of it, because I was still too blurred by contact with the physical. Yet spiritually and mentally I was very much at peace.[1]

But at least as often, if not more often, there is no confusion—quite the opposite. In these cases the spirit body immediately exhibits a heightened awareness of every detail. Many NDEs cited by Kenneth Ring make it clear that the subject's perception was heightened and enhanced, sometimes verging on an omniscient perspective.

Take the case of Craig, who had an NDE when he nearly drowned. Describing the event, he wrote,

> All of a sudden, I noticed a floating sensation, as if I were rising. I was shocked to find that I was floating upwards into the open air above the river. I remember vividly the scene of the water level passing before my eyes. Suddenly I could see and hear as never before. The sound of a waterfall was so crisp and clear that it just cannot be explained by words. Earlier that year, my right ear had been injured when somebody threw an M-80 into a bar where I was listening to a band, and it exploded right next to my head. But now I could hear perfectly clearly, better than I ever had before. My sight was even more beautiful. Sights that were close in distance were as clear as those far away, and this was at the same moment, which astounded me. There was no

blurriness in my vision whatsoever. I felt as if I had been limited by my physical senses all these years, and that I had been looking at a distorted picture of reality.[2]

A similar report of enhanced perception was given by a man who had an out-of-body experience (not an NDE) while dancing on stage.

> Suddenly, without a moment's warning, I found myself in steel rafters near the ceiling of the room. I was aware of the gloom of the girders rising up through the shadows, and looking down on the spectacle below, I was startled to see that my vision had changed: I could see everything in the room—every hair on every head, it seemed—all at the same time. I took it all in, in a single omnipresent glance: hundreds of heads arranged in wavering rows of portable chairs, a half-dozen babies sleeping in laps, hairs of many different colors, shining from the light on stage. Then my attention shifted to the stage, and there we were in multicolored leotards, whirling about in our dance, and there I was—there I was—face-to-face with [his dancing partner].[3]

Compare this to a woman with pneumonia who lost consciousness:

> I was hovering over a stretcher in one of the emergency rooms at the hospital. I glanced down at the stretcher, knew the body wrapped in blankets was mine, and really didn't care. The room was much more interesting than my body. And what a neat perspective. I could see everything. And I do mean everything! I could see the top of the light on the ceiling, and the underside of the stretcher. I could see tiles on the ceiling and the tiles on the floor, simultaneously: three hundred degree spherical vision. And not just spherical. Detailed! I could see every single hair and the follicle out of which it grew on the head of the nurse standing beside the stretcher. At the time, I knew exactly how many hairs there were to look at. But I shifted focus. She was wearing glittery white nylons. Every single shimmer and sheen stood out in glowing detail, and once again, I knew exactly how many sparkles there were.[4]

P.M.H. Atwater had three NDEs and later became an NDE researcher herself. In *We Live Forever* she describes her second experience, which began when she passed out from a burst blood clot.

> I simultaneously saw and experienced my body as it lay supine, face up, on the dining-room floor ... I witnessed myself in spirit form begin to lift ...
>
> I floated up to the light fixture [on the ceiling] ... I noted how superbright everything was and how much better my faculties worked ... I floated back down to the body on the floor and hovered, studying the body shell I had once inhabited.

She adds, "It's as if I suddenly had 360-degree, X-ray vision, and I could see everything all at once, inside and outside."[5]

In *Dying to be Me*, Anita Moorjani writes,

> Although my physical eyes were closed, I seemed to be acutely aware of every minute detail that was taking place around me and beyond. The sharpness of my perception was even more intense than if I'd been awake and using my physical senses. I seemed to just know and understand everything—not only what was going on around me, but also what everyone was feeling, as though I were able to see and feel through each person ...
>
> I began to feel weightless and to become aware that I was able to be anywhere at any time ... and this didn't seem unusual. It felt normal, as though this were the real way to perceive things.[6]

Anita also somehow overheard a dialogue between her husband and a doctor many yards down the hall, well outside her normal range of hearing. She even perceived the fact that her brother was on an airplane flying to see her. We'll look at other examples of "veridical NDEs" momentarily.

Here are two examples of enhanced perception in NDEs from Robert Crookall's files:

- Case No. 767—Mrs. Olga Adler. "I saw my husband and baby. Somehow I could not bring myself to look down at my own bed because, if my body were lying there, I didn't want to see it. I looked up instead and, strangely enough, the roof was no longer there—I could see outdoors: my vision had somehow expanded and sharpened ... Everything was clear and beautiful."
- Case No. 776—Mary Swainson. "I was seventeen and at boarding school at the time of a severe 'flu epidemic. When my temperature rose to 105°, they moved me to a

separate room for I was seriously ill. I remember the experience of delirium. I mention this because a part of me was aware of my state as being confused, and it was completely different from what happened next. I then came out of my body, not only into clear consciousness, but into a more intense livingness than anything I had previously experienced. There was an awareness of expansion, of immense well-being and clarity, of joy and meaning. I remember thinking, 'If this is death, how wonderful, how easy, how natural.'"[7]

Janice Holden, a professor at the University of North Texas, distributed a questionnaire to people who had reported NDEs that included awareness of their physical surroundings. She received 63 replies.

Seventy-nine percent of her sample reported having clear visual perceptions, and a comparable percentage also stated that it was distortion-free, in color, and involved ... a panoramic field of vision. Furthermore, 61% of her cases claim that they had a complete and accurate memory of the physical environment, and a like percentage even said they could read during [the out-of-body portion of their NDE]![8]

Eyeless vision in NDEs

People who suffer from poor vision suddenly find themselves seeing perfectly in an NDE. Kenneth Ring reports the NDE of Harold Jaffe, who at age 21 underwent surgery during the Korean War. In a terse, elliptical style, Jaffe recalls his experience:

Spinal column surgery ... Ineffective spinal anesthesia in midsurgery required rapid use of gas/shots from a panic situation. I heard later that the combination "went green," i.e. sour. I recall lapsing into unconsciousness (having been awake and alert during the first hour of surgery). I "sensed" my heart stopping—thought, "HEY, you guys are losing me." The next moment I was "floating" against the canvas roof of the O.R. tent, looking down on "me" stretched out on the table, face down, still being operated on.

The surgeon was alerted to cardiac arrest; several people shouted at once. A heavy, muscular black Air Force sergeant rushed in on call. "I'm not clean, sir," he said. "To hell with that, flip this man over!" He waited for a second for the surgeon to pack the wound, then fork-lifted me onto my back. I clearly "saw" an x-shaped scar on the top of the sergeant's scalp—even though my vision without glasses is 20/400. The medical team frantically worked on my body to resuscitate me. I saw the anesthesiologist (female, lieutenant, Air Force) wiping tears, shaking her head, saying, "[expletives] he's gone!" I "yelled" to her that I was still here, but she couldn't hear me ...

I felt myself being sucked back. Many days later I regained consciousness ... Weeks later I spoke of my experience to my surgeon, hoping he wouldn't think I was crazy and declare me Section 8. Surprised that I could describe every detail of my "death" and [be] aware of the black corpsman's x-shaped scar on his scalp, my doctor only shrugged and said, "Well, nothing surprises me anymore."[9]

Ring also quotes a 48-year-old woman with even worse eyesight, who suffered postsurgical complications in 1974.

Bang, I left! The next thing I was aware of was floating on the ceiling. And seeing him [i.e., her doctor] down there, with his hat on his head, I knew who he was because of the hat ... It was so vivid. I'm very nearsighted, too, by the way, which was another one of the startling things that happened when I left my body. I see at fifteen feet what most people see at four hundred ... They were hooking me up to a machine that was behind my head. And my very first thought was, "Jesus, I can see! I can't believe it, I can see!" I could read the numbers on the machine behind my head and I was just so thrilled ...

Things were enormously clear and bright ... From where I was looking, I could look down on this enormous fluorescent light ... And it was so dirty on top of the light ... I was floating above the light fixture ... and it was filthy. And I remember thinking, "Got to tell the nurses about that." [10]

The woman said that, upon her recovery, she was allowed to return to the operating room, where she confirmed that the numbers were correct. Unfortunately, the only person she told was her anesthesiologist, who had since relocated, and Ring was not able to find him.

Even more intriguing are cases of patients who are actually blind, yet who report visual perceptions in their NDEs. Kenneth Ring and Sharon Cooper wrote a whole book on this subject, *Mindsight*. One of their cases involved Brad Barrows, blind from birth because of a prenatal defect. In 1968, while residing at the Boston Center for Blind Children, eight-year-old Brad became feverish and suddenly had trouble breathing.

> He became aware that he was slowly lifting up from the bed. "It was," he said, "as if my being was slowly floating up through the room." He remembers, when he was close to the ceiling, seeing his apparently lifeless body on the bed. He also saw his blind roommate get up from his bed and leave the room to get help. (His roommate later confirmed this, Brad said.)
>
> Next, he found that he was able to penetrate the second floor ceiling of his room and ... soon found that he "was going straight up toward the roof of the building, actually up and over it." ... Once he had emerged from the building, he discovered that he could see quite clearly ...
>
> He noticed that the sky was cloudy and dark. There had been a snowstorm the day before, and Brad could see snow everywhere except for the streets that had been plowed, though they were still slushy. Brad could also observe the snow banks that the plows had created. He saw a streetcar go by. Finally, he recognized the playground used by the children of his school and a particular hill he used to climb nearby.
>
> When asked if he "knew or saw" these things, he said, "I clearly visualized them. I could suddenly notice them and see them ... I remember ... being able to see quite clearly."[11]

Helen Keller fully expected to see in the next life, as she explained in her 1927 book *My Religion*:

> My faith never wavers that each dear friend I have "lost" is a new link between this world and the happier land beyond the morn ... I cannot understand why anyone should fear death. Life here is more cruel than death. Life divides and estranges, while death, which at heart is life eternal, reunites and reconciles. I believe that when the eyes within my physical eyes shall open upon the world to come, I shall simply be consciously living in the country of my heart.[12]

Out-of-body perception can go far beyond the ordinary senses. Raymond Moody relates the story of a doctor in South Dakota who was involved in a minor car accident on his way to the hospital. Still worrying about possible legal consequences, he arrived at the ER, where he resuscitated a man in cardiac arrest.

The next day, the man he had rescued told him a remarkable story: "While you were working on me, I left my body and watched you work." ...

In precise detail, he told the doctor how the instruments looked and even in what order they were used. He described the colors of the equipment, shapes, and even settings of dials on the machines.

But what finally convinced this young cardiologist that the man's experience was genuine was when he said, "Doctor, I could tell that you were worried about that accident. But there isn't any reason to be worried about things like that. You give your time to other people. Nobody is going to hurt you."

Not only had this patient picked up on the physical details of his surroundings, he had also read the doctor's mind.[13]

Verifiable details in NDEs

As we've seen in more than one case, it's sometimes possible to verify the observations made during an NDE.

A 49-year-old man had a heart attack so severe that after 35 minutes of vigorous resuscitation efforts, the doctor gave up and began filling out the death certificate. Then someone noticed a flicker of life, so the doctor continued his work with the paddles and breathing equipment and was able to restart the man's heart.

The next day, when he was more coherent, the patient was able to describe in great detail what went on in the emergency room. This surprised the doctor. But what astonished him even more was the patient's vivid description of the emergency room nurse who hurried into the room to assist the doctor.

He described her perfectly, right down to her wedge hairdo and her last name, Hawkes. He said that she rolled this cart down the hall with a machine that had what looked like two Ping-Pong paddles on it (an electroshocker that is basic resuscitation equipment).

When the doctor asked him how he knew the nurse's name and what she had been doing during his heart attack, he said that he had left his body and—while walking down the hall to see his wife—passed right through nurse Hawkes. He read the name tag as he went through her, and remembered it so he could thank her later.[14]

While veridical NDEs constitute a small minority of documented cases, a fair number have been reported over the years. Some have even become famous. One of the best-known involves Maria's shoe.

The case was reported by Seattle social worker Kimberly Clark. A migrant farm worker named Maria, hospitalized at Harborview Medical Center, told Clark that during cardiac arrest she left her body and ascended to the third floor, where she observed a running shoe inexplicably left on a ledge. Clark was curious enough to investigate. She discovered that the shoe was in fact there, and that it matched Maria's description. Moreover, because of its position on the ledge, it could not be clearly seen through the window. Clark writes,

> The only way she could have had such a perspective was if she had been floating right outside and at very close range to the tennis shoe. I retrieved the shoe and brought it back to Maria; it was very concrete evidence for me.[15]

Oddly enough, this is not the only veridical NDE with a shoe as its focus. A 1985 case involved a woman at Hartford Hospital who had been resuscitated. Kathy Milne, the nurse who investigated the case, reports:

> She told me how she floated up over her body, viewed the resuscitation effort for a short time, and then felt herself being pulled up through several floors of the hospital. She then found herself above the roof and realized she was looking at the skyline of Hartford. She marveled at how interesting this view was, and out of the corner of her eye, she saw a red object. It turned out to be a shoe ...
>
> I was relating this to a resident, who, in a mocking manner, left. Apparently, he got a janitor to get him onto the roof. When I saw him later that day, he had a red shoe and became a believer, too.[16]

In a follow-up investigation, Kenneth Ring asked Milne whether she had ever heard of the case of Maria's shoe. She had not.

There's yet another shoe-related incident. In 1982, a nurse named Joyce Harman

> returned from work after a vacation. On that vacation, she had purchased a new pair of plaid shoelaces, which she happened to

be wearing on her first day back at the hospital. That day, she was involved in resuscitating a patient, a woman she didn't know. The resuscitation was successful, and the next day, Harmon chanced to see the patient ...

The patient, upon seeing Harmon, volunteered, "Oh, you're the one with the plaid shoelaces!"

"What?" Harmon replied, astonished. She says she distinctly remembers feeling the hair on her neck rise.

"I saw them," the woman continued. "I was watching what was happening yesterday when I died. I was up above."[17]

From the 1970s comes an evidential case not involving footwear. A clinical instructor named Sue Saunders

> was helping in the emergency room to resuscitate a sixty-ish man whose electrocardiogram had gone flat. Medics were shocking him repeatedly, with no results. Saunders was trying to give him oxygen. In the middle of the resuscitation, someone else took over for her and she left.
>
> A couple of days later, she encountered this patient in the cardiac unit. He spontaneously commented, "You looked so much better in your yellow top."
>
> She, like Harmon, was so shocked at this remark she got goosebumps, for she *had* been wearing a yellow smock that day.
>
> "Yeah," the man continued, "I saw you. You had something over my face, and you were pushing air into me. And I saw your yellow smock."
>
> Saunders confirmed that she had had something over her face—a mask—and that she had worn the yellow smock while trying to give him oxygen, while he was unconscious and without a heartbeat.[18]

A man named Howard, who suffered cardiac arrest and had to be resuscitated, described an NDE that took place while he was unconscious:

> I felt myself rising up through the ceiling and it was like I was going through the structure of the building. I could feel the different densities of passing through insulation. I saw wiring, some pipes and then I was in this other room.
>
> It looked like a hospital but it was different ... It was very quiet and it seemed like no one was there. There were individual

rooms all around the edge and on some of the beds were these people, except they were not people, exactly. They looked like mannequins and they had IVs hooked up to them but they didn't look real. In the center was an open area that looked like a collection of work stations with computers.

Dr. Lauren Bellg, a critical care physician, describes herself as stunned when she heard this. She writes,

> I stole a look at the nurse who looked equally surprised. What we knew that Howard didn't, is that right above the ICU is a nurse-training center where new hires spend a few days rotating through different scenarios. There are simulated hospital rooms around the perimeter with medical mannequins on some of the beds. In the center there is indeed a collection of workspaces with computers.[19]

The patient also repeated statements made by Bellg during the resuscitation effort, when he was being defibrillated, and accurately reported who was present during the event.

Michael Sabom recalls an interview with Pete Morton, a 53-year-old Air Force veteran:

> He told me he had left his body during his first cardiac arrest and had watched the resuscitation. When I asked him to tell me what exactly he saw, he described the resuscitation with such detail and accuracy that I could have later used the tape to teach physicians.
>
> Pete remembered seeing a doctor's first attempt to restore his heart. "He struck me. And I mean he really whacked me. He came back with his fist from way behind his head and he hit me right in the center of my chest." Pete remembered them inserting a needle into his chest in a procedure that he said looked like "one of those Aztec Indian rituals where they take the virgin's heart out." He even remembered thinking that when they shot him they gave him too much voltage. "Man, my body jumped about two feet off the table."[20]

The last detail is significant because, even today, and certainly at the time of Sabom's investigation, Hollywood depictions of CPR would not show the patient jumping "two feet off the table," although in real life this does happen.

In his memoir, Bruce Greyson recounts this highly evidential NDE:

> Jack Bybee was hospitalized with severe pneumonia at age 26, in his native South Africa ...
>
> "I had been taken very ill, and was three to four weeks in an oxygen tent... I was friendly (read 'flirting,' when I could be) with a nurse from the farmlands of the Western Cape. She had told me it was her twenty-first birthday that weekend, and that her parents were coming in from the country to celebrate. She fluffed up my pillows, as she always did. I held her hand to wish her a happy birthday, and she left.
>
> "In my NDE, I met Nurse Anita on the other side. 'What are you doing here, Anita?' I asked. 'Why, Jack, I've come to fluff your pillows, of course, and to see that you are all right. But, Jack, you must return, go back. Tell my parents I'm sorry I wrecked the red MGB. Tell them I love them.'
>
> "Then Anita was gone—gone through and over a very green valley and through a fence, where, she told me, 'there is a garden on the other side. But you cannot see it. For you must return, while I continue through the gate.'
>
> "When I recovered, I told a nurse what Anita had said. This girl burst out into tears and fled the ward. I later learned that Anita and this nurse had been great friends. Anita had been surprised by her parents, who loved her dearly and had presented her with a red MGB sports car. Anita had jumped into the car, and in her excitement raced down the mountain, De Waal Drive, along the slopes of Table Mountain, into 'Suicide Corner' and a concrete telephone pole.
>
> "But I was 'dead' when all that happened. How could I possibly know these facts? I knew them as stated above. I was told by Anita in my experience."[21]

In 1938 E.L. Huffine crashed his private plane in a field. Later he recounted the experience in an article called "I Watched Myself Die." The excerpt begins immediately after the impact of the crash.

> Now comes the part of the experience which was so strange, and yet so beautiful. With that blow on my head, I was suddenly observing the whole scene from about fifty feet away from the plane. I saw Roselyn [his wife] struggling to unfasten the safety belt which still held her. Hot vapor burst from the engine. At last Roselyn pulled free onto the ground. There was another form on the ground too. I knew it was mine, but it did not

contain the consciousness with which I was observing all that was happening. Roselyn was dragging the body away from the smoking plane, but I watched with indifference.

It was such a profound revelation! I felt myself as clear as light. There was no sense of pain, only a feeling of completeness and well-being.

I saw cars pouring into the field from the highway, people milling about, talking excitedly. I could hear distinctly every word that was said. My attention was particularly drawn to a man and a woman far out at the edge of the crowd.

"Well, he must have been a wild one!" the woman was saying. "It's no more than he deserved! Only birds are supposed to fly!"

Huffine was revived by a friend who applied artificial respiration, shook him violently, and shouted his name. The friend helped him upright, and Huffine "felt a curious drive" to address the couple he had noticed earlier.

"I heard what you said about me," I told the woman.

The woman looked startled; they were standing well out of earshot from where my body had lain. "I didn't say anything."

I repeated what I had heard. She turned ashen and fled to her car.[22]

Probably the most famous veridical NDE is the Pam Reynolds case, first reported by Michael Sabom in *Light and Death*. Reynolds underwent a challenging surgical procedure that required stopping her heart and lowering her body temperature—in effect, putting her in a state of suspended animation almost indistinguishable from death. The deepest parts of her NDE *may* have occurred while she was in this condition, although it's impossible to be sure. The early part of her NDE, which included verifiable details, took place before her heart was stopped; even so, she was heavily sedated, her eyes masked, and her ears occluded with earplugs that made continuous loud clicking noises.

Reynolds told Sabom about the start of her NDE:

The next thing I recall was the sound: It was a natural *D*. [Reynolds was a professional musician.] As I listened to the sound, I felt it was pulling me out of the top of my head. The further out of my body I got, the more clear the tone became. I had the impression it was like a road, a frequency that you go on ... I remember seeing several things in the operating room when I was looking down. It was the most aware that I think that I have ever been in my entire life ... I was metaphorically sitting on Dr. Spetzler's shoulder. It was not like normal vision. It was brighter and more focused and clearer than normal vision ...

The [surgical] saw thing that I hated the sound of looked like an electric toothbrush and it had a dent in it, a groove at the top where the saw appeared to go into the handle, but it didn't ... And the saw had interchangeable blades, too, but these blades were in what looked like a socket wrench case.[23]

The description of the saw and its blades was correct, as were other highly specific details.

As we might expect after learning how far afield the double can travel, verifiable observations in an NDE are not limited to the person's immediate surroundings. Dr. Melvin Morse was on duty in the ER when seven-year-old Katie was brought in. She had been found floating face-down in a swimming pool, and though Morse was able to resuscitate her, she suffered from severe swelling of the brain and other injuries. Nevertheless, she made a full recovery.

Upon meeting Morse in his office, Katie

turned to her mother and said, "That's the one with the beard. First there was this tall doctor who didn't have a beard, and then he came in." Her statement was correct. The first into the emergency room was a tall, clean-shaven physician named Bill Longhurst.

Katie remembered more. "First I was in the big room, and then they moved me to a smaller room where they did X-rays on me." She accurately noted such details as having "a tube down my nose."

So far, this isn't much different from other cases we've looked at. But later in her NDE ...

Katie was given a glimpse of her home. She was allowed to wander throughout the house, watching her brothers and sisters play with their toys in their rooms. One of her brothers was playing with a G.I. Joe, pushing him around the room in a jeep. One of her sisters was combing the hair of a Barbie doll and singing a popular rock song. She drifted into the kitchen and watched her mother preparing a meal of roast chicken and rice.

Then she looked into the living room and saw her father sitting on the couch staring quietly ahead. She assumed he was worrying about her in the hospital.

Later, when Katie mentioned this to her parents, she shocked them with her vivid details about the clothing they were wearing, their positions in the house, even the food her mother was cooking.[24]

Conclusion

A wealth of testimony from more than one line of investigation indicates that the newly separated nonphysical body enjoys heightened sensory perceptions.

If this is so, we might expect supernormal perceptions even in people who have not yet left the body but are on the verge of doing so. As you'll see, this is exactly what we find.

CHAPTER FIVE:
Deathbed Visions

IN *CRIME AND PUNISHMENT*, Svidrigailov and Raskolnikov engage in a brief conversation about ghosts.

> "I didn't ask you whether you believe that ghosts are seen, but whether you believe that they exist."
>
> "No, I won't believe it!" Raskolnikov cried, with positive anger.
>
> "What do people generally say?" muttered Svidrigailov, as though speaking to himself, looking aside and bowing his head. "They say, 'You are ill, so what appears to you is only unreal fantasy.' But that's not strictly logical. I agree that ghosts only appear to the sick, but that only proves that they are unable to appear except to the sick, not that they don't exist."
>
> "Nothing of the sort," Raskolnikov insisted irritably.
>
> "No? You don't think so?" Svidrigailov went on, looking at him deliberately. "But what do you say to this argument (help me with it): ghosts are, as it were, shreds and fragments of other worlds, the beginning of them. A man in health has, of course, no reason to see them, because he is above all a man of this earth and is bound for the sake of completeness and order to live only in this life. But as soon as one is ill, as soon as the normal earthly order of the organism is broken, one begins to realize the possibility of another world; and the more seriously ill one is, the closer becomes one's contact with that other world, so that as soon as the man dies he steps straight into that world. I thought of that long ago. If you believe in a future life, you could believe in that, too."
>
> "I don't believe in a future life," said Raskolnikov.[1]

Svidrigailov is wrong on one point. As we've observed in cases of crisis apparitions, ghosts are not seen exclusively by people who are ill. Moreover, such experiences are by no means limited to occasions of crisis on the part of the dying or newly deceased. They can happen at any time. Through surveys and interviews, Erlendur Haraldsson determined that 14% of Icelanders had experienced visual apparitions of the dead, while another 17% reported auditory, olfactory, or tactile impressions.[2] A survey of the population of Charlottesville, Virginia, determined "that 7.5% of 622 respondents claimed to have had the visual impression of an apparition."[3]

Nor are such visions new, as C.V. Wedgwood reports, a tad sardonically, in her book *The Thirty Years War*.

> A prince of Anhalt, an intelligent and sober young man, recorded the seeing of phantoms in his diary without a flicker of surprise or incredulity. The Electoral family of Brandenburg believed firmly in the "White Lady" who appeared to warn them of approaching death and who on one occasion had dealt such a box on the ear to an officious page who had incommoded her that he died soon after.[4]

Nevertheless, Svidrigailov's basic argument seems logical enough. As the dying person releases his hold on life, it makes sense that he would open his perceptions to the new reality that awaits him. If so, he might be expected to see not only his own spirit form, but the spirits of others who've gone before him.

Such cases have been documented—many of them. Like crisis apparitions, they are common enough to have earned their own designation: "deathbed visions."

The first deathbed vision study by William Barrett, published in 1926, collected a number of intriguing accounts, not all of which were directly investigated. Here are some typical examples. A case that originally appeared in the journal *Light* in April, 1906, recounts the death of a young mother.

> "My first desire now is to go ... I see people moving—all in white. The music is strangely enchanting. Oh! here is Sadie; she is with me—and—she knows who I am." Sadie was a little girl she had lost about ten years before. "Sissy!" said the husband, "you are out of your mind." "Oh, dear! why did you call me here again?" said the wife, "now it will be hard for me to go away again; I was so pleased while there—it was so delightful—so soothing." In about three minutes the dying woman added, "I am going away again and will not come back to you even if you call me."
>
> This scene lasted for about eight minutes, and it was very plain that the dying wife was in full view of the two worlds at the same time, for she described how the moving figures looked in the world beyond, as she directed her words to mortals in this world.[5]

A certain Dr. Wilson of New York wrote of the death of a patient named James Moore:

> Then something which I shall never forget to my dying day happened, something which is utterly indescribable. While he appeared perfectly rational and as sane as any man I have ever seen, the only way that I can express it is that he was transported into another world ... He said in a stronger voice than he had used since I had attended him, "There is Mother! Why, Mother, have you come here to see me? No, no, I'm coming to see you. Just wait, Mother, I am almost over. I can jump it. Wait, Mother." On his face there was a look of inexpressible happiness, and the way in which he said the words impressed me as I have never been before.[6]

During a fatal bout of "bilious fever," ten-year-old Daisy Dryden of Yuba County, California, had visionary experiences that were unusually long-lasting and vivid.

> Two days before she left us, the Sunday School Super-intendent came to see her ... When he was about to leave, he said, "Well, Daisy, you will soon be over the 'dark river.'" After he had gone, she asked her father what he meant by the "dark river." He tried to explain it, but she said, "It is all a mistake; there is no river; there is no curtain; there is not even a line that separates this life from the other life." And she stretched out her little hands from the bed, and with the gesture said, "It is here and it is there; I know it is so, for I can see you all, and I see them there at the same time." We asked her to tell us something of that other world and how it looked to her, but she said, "I cannot describe it; it is so different, I could not make you understand."[7]

From deathbed visions of a century ago, we proceed to a case reported in 2021 by hospice social worker Scott Janssen. This one requires some backstory. Janssen's patient was an elderly World War II veteran who had been traumatized by the large loss of life during a particular combat operation. The night after this battle, unable to sleep, he had seen a man sitting on the end of his cot. "He was wearing a World War I uniform," the patient told Janssen, "with one of those funny helmets. He was covered in light, like he was glowing in the dark ... He was looking at me with love. I could feel it. I'd never felt that kind of love before." The patient somehow sensed that "all the pain and cruelty wasn't what was real." Instead, the reality was "that no matter how screwed-up and cruel the world looks, on some level, somehow, we are all loved. We are all connected."

There were a few other such visits by the same phantom figure, but they stopped when the war ended. Years later, the patient found an old family photo labeled *Uncle Calvin, killed during World War I, 1918*. "It was the same guy," the patient said.

But that wasn't the end of his story. While in hospice, the patient confided to Janssen, "He's back ... Saw him last night on the foot of my bed. He spoke this time ... He's going to help me over the hill when it's time to go."[8]

The New York Times ran an interesting piece by Jan Hoffman in 2016, detailing research into deathbed visions:

> Donna Brennan, a longtime nurse with Hospice Buffalo, recalled chatting on the couch with a 92-year-old patient with congestive heart failure. Suddenly, the patient looked over at the door and called out, "Just a minute, I'm speaking with the nurse."
>
> Told that no one was there, the patient smiled, saying it was Aunt Janiece (her dead sister) and patted a couch cushion, showing "the visitor" where to sit. Then the patient cheerfully turned back to Mrs. Brennan and finished her conversation."[9]

An old case, dating prior to 1918, also shows the ability of the dying to switch effortlessly between physical and nonphysical perceptions. Dr. E.H. Pratt describes the death of his baby sister Hattie:

> She knew she was passing away, and was telling our mother how to dispose of her little personal belongings among her close friends and playmates, when she suddenly raised her eyes as though gazing at the ceiling toward the farther side of the room, and after looking steadily and apparently listening for a short time, slightly bowed her head, and said, "Yes, Grandma, I am coming, only wait just a little while, please."
>
> Our father asked her, "Hattie, do you see your grandma?"
>
> Seemingly surprised at the question she promptly answered, "Yes, Papa, can't you see her? She is right there waiting for me." At the same time she pointed toward the ceiling in the direction in which she had been gazing. Again addressing the vision she evidently had of her grandmother, she scowled a little impatiently and said, "Yes, Grandma, I'm coming, but wait a minute, please."

She then turned once more to her mother, and finished telling her what of her personal treasures to give to different ones of her acquaintances. At last giving her attention once more to her grandma, who was apparently urging her to come at once, she bade each of us goodbye ... She then fixed her eyes steadily on her vision but so faintly that we could but just catch her words, said, "Yes, Grandma, I'm coming now."[10]

She died immediately afterward.

As noted by the *Times*, such cases illustrate a key difference between deathbed visions and delirium-produced hallucinations. A delirious patient cannot interact normally with the people around him, while a person having a deathbed vision is perfectly able to function on both levels at once. Moreover, delirium is characterized by agitation and fear, while deathbed visions are typically (though not invariably) experienced as calming, even joyful.

There are other differences. A recent study of deathbed visions in Ireland compared patients who were heavily medicated and/or suffering a fever with those who weren't. *The Irish Times* reports:

> One common sense explanation may be that the visions are drug- or fever-induced hallucinations. But 68 per cent of respondents agreed, or strongly agreed, that [deathbed visions] have different qualities from such hallucinations.
>
> [Researcher Una] MacConville says there appears to be a difference in the quality of the visions: they appear with greater clarity, and they are experienced as meaningful, with significant associations, rather than random, as they would be in drug-induced cases.[11]

The patients themselves nearly always regard the experience as real, a point made by the *New York Times* article:

> Nearly 90 percent of the patients in the studies reported having at least one near-death dream or vision, and 99 percent of those believed the dreams or visions to be real. About 50 percent of the experiences occurred while the person slept, 16 percent while they were awake, and the rest while both asleep and awake ...
>
> Previous studies suggest that as many as 60 percent of conscious dying patients experience end-of-life dreams and visions, but the actual number likely is higher because the

phenomenon is considered underreported by patients and family members for fear of embarrassment.[12]

Though some dying patients do hallucinate, especially when given certain medications, there is also evidence that the last moments of life can be accompanied by unusual clarity of thought. This phenomenon, known as terminal lucidity, is well known.

Michael Nahm and Bruce Greyson write: "In one study of end-of-life experiences, 70% of caregivers in a nursing home reported that during the past five years, they had observed patients with dementia becoming more lucid a few days before death. Members of another palliative care team confirmed that such incidents happen regularly."[13]

In another article, Michael Nahm observes the historical longevity of this belief: "Hippocrates, Plutarch, Cicero, Galen, Avicenna, and other scholars of classical times noted that symptoms of mental disorders decrease as death approaches ... All of them held the view that the soul remains basically intact when the brain is affected by physical malfunction and disturbance of the mind. Therefore, they believed that during and after death, the soul was freed from material constraints, regaining its full potential."[14]

I've been told of a few deathbed visions. In one case, a medical doctor described his father's recent death after an illness. In his last minutes, the father became visibly happy. He pointed into space and declared that "two men with white light around them" were "coming toward" him. "Right over there," he said, his demeanor reflecting complete peace. Immediately after this, he rested his head on the pillow and died. The doctor took great comfort in having witnessed this experience.

Verifiable deathbed visions

Comforting or not, such stories can always be dismissed as fantasies, no matter how real they seem to the patients. But what if the dying person sees a vision of someone not known to have died? Often called "Peak in Darien"[15] cases, such accounts are inherently more evidential.

At the start of his book, Barrett relates a story told to him by his wife, Lady Florence Barrett, a pioneering surgeon in an era when female physicians were nearly unknown. Her story involves a young woman, Mrs. B, who was dying of post-delivery complications.

She lay looking up towards the open part of the room, which was brightly lighted, and said, "Oh, don't let it get dark—it's getting so dark ... Darker and darker." Her husband and mother were sent for.

Suddenly she looked eagerly towards one part of the room, a radiant smile illuminating her whole countenance. "Oh, lovely, lovely," she said. I asked, "What is lovely?" "What I see," she replied in low, intense tones. "What do you see?" "Lovely brightness—wonderful beings." It is difficult to describe the sense of reality conveyed by her intense absorption in the vision.

Then—seeming to focus her attention more intently on one place for a moment—she exclaimed, almost with a kind of joyous cry, "Why, it's Father! Oh, he's so glad I'm coming; he is so glad. It would be perfect if only W (her husband) could come too."

Hospital matron Miriam Castle continues the story:

Her husband was leaning over her and speaking to her, when pushing him aside she said, "Oh, don't hide it; it's so beautiful." Then turning away from him towards me ..., Mrs. B said, "Oh, why there is my Vida," referring to a sister of whose death three weeks previously she had not been told. Afterwards the mother, who was present at the time, told me, as I've said, that Vida was the name of the dead sister of Mrs. B's, of whose illness and death she was quite ignorant, as they had carefully kept this news from Mrs. B owing to her serious illness.

The patient's mother Mary Clark confirmed this account, stating that the patient, with "rather a puzzled expression," turned to her and said, "He has Vida with him ... Vida is with him."[16]

Accounts like this are not rare even today. In their 1993 book *Final Gifts*, hospice nurses Maggie Callanan and Patricia Kelley report the case of an elderly Chinese lady, terminally ill with cancer, who

dreamed often of her husband, who had died some years before.

"I will join him soon," she said.

But one day [she] seemed very puzzled.

"Why is my sister with my husband?" she asked. "They are both calling me to come."

"Is your sister dead?" I asked.

"No, she still lives in China," she said. "I have not seen her for many years."

When I related this conversation to the daughter, she was astonished and tearful.

"My aunt died two days ago in China," [the daughter] said. "We decided not to tell Mother—her sister had the same kind of cancer."[17]

The same authors relate a case involving Peggy, a young woman dying of lymphoma, who seemed "bright, radiant, and ... unusually active" when she spoke to her nurse one day.

"Let me tell you what happened to me," Peggy said. "I was lying here in bed yesterday, sort of drifting in and out of sleep, and remembering back to a happy time in my childhood. My brother and I were taken in by my aunt during a time that my parents were having financial difficulty. I really loved my aunt, she was wonderful—so loving to both of us. It was just a very happy time for me. I still love her a lot. I woke up with a start when I felt a warm, caring hand on my shoulder. I looked around behind me and there was my aunt smiling at me as she touched me. It made me feel so good and safe."

"Where is your aunt?" the nurse asked.

"She lives in Massachusetts," Peggy said. "I haven't seen her in a long time because she's sick. But I felt her with me off and on all day; it made me feel so good! Last night my uncle called to say she died yesterday—and at the same time that I was first aware of her being with me! And then today I woke up and she was touching me again!"[18]

Bruce Greyson contributed an article to *Anthropology & Humanism*, a journal of the American Anthropological Association. "Seeing Dead People Not Known to Have Died" lists many veridical deathbed vision cases, more than I can list. The material in quotes consists of Dr. Greyson's summaries.

- One very early case was written up by Dr. Henry Atherton in 1680. The doctor's teenage sister, "who had been sick for a long time, was thought to have died. Indeed, the women attending to her saw no breath when they held a mirror to her mouth and saw no response when they put live coals to her feet. Nevertheless, the girl recovered and related a vision of visiting heaven, which her relatives dismissed as 'dream or fancy.' The girl then insisted that she had seen several people who had died after she had lost consciousness. One of those she named was thought to be still alive; however, her family subsequently sent out inquiries and confirmed that the girl was correct."

- In 1889 pioneering psi researchers Edmund Gurney and F.W.H. Myers "described the case of John Alkin Ogle, who, an hour before he died, saw his brother who had died 16 years earlier, calling him by name. Ogle then called out in surprise, 'George Hanley!'—the name of a casual acquaintance in a village forty miles away—before expiring. His mother, who was visiting from Hanley's village, then confirmed that Hanley had died ten days earlier, a fact that no one else in the room had known."

- Another early psi researcher, James Hyslop, wrote in 1908 about a case involving two children both suffering from diphtheria. "Jennie, age eight, died on a Wednesday, a fact that was intentionally kept hidden from her friend Edith. At noon on that Saturday, Edith selected two of her photographs to be sent to Jennie, providing evidence that she still thought Jennie to be alive. Shortly thereafter she lapsed into unconsciousness, but that evening she awakened and spoke of seeing deceased friends. Then suddenly she said to her father, in great surprise, 'Why, papa, I am going to take Jennie with me!' She then reached out her arms and said, 'O, Jennie, I'm so glad you are here,' lapsed back into unconsciousness, and died."

- In 1949, Natalie Kalmus, one of the developers of the Technicolor process, wrote about her sister Eleanor's deathbed vision. In her final moments, Eleanor "began calling out the names of deceased loved ones whom she was seeing. Just before she died, she also saw a cousin named Ruth and asked, 'What's she doing here?' Ruth had died unexpectedly the week before, and Eleanor, because of her condition, had not been told."[19]

If people on the verge of dying can see the newly deceased, what about people who actually do "die" and are resuscitated? This story was told to Raymond Moody, who later confirmed it with the physicians who attended the patient:

> I was terribly ill and near death with heart problems at the same time that my sister was near death in another part of the same hospital with a diabetic coma. I left my body and went into the corner of the room, where I watched them work on me down below.
>
> Suddenly, I found myself in conversation with my sister, who was up there with me. I was very attached to her, and we were having a great conversation about what was going on down there when she began to move away from me.
>
> I tried to go with her but she kept telling me to stay where I was. "It's not your time," she said. "You can't go with me because it's not your time." Then she just began to recede off into the distance through a tunnel while I was left there alone.
>
> When I awoke, I told the doctors [sic] that my sister had died. He denied it, but at my insistence, he had a nurse check on it. She had in fact died, just as I knew she did.[20]

Outside observers

How about people in attendance on the dying person? Though perfectly healthy themselves, do they ever see such visions? Yes, occasionally.

William Barrett quotes a letter to the Journal *Psychica*, by a certain Z.G., whose identity was known to the editor but withheld from the public.

> I lost my daughter when she was seventeen years of age; ... A fortnight before her death, one evening when I was leaning over the head of her bed, I asked her what she was thinking of, seeing her absorbed. She replied, "Little mother, look there," pointing to the bed-curtains. I followed the direction of her hand and saw a man's form, completely white, standing out quite clearly against the dark curtain ... I had the weakness to declare to her, "I see nothing"; but my trembling voice betrayed me doubtless, for the child added with an air of reproach, "Oh, little mother, I have seen the same thing for the last three days at the same hour; it's my dear father who has come to fetch me."[21]

Another case:

> Two women watching by their dying sister, Charlotte, saw a bright light and within it two young faces hovering over the

bed, gazing intently at Charlotte; the elder sister recognized these faces as being two of her brothers, William and John, who had died when she was young. The two sisters continue to watch the faces till they gradually "faded away like a washed-out picture," and shortly afterwards their sister Charlotte died.[22]

A more detailed and evidential case was provided by Professor W.C. Crosby. It involves Mrs. Carolyn Rogers, 72, a twice-married widow, and Mary Wilson, a professional nurse in attendance on her.

> Between 2 and 3 a.m., ... while she was resting on the settee, but wide awake, [Mrs. Wilson, the nurse] happened to look toward the door into the adjoining chamber and saw a man standing exactly in the doorway, the door being kept open all the time. He was middle-sized, broad-shouldered, with shoulders thrown back, had a florid complexion, reddish-brown hair (bareheaded) and beard, and wore a brown sack overcoat, which was unbuttoned. His expression was grave, neither stern nor pleasant, and he seemed to look straight at Mrs. Wilson, and then at Mrs. Rogers without moving. Mrs. Wilson supposed, of course, that it was a real man, [and] tried to think how he could have got into the house. Then, as he remained quite motionless, she began to realize that it was something uncanny, and becoming frightened, turned her head away and called her daughter, who was still asleep on the couch, wakening her. Looking back at the door after an interval of a minute or two the apparition had disappeared; both its coming and going were noiseless ...
>
> In the morning Mrs. Rogers' niece, Mrs. Hildreth, who lives in the neighborhood, and has known Mrs. R. and her family for many years, called at the house. Mrs. Wilson related her experience to her and asked if the apparition resembled Mr. Rogers, and Mrs. Hildreth replied emphatically that it did not. (All who knew Mr. Rogers are agreed on this point.) ... Mrs. Hildreth said that Mrs. Wilson's description agreed exactly with Mr. Tisdale, Mrs. Rogers' first husband. Mrs. Rogers came to Roslindale after marrying Mr. Rogers, and Mrs. Hildreth is the only person in that vicinity who ever saw Mr. Tisdale; and in Mrs. Rogers' house there is no portrait of him or anything suggestive of his personal appearance.[23]

To round things out, and as a reminder that not all final visions are joyous, here's a historical anecdote from Anthony Everitt's biography *Augustus*. After a long reign, the Roman emperor lay on his deathbed. "Just before he died, his wits seemed to wander, for he suddenly cried out in terror: 'Forty young men are carrying me off!'"[24]

The story can't be verified, but considering how many of his countrymen Augustus put to death in his quest for the throne, I'm not sure his wits did wander. He may have been seeing his immediate future all too clearly.

Conclusion

Deathbed visions have been reported by reliable witnesses, including trained medical workers, from time immemorial. They often play a crucial role in ameliorating the distress and fear that can accompany the dying process.

CHAPTER SIX:
NDEs throughout History

Accounts of separating from the body may be sidelined as fringe phenomena in our culture, but they are openly acknowledged in others. Kenneth Ring quotes a 19th-century missionary's account of the Tahitian belief that at death

> the soul [was] drawn out of the body, whence it was borne away, to be slowly and gradually united to the god from whom it had emanated ... The Tahitians have concluded that a substance, taking human form, issued from the head of the corpse, because among the privileged few who have the blessed gift of clairvoyance, some affirm that, shortly after a human body ceases to breathe, a vapor arises from the head, hovering a little way above it, but attached by a vapory cord. The substance, it is said, gradually increases in bulk and assumes the form of an inert body. When this has become quite cold, the connecting cord disappears and the dis-entangled soul-form floats away as if borne by invisible carriers.[1]

Such accounts can be traced far back in history. The ancient Egyptians believed that each person was born with a ka or spirit double, which followed him like a shadow. Egyptologist Adolf Erman describes the ka as "an independent spiritual being, living within the man, and through its presence bestowing upon the man 'protection, intelligence, purity, health, and joy.' No man nor god was conceivable without his ka, which grew up with him and never left ... After the death of the man, just as during his lifetime, the ka was still considered to be representative of his human personality."[2]

The idea may well have originated from sightings of apparitions (the ka was said to return periodically to the dead person's tomb, much like a haunting spirit) or from clairvoyant perception of the spirit body hovering over the dying person.

As old as it is, Egyptian civilization was predated by ancient Sumer in present-day Iraq. Assyriologist and philologist Irving Finkel tells us that this culture's cuneiform literature on ghosts "goes back in time to the third millennium BC" and proliferates in later centuries. "The written works of the Mesopotamians of ancient Iraq: Sumerians, Babylonians and Assyrians ... [offer] a complete, functional and in no way alien human system that covers death, burial, afterlife and, above all, ghosts."[3]

More recent, and also far more sophisticated, are the teachings of the Bardo Thödol, known colloquially as the *Tibetan Book of the Dead*, which probably dates to the eighth century AD. Peter and Elizabeth Fenwick observe:

> The stages of the near-death experience bear a remarkable similarity to teachings in the *Tibetan Book of the Dead* concerning what happens during dying and after death ... The Tibetan *bardos* ... are the states of living, of dying and of "becoming"—the state you enter after death.
>
> It is the transition from the *bardo* of dying to the *bardo* of becoming which carries many parallels with the NDE. As dissolution or death dawns, you enter a black experience which has many features of the tunnel [seen in many NDEs]. You then move into an area of light, "a great expanse of light beyond birth or death." After death individuals stay around the place of death and can witness what is happening in much the same way as happens in the out-of-body experience of the NDE. They can see living relatives but are unable to communicate with them. The body tends to become idealized, as we have seen happens in some NDEs."[4]

NDEs continue to be reported around the globe. In *The Next World*, Gregory Shushan presents many such accounts from different cultures, past and present. He writes,

> Accounts of NDEs can be found in purportedly documentary texts from ancient Greece and Rome, the ancient Near East, Medieval to modern Europe, Ancient to modern China, India, and Japan, Pre-Columbian Mesoamerica and modern Mexico, 18th-and 19th-century United States, 12th-century to modern Tibet, modern Thailand and the Philippines, and in the indigenous societies of the Pacific, Asia, the Americas, and Africa.[5]

A detailed NDE from 19th-century Hawaii involves a Kona woman, Kalima, who spontaneously revived during her own funeral. Kalima said, "I died, as you know. I seemed to leave my body and stand beside it, looking down on what was me. The me that was standing there looked like the form I was looking at, only, I was alive and the other was dead. I gazed at my body for a few minutes, then turned and walked away." She passed through ghostly villages, encountering various deceased people known to her. She "felt so full of joy, too, that my heart sang within me, and I was glad to be dead." She was feeling "happier every minute," until she was ordered to return to her body, a prospect she greeted with disgust. "I looked at [her body] and hated it. Was that my body? What a horrid, loathsome thing it was to me now, since I had seen so many beautiful, happy creatures! Must I go and live in that thing again?" A witness said that for the rest of her earthly life, Kalima "never ceased to regret coming back to her body."[6]

Among many other accounts, Shushan also reports a Maori NDE from the early 1960s. "A woman named Nga revived as her body was being taken for burial. She described an OBE in which she hovered above her head before exiting the room" and moving to the threshold of the spiritual world. And there is the case of "a Buddhist monk, born in 1908," who recalled his death in a past life. He witnessed "his own body being cremated. He claimed that his state of awareness was such that he could 'see in all directions' at once."[7] As we have seen, panoramic vision is sometimes reported in NDEs.

Religious traditions and NDEs

Some religious traditions almost certainly are derived, in part, from near-death experiences. Gregory Shushan observes:

> In Hawaii, information about the afterlife originated with people "who have been brought back to life from the dead." ... Many people who had died and come to life again ... Even some people of this age, who have swooned or perhaps lain dead for a few hours or half a day, have related their [afterlife] experiences ... The reason they were believed was because so many had died and come to life again and had told innumerable stories about these places ...
>
> Samoan afterlife beliefs were "confirmed by ... accounts of men going to the other world and returning again to this one." ...
>
> These examples substantiate and psychologist Holger Kalweit's ... generalization that individuals across cultures claim that they gained their knowledge of the afterlife "from the experiences of those who have returned [NDErs] and from shamans."[8]

Shamans themselves typically undergo vision quests as part of their training. Such experiences can be induced by fasting, sweating, or the use of hallucinogenics such as peyote. The resulting accounts sometimes bear intriguing parallels to NDEs. Other shamanic visions essentially *are* NDEs, as in the case of the Oglala Sioux shaman Black Elk, whose life-changing vision took place during a serious illness when he hovered on the edge of death.[9]

In short, a close approach to death, followed by a return, can play an important role in raising awareness of the afterlife and our spiritual nature.

Other cultural implications

Is it possible that these phenomena play an even larger role in our culture? Throughout history there have been stories of people carried off to a secret realm of fairies, elves, leprechauns, and so forth, where they were subjected to various indignities before their release or escape. Could some of these stories have their origin in experiences outside the body?

These diminutive folkloric figures bear a certain resemblance to the fabled "little green men" of UFO lore—known by aficionados as "grays." This parallel has led some writers, notably Jacques Vallee, D. Scott Rogo, and John Mack, to suggest a paranormal dimension to UFO encounters.

In his book *Abduction,* Mack says "abductees" often report that their experiences began with a humming or buzzing sensation; they then found themselves floating out of bed. If they tried to rouse the person sleeping in bed with them, they would find the person unresponsive. Often they would float through the house, even passing through walls. Frequently they reported heightened senses, the feeling that the experience was more real than ordinary reality. Aliens were sometimes perceived as luminous beings capable of telepathic communication. In some cases an abductee reported becoming aware of a lifelong relationship with an alien who had served the kind of role assigned, in a more overtly spiritual context, to a "spirit guide." Moreover, some abductees saw flashes of past lives during their experience, while others felt they were being given a glimpse of omniscient knowledge. Some reported seeing Earth from space, or having visions of impending global catastrophe, usually of an ecological kind.

I'm far from the first person to point out that this prototypical "abduction experience" doesn't sound like a physical event at all. It sounds as if the person's astral body left the physical body, moved around on the physical plane for a while, and then embarked on an adventure similar to the wilder outings reported by Robert Monroe. All these details—weightlessness, passing through walls, luminous beings, telepathy, guides or guardians, past lives, universal knowledge, and prophecies of global disaster—abound in both OBEs and NDEs, as we have already seen in part and will see in more detail later.

Again I'm reminded of the problem of analytic overlay, discussed in Chapter 2. In an "abduction," the person caught up in a baffling new experience perhaps perceives a sense of motion, brightness, smooth surfaces, unfamiliar or inhuman presences—and, relying on pop-culture tropes, connects these dots to conclude, "I'm being pulled by a tractor beam into a spaceship filled with extraterrestrials." Likewise, in an earlier era, the same perceptions could have been interpreted as being carried off by the fairy folk, in accordance with prevailing beliefs of the time.

In any event, I see no reason to think that so-called abductees *physically* entered spaceships, were subjected to invasive surgery, learned about human-alien hybrid breeding experiments, or encountered reptilian creatures and small gray aliens with bulbous heads.

> Some abductees claim to have marks on their bodies suggestive of physical tampering. Even if these claims are true, I'm not sure they prove much. The unconscious mind has remarkable powers in this regard, as noted by Guy Lyon Playfair in a discussion of experiments in hypnosis conducted by psychiatrist Léon Chertok:
>
>> Chertok showed that wounds can not only be healed by suggestion, but also caused by it. He managed to produce a handsome blister on the arm of patient by placing a coin on it and suggesting that it was very hot, which it was not. An intriguing detail was that the patient reported feeling no sensation of heat at all, and yet her skin reacted as if something extremely hot had indeed come into contact with it—on the exact spot where the coin had been placed ... Chertok saw this as "irrefutable proof of the

influence of the mind on physiological processes," and wondered why this was still not fully acknowledged "in spite of the accumulation of data."[10]

The strange marks reported by abductees may be unconscious manifestations of their belief in the physical reality of their experience. The stigmata suffered by some highly religious persons probably fall into the same category.

Conclusion

If OBEs and NDEs lie at the root of much of our folklore, then the universal symbolic language explored by James Fraser, Carl Jung, and Joseph Campbell, which so deeply informs our public and private narratives, may have originated in these phenomena. Religion itself may be no more than a formal, ritualized system designed to make sense of experiences outside the body. And since the earliest civilizations, such as Sumer and Egypt, were erected largely on a religious foundation, we might go so far as to say that the double's separation from the physical body has been a key factor in the civilizing of mankind.

CHAPTER SEVEN:

How Is It Possible?

IN THE MATERIALIST WORLDVIEW, NDEs are purely imaginary, the products of a disrupted or dying brain. This hypothesis has gone through many changes over the years; currently the most popular version involves so-called bursts, surges, or spikes of electrical activity observed in the dying brains of lab rats.

The trouble is that these "spikes" are large only in comparison to the near-flatline condition immediately preceding and following them. By comparison with normal brain activity, they are extremely minute—too small even to be detected by a standard EEG. (They can be picked up only by electrodes implanted in the brain itself.) They're extremely short-lived and restricted to very narrow bands of the electromagnetic spectrum.

Given that the most widely accepted models of brain functioning posit widespread "global" information processing as a precondition for awareness, it's hard to see how brief, narrow, isolated, low-level bursts can account for the persistence of consciousness.

These points were part of the rebuttal to one of the rat studies offered by Bruce Greyson, Edward F. Kelly, and W.J. Ross Dunseath:

> [T]he activity observed following cardiac arrest represents a tiny fraction of the total neuroelectric power present just before arrest ..., and thus it is misleading to describe these rat brains as being "hyperaroused." All that can be concluded is that activity of unknown functional significance occurred at a few places in the EEG frequency spectrum in the context of near-total obliteration of activity accompanying the waking state. The pertinent question here is not whether there is any brain electrical activity at all after cardiac arrest, but whether there is activity of the type currently thought to be necessary for conscious experience ...
>
> [M]any reports of near-death experiences include verifiable perceptions by the experiencer that are anchored to specific time periods far longer than 30 [seconds] after cardiac arrest, the duration of the electrical surge in this study.[1]

More recently, neuroscientist Sam Parnia supervised a challenging series of experiments in which brain activity was measured not in rodents, but in human patients undergoing CPR after heart failure.

> Brain activity was measured at two- or three-minute intervals, when doctors had to stop chest compressions or electric shocks to see if the patient's heart would restart, Parnia said.
>
> "There was no movement. It was a silence. That's when we would take measurements to see what's happening. We found the brains of people who are going through death have flatlined, which is what you would expect …
>
> "But interestingly, even up to an hour into the resuscitation, we saw spikes—the emergence of brain electrical activity, the same as I have when talking or deeply concentrating."

Bruce Greyson, who took issue with the rodent studies, also has doubts about the human trials, saying,

> This latest report of persistent brain waves after cardiac arrest has been blown out of proportion by the media. In fact, [Parnia's] team did not show any association between these brain waves and conscious activity …
>
> That is, those patients who had near-death experiences did not show the reported brain waves, and those who did show the reported brain waves did not report near-death experiences …
>
> All [the study] has shown is that in some patients there is continued electrical activity in the head that occurs during the same period that other patients report having NDEs.[2]

Parnia concedes that patients who reported an NDE could not be matched specifically with those who showed electrical activity during CPR. He attributes this to the small sample size; out of 567 patients, only 53 were resuscitated, of whom only 28 were interviewed. In all, eleven patients reported some form of awareness, but only six reported an NDE.

These studies are certainly interesting, but the results do not, as yet, add up to anything like a neurological explanation of NDEs. The same holds true for oxygen deprivation, endorphin release, and memories of the birth canal (supposedly linked to the common NDE account of going through a tunnel toward a light).[3] It's also worth noting that the dying brain hypothesis, in any of its forms, cannot explain the similar phenomena reported in OBEs, which usually involve people in perfectly good health. Nor can it explain veridical NDEs.

Well, maybe the NDE never happened at all. Some critics have suggested that NDEs can be written off as nothing more than false memories.

At least one scientific study indicates otherwise. Researchers at the Coma Science Group analyzed people's memories of NDEs, comparing them to so-called flashbulb memories ("vivid and long-lasting memories of the circumstances in which one learned about a shocking public event") and autobiographical memories (mental narratives). They found that

> NDE verbal recollections include a higher overall amount of details and a higher amount of internal/episodic details than flashbulb and autobiographical memories. More precisely, they comprise more event and perceptual internal details. Moreover, we found that flashbulb memories are associated to a lower intensity of feelings while remembering and a lower personal importance, and are less reactivated and less susceptible to be remembered from a first person perspective. Finally, NDE memories are more central than autobiographical memories, which in turn are more central than flashbulb memories. Besides, more central events contain more episodic verbal details. Overall, our results fall in line with existing literature that highlights the uniqueness of NDE memories.[4]

Though the study does not rule out the possibility that the NDE is an especially vivid hallucination, it suggests, at the very least, that NDEs are qualitatively different from ordinary fantasies.

Skeptics sometimes argue that NDEs in the operating room are the result of "anesthesia awareness," a known phenomenon in which an improperly sedated patient becomes conscious of the events around him. But anesthesia awareness is defined by very different symptoms than the typical NDE. This contrast is best illustrated by the case of a fifteen-year-old boy who underwent both types of experience at different times. While under anesthesia for an operation, the boy heard music and the doctor's voice. He saw three big lamps above him and felt as if someone was moving him onto his left side on the operating table. He also felt an injection in his hip. All these perceptions were accurate.

However, while being interviewed, the boy also spontaneously described an experience that occurred three years earlier during a similar operation. The boy reported the prior experience this way:

I was sleeping and suddenly I felt awake and had the impression that I was leaving my body through my head ... I could see from above my whole body lying on the back on the operating table, and surrounded by many doctors. I felt as being above my physical body ... and I was lying face down ... I was like a spirit ... without my own arms and legs ... and I was floating under the ceiling of the room. Initially, while feeling detached from my real body, I felt a little bit scared and weird ... but then I had a sensation of lightness ... and I felt relaxed and comfortable ... I had the impression that everything was real ... I distinguished the operating room and the surgeons ... I then saw a dark tunnel in front of me ... and I felt attracted to it ... I passed through the tunnel very fast and at its end I saw ... a bright light ... that did not hurt my eyes ... As I was passing through the tunnel ..., I heard noises ... which sounded like when you are watching TV without a program ..., then these noises became voices ... Suddenly I felt again attracted to my body, in which I went again through my head. At this time point, the experience was over and I was asleep.[5]

Upon waking up, he "felt disappointed as he did not have enough time to see what was going on at the end of the tunnel."

Note how different the two events were. In the episode of anesthesia awareness, he remained in the body, so to speak. He felt his body being moved and poked. In the NDE, on the other hand, he had an out-of-body experience and was "like a spirit." The first experience sounds uncomfortable and disconcerting; the second was so pleasant that the boy wished it had gone on longer.

In short, this case—along with many others—suggests that anesthesia awareness bears little resemblance to an NDE. And there remain those baffling verifiable details reported by NDErs. How to explain those? Sometimes, the approach is simply to explain them away with the wave of a hand.

Consider anesthesiologist Gerald Woerlee's analysis. He acknowledges that accurate information has been provided by patients who were apparently unconscious or even seemingly lifeless. But their accounts, he insists, cannot be taken at face value:

Observers see with physical light waves, and hear with physical sound waves. But the supposedly disembodied consciousness of a person undergoing an out of body experience is immaterial, and this has major provable consequences.

The immaterial disembodied consciousness of a person

> undergoing an out of body experience does not interact with physical matter at all, because it can depart from the body, actually passing through the solid matter of the body, and even pass through solid walls. Accordingly, the disembodied consciousness cannot possibly hear, because it would also have no interaction with sound waves in air ...
>
> The disembodied consciousness of a person undergoing an out of body experience is invisible and has no interaction with physical matter. These things mean it cannot be seen, and cannot be photographed or imaged at any wavelength of the electromagnetic spectrum. Accordingly, the disembodied consciousness of a person undergoing an out of body experience does not interact with light at all, which means it cannot possibly see anything ...
>
> An immaterial consciousness cannot see and hear, which means that people undergoing out of body experiences hear with their ears, see with their eyes, and build images of all that occurs within their minds.[6]

This argument is a textbook example of the logical fallacy of question-begging:

> The fallacy of begging the question occurs when an argument's premises assume the truth of the conclusion, instead of supporting it. In other words, you assume without proof the stand/position, or a significant part of the stand, that is in question. Begging the question is also called arguing in a circle.[7]

In this case, Woerlee is saying, in effect, that out-of-body perception is impossible because only in-the-body perception is possible. The second part of the statement is merely a restatement of the first part. Clearly, the whole point at issue is whether some form of consciousness, which includes perception, can operate independent of the physical body (and the physical senses). Nothing Woerlee has written can establish that such perception does not take place, since, clearly, if it does take place, it will function in some manner that is not yet understood.

In addition to begging the question, Woerlee equivocates on the meaning of "conscious" and "unconscious."

> An out of body experience is indisputably a conscious experience. After all, an unconscious person has no experiences. An unconscious person hears nothing, sees nothing, and experiences

nothing. So even though the physical body of a person undergoing an out of body experience is seemingly unconscious, they are nonetheless very conscious, and only appear unconscious ... Accordingly, veridical perceptions of seeing things, people and events, as well as hearing sounds and speech during out of body experiences are due to the apparently unconscious person actually seeing and hearing these things.[8]

No one denies that people having NDEs are conscious in the sense that their consciousness is still operating. Indeed, this is the whole point of the extensive NDE literature. The contention of survivalists, however, is that the person's mind remains conscious even though his body is inert and unconscious. In other words, a distinction is drawn between being *physically* unconscious and being *mentally* unconscious. But from the materialist point of view, this is a distinction without a difference; there simply cannot be any such thing as nonphysical awareness.

If this were true, then all psychic phenomena involving extrasensory perception would be invalidated. No doubt Woerlee would embrace this conclusion, but to do so, he would have to dismiss a great deal of evidence to the contrary.

The ganzfeld

The most compelling evidence of ESP is a decades-long, international series of tests collectively known as the ganzfeld experiments. As parapsychologist Dean Radin explains, the ganzfeld is "a mild form of unpatterned sensory stimulation originally developed by gestalt psychologists to study the nature of perception and visual imagery."[9]

In ganzfeld tests, the subject is isolated from most sights and sounds—the eyes are covered, and the ears are fitted with headphones that play "pink noise," similar to the sound of rushing water. She relaxes into a semi-trance and then reports whatever images come into her mind while a "sender" in another room concentrates on sending a target image selected at random from four possibilities.

The subject's chance of hitting upon the correct image is one in four or 25%, but the ganzfeld tests cumulatively show a success rate of around 32%. That may not sound like much, but given the number of tests conducted, the result is statistically significant—in fact, very significant. Radin writes,

From 1974 through 2004, some 88 ganzfeld experiments had been reported. Those studies involved 1,008 hits and 3,145 trials, for a combined hit rate of 32 percent as compared to the chance-expected 25 percent. This 7 percent positive effect would occur by chance with odds of *29 million trillion to 1* ...

When we update the meta-analysis with studies published through 2010, we find 1,323 hits in 4,196 trials, for a combined hit rate of 31.5 percent. The new data increase the overall odds against chants from a mere 29 million trillion to 1 in 2004 to a stunning *13 billion trillion* to 1 ...

Since [1974] seven meta-analyses have been performed ... Six reported statistically significant evidence with odds against chance ranging from a modest 20 to 1 to over a trillion to 1 ...

[This result] indicates that telepathy has been successfully repeated in many different laboratories, with different investigators and participants in different cultures, over nearly four decades. Persistent, successful repeatability, including by disbelieving skeptics, is as real as it gets in science.[10]

There's even more to the story. When senders and receivers were emotionally close to each other, the average hit rate climbed to 37%. Parents and their children scored 43.55. Siblings scored an incredible 71.4%.[11]

Skeptics have been unable to punch holes in these data. Even the outspoken skeptic Richard Wiseman has stated,

> I agree that by the standards of any other area of science that remote viewing is proven, but [this] begs the question: do we need higher standards of evidence when we study the paranormal? I think we do.[12]

Wiseman later clarified that he didn't mean to single out remote viewing: "It is a slight misquote, because I was using the term in the more general sense of ESP—that is, I was not talking about remote viewing per se, but rather Ganzfeld, etc. as well. I think that they do meet the usual standards for a normal claim, but are not convincing enough for an extraordinary claim."[13]

Of course, this raises the question of how to distinguish an ordinary claim from an extraordinary one. It's hard to escape the conclusion that the extraordinary claims are simply the ones that skeptics don't like. It's also hard to avoid thinking that the skeptics will keep moving the goalposts, demanding more and more evidence for "extraordinary" claims, and never pronouncing themselves satisfied.

Remote viewing

In his original quote, Wiseman mentioned remote viewing, which, as we've seen, is another term for clairvoyance—the ability to see things at a distance without the use of the known senses. Numerous experiments in remote viewing have been conducted, including those carried out under the auspices of the Stargate Project, a long-running government program driven by concerns over potential military applications of psi. Contrary to popular belief, Stargate was not shut down because of a lack of positive results, but rather because the positive results, while undeniable, were deemed too sporadic and unpredictable to be of practical use—a continuing issue with all forms of psi.

An interesting quirk of remote viewing is that sometimes the target location is accurately described according to its appearance many years ago, or even its appearance at some point in the future (later confirmed). This can happen even when the remote viewer is not consciously attempting to access a different time period. Some remote viewers specialize in retrocognition—seeing the past—in order to assist archaeologists. Stephan A. Schwartz's books, such as *The Secret Vaults of Time* and *The Alexandria Project*, detail his successful experiments in what he calls "psychic archaeology"—the use of psychics to find or identify ancient sites and artifacts.

One such case involves psychic George McMullen, who worked with archaeologist J. Norman Emerson. At a certain Canadian site, diggers were unable to find the palisade, or perimeter fence, which is known to surround most Ontario Indian villages. "This wooden fence ... is an archaeologist's first priority," writes Schwartz, "since it gives some idea of the size of the site."

Two years had been spent digging, without resolving this issue. Then George McMullen came to the site. Within minutes, he announced that much of the palisade

> was now covered by the eight- to ten-foot deep gravel pile. However, if Reid [the lead archaeologist] would dig to the east of the gravel, in a small ravine at the field edge, he would not only find it, but would also discover an entrance shaped like a "cattle gate." ... McMullen paced off the area, indicating a palisade that cut off the space between two ravines.

McMullen described a type of palisade that had never been identified before. He also said that it did not completely encircle the village, but ran along only part of the perimeter. Both of these claims ran counter to expectations and were met with doubt. But McMullen was right, as the diggers quickly established. The site

> had a palisade and [McMullen's] psychic line exactly overlay a course that excavation showed to be correct for all but three feet at the lower east end. His description of the entranceway ("like a cattle gate") was equally impressive, and accurate in location to within less than twelve inches.
>
> Furthermore, his reconstruction of its purpose, which was not for defense but "like a snow fence," was borne out ...
>
> No such palisade had ever been found and there was no reason to believe one existed. Yet Reid's fieldwork proved the psychic completely accurate.

Another question plaguing the archaeological team was the location of the west wall of House I. All that had been found were "seemingly random post molds [impressions in the ground left by disintegrated posts] ... No discernible line could be traced."

Regarding this issue,

> George was equally explicit. He said the wall Reid was searching for would be found running parallel to the medial hearths (fire pits) fifteen feet to the west ... The southern end of the house was fifty feet distant from the gravel deposit.

And what do you know? "The west wall was just where McMullen said it would be, and the position of the end of the house was 'within eighteen inches of its predicted location.'"

There's more:

> A week later McMullen returned ... and located what he described as a "different house" ... probably a ceremonial structure. This second and totally unexpected house [later called House II] was located by McMullen in an area that, because of its heavy brush and gravel spillover, had never been excavated ...
>
> [McMullen's] outline of this building ... was if anything more accurate ... his dimensions and wall lines were exact.[14]

House II not only proved to be where McMullen had indicated, but, as predicted, it was determined to have been a ceremonial structure.

In short, McMullen discovered a new type of perimeter fence, the west wall of House I, and all of House II, describing each of these accurately, and accomplished all of this in a few hours. Trained archaeologists had worked the site for two previous seasons without finding these things, so clearly there was nothing obvious about their location.

McMullen identified other structures at other sites. Other psychics have been involved in archaeological research, as well. Schwartz's books contain chapter after chapter of documented cases.

> Stephan Schwartz was also involved in an experiment conducted after the Iraq War, when Saddam Hussein was on the run. In "Finding Saddam Hussein: A Study in Applied Remote Viewing," he describes how an impromptu team of 47 first-time remote viewers predicted where and how the ousted dictator would be found.
>
> The experiment, conducted on November 3, 2003, produced the following results: Saddam would be discovered "beneath an ordinary looking house … on the outskirts of a small village … near Tikrit" (Saddam's hometown). He would be in "a hiding place … like a cavern or a 'carved out space' … not visible but hidden underneath something … [with a] vent tube built into [it]." Moreover, when found, Saddam would look "like a homeless person … ratty … unkempt … [with a] salt and pepper beard … wild [hair] … disheveled [appearance]." He would have only "two or three supporters with him at the time of his discovery," he would be armed "but would put up no resistance," would "have a quantity of money with him," and would be "defiant but [would] not put up any resistance [but would be] tired and dispirited."[15]
>
> Schwartz himself expected a different outcome. He thought Saddam, like deposed dictator Idi Amin of Uganda, would be discovered living in Saudi Arabia in relative luxury. In any event, the predictions were sealed in a notarized envelope and stored in an archive. On December 13,

Saddam was captured, and within a short time the details came out. They matched the remote viewers' predictions quite closely. Saddam was indeed found in a small village near Tikrit, hiding in his so-called "spider hole" (as the media dubbed it) equipped with a vent pipe. He had a long salt-and-pepper beard and an overall disheveled appearance. Two people were with him. He had a box of money containing hundred dollar bills in US currency. Though armed with a pistol, he put up no resistance. The Lieutenant General in command of US forces in Baghdad described him as "a tired man, and also a man resigned to his fate."

Skeptics often say that if psi were real, the US military would be using it. But who knows? Maybe they are. The Stargate Project was classified for decades, and few people knew of the work while it was going on. Could the same thing be true today?

Games of chance

Another common objection to ESP is that if it were real, people with this talent would play the lottery, repeatedly beating the odds, winning big prizes again and again. Nobody ever does this; hence, there's no ESP.

It might sound convincing, except for one inconvenient fact: there are quite a few cases of individuals who've won big jackpots multiple times.

The most famous repeat winner is Joan Ginther, who won the lottery jackpot four times—in 1993, 2006, 2008, and 2010. She raked in a total of $20.4 million. The odds of winning were never better than 1 in 900,000 and ran as low as 1 in 15.8 million for the 1993 ticket. Because she has a degree in math and was known to buy a lot of tickets, it's sometimes suggested that she used some kind of system. But lottery expert Gail Howard demurs, noting that Ginther won three of her four big prizes with scratch-off tickets. "As far as I know, there's no way to beat the odds with scratch-offs," Howard says.[16]

A Canadian man, Seguro Ndabene, won five jackpots in five years: $1 million, $100,000, $1 million, $50,000, and $17 million. Total: $19.5 million.[17]

Keith Selix, who won $81,000 on three separate picks, attributed his success to his deceased wife. "I'm still thinking that I'm being led from up above," he said after his third win. Though his winnings are a far cry from the millions racked up by Ginther and Ndabene, they're still impressive; he had to beat odds of 1 in 89,775 for one win, the same odds (playing the same game) for his second win, and odds of 1 in 119,700 for his remaining win.[18]

CNBC has more:

> Lottery ticket sales generate roughly $80 billion of revenue annually in the US, as players hope to become the latest person who beat the odds to win a once-in-a-lifetime jackpot.
>
> But, for some especially lucky people, that once-in-a-lifetime luck inexplicably strikes more than once.
>
> In fact, there are many recent stories of people who have been lucky enough to win the lottery multiple times—whether it's a $1,000 prize or a $1 million jackpot.
>
> In May, 72-year-old Peggy Dodson won a $1 million jackpot from a "Max-a-Million" scratch-off lottery ticket that she bought at the same Pennsylvania convenience store where she'd purchased another scratch-off ticket that turned out to be a $100,000 winner just two years earlier ...
>
> When Janet Pflaumer-Phillips, 59, won $1 million from a "Diamond Millions" scratch-off lottery ticket last month, it was technically her first big lottery win. But if you count the two times her husband, Kevin Phillips, won his own separate $1 million prizes (in 2014 and 2016), then that made three wins for the couple overall, and a total of $3 million ...
>
> And Eugene Martellio, of Vineland, N.J., won a $3 million grand prize playing the "CA$H OUT" scratch-off lottery game in April, just two years after winning more than $730,000 from a Jersey Cash 5 lottery drawing.[19]

Of course, I don't know if any of these people actually used some form of precognition—or, in Mr. Selix's case, spirit guidance—to obtain these payouts. But when skeptics say that if ESP exists, repeat lottery winners would be expected, the obvious riposte is that repeat winners are hardly unheard of.

Conclusion

If healthy, living persons can obtain information without the use of their physical senses, there's no reason why the sick and the dying cannot obtain information the same way. In fact, as reliance on the physical body diminishes, it would make sense that extrasensory channels of perception would open up. As Dostoevsky's Svidrigailov said,

> As soon as one is ill, as soon as the normal earthly order of the organism is broken, one begins to realize the possibility of another world; and the more seriously ill one is, the closer becomes one's contact with that other world.

CHAPTER EIGHT:
The Double

AT THIS POINT, I think enough testimony from a sufficient variety of sources has been presented to establish the strong possibility, at least, of a nonphysical counterpart to the physical body—a "spirit double" that commences permanent separation during the dying process, and can initiate temporary separation on other occasions.

This mysterious double is bound to the physical body by cordlike extensions, broken only at the moment of death. The nexus of consciousness switches from the physical body to the double, sometimes after a brief blackout. Freed of physical limits, perception becomes more acute and more wide-ranging, encompassing paranormal abilities such as clairvoyance and telepathy.

The double can be seen by others if they are sufficiently sensitive to psychic impressions. Such sightings are probably the basis of much religious belief, just as doubles that were temporarily separated may be the basis for much of our folklore, both past (abduction by "little people") and present (abduction by "aliens").

But what exactly *is* this elusive double? What is its nature? What is its ultimate purpose?

A lengthy discussion is provided in Geraldine Cummins's *Beyond Human Personality*. Cummins was a medium who produced a good deal of channeled literature, notably *Swan on a Black Sea*, often cited as one of the most evidential examples of channeling.

Decades before *Swan*, Cummins produced two books allegedly dictated to her by the deceased psychical researcher, psychological theorist, and classicist F.W.H. Myers. *Beyond Human Personality* was the second of the two.

According to this material, the etheric double is a secondary body serving a vital role as an interface between the mind (or soul) and the physical body. As "Myers" says, "The soul has to work through the medium of the double and never directly commands matter. Always there is this unifying body which comes between the self and his outward appearance in the material world."[1]

The double is active at all times, but functions independently of the physical body only on certain occasions, such as when the physical body is asleep or comatose. The rest of the time, the etheric body is closely entwined with the physical body.

Myers is emphatic in saying that the deceased person continues to have a body:

> When discussing the survival of human personality, the student should discard the idea of any bodiless creation ...
>
> There is a body vibrating at a slightly higher rate of intensity which accompanies the human being from birth till death—a body invisible to the eye, which receives the soul or conscious intelligence during sleep—a body which, at all times, acts as intermediary between the intellect, imagination and the physical shape ...
>
> Further, this double is in the likeness of the visible manifestation of the man. So similar are they in appearance, they might be described as twins if they could be visualized together. The double, indeed, reflects the impressions of its companion, receives the memories registered by the senses and imprints those impressions on its brain-substance, which connects it with the mental representations that are, indeed, the very stuff of memory ...
>
> On this basic structure the student may build up his arguments when he engages the materialist in discussion. He can account, for instance, for loss of memory in the ageing man or woman, by the fact that the soul can no longer effectively impress the deteriorating physical brain. The machine is too worn to be responsive. On the other hand, the memory of the individual is retained and registered very fully in the unifying body. This body does not imitate its companion and gradually decay as the years pass. In my previous book [*The Road to Immortality,* also channeled by Cummins] I have called it the "husk," for it contains and shelters the nascent manifestation which is to be eventually the body of the soul in the world after death.
>
> During the whole of a man's life, this potential expression of personality is forming in the etheric womb, is growing during the span of twenty, fifty, seventy years, whatever may be the term of his sojourn on earth ...
>
> The double holds the physical body within its grip and is a power for integration. Even when the human being sleeps and the former no longer occupies the material shape, the latter is controlled by a fine web, by certain threads and two cords which unite it to its finer semblance ...
>
> Now, when the ordinary man is fully awake, his unifying body rests within the physical shape. The two forms fit into each other and pervade each other exactly. But, as soon as a man

becomes drowsy, the double tilts outwards; and one who can see with the inner eye will perceive a pale form which has, perhaps, half emerged from the actual material body. If a shock or noise rouses its owner, instantly it slips back within the physical manifestation of the individual.[2]

Esotericist Charles Hampton makes the same point:

> During earth life the etheric double is coterminous with the nervous system as well as enveloping it. In outline, in form and feature, it is a replica or double of the physical body in matter finer and more tenuous than the finest gaseous substance, yet it is still physical matter ... The etheric double disintegrates or dematerializes once it is abandoned. It never was intended to be a vehicle of consciousness. Its function was to convey vitality to the body through the nervous system ... Death means that the etheric double is disunited from the nervous system, but the double is no more to be preserved then the physical is; it is part of the physical and will disintegrate. Immediately on awakening in the astral world the etheric matter fades out like mist.[3]

The double, then, is not just superficially identical to the physical body. It's an exact duplicate, containing (so we are told) all the same organs, vessels, nerves, and so forth, including, of course, an etheric brain. Or, to put it in more modern terms, the double is a matrix of the same information that constitutes the physical body, and the separation of the double entails a transference, so to speak, of this data set from one location to another, rather like copying a computer file. (Thus giving a new twist to the expression "uploading to the cloud.")

However we understand it, the newly deceased person feels himself reborn in a body that's essentially identical to the earthly body, but without earthly weaknesses and flaws—a body that is familiar, yet different; one's own, yet new. Or as St. Paul put it in I Corinthians:

> The body that is sown is perishable, it is raised imperishable; it is sown in dishonor, it is raised in glory; it is sown in weakness, it is raised in power; it is sown a natural body, it is raised a spiritual body ...
>
> And just as we have borne the image of the earthly man, so shall we bear the image of the heavenly man.[4]

If the "Myers" communication is accurate, then what Andrew Jackson Davis saw was not an original formation of the etheric double but its reformation after separating from the physical body. The etheric double, which previously served mainly as the interface between the mind and the physical body, becomes the only vehicle through which the person's mind operates, now that the physical vehicle is defunct.

In *The Supreme Adventure*, Robert Crookall essentially agrees with "Myers" in arguing that some kind of "body" is necessary even at higher levels of spiritual development. He specifies four bodies, initially intertwined, not unlike nested dolls. They are:

1. The physical body—the one we use during our earthly incarnation
2. The energy body (which Crookall calls "the vehicle of vitality," and which other authors call the astral body, astral shell, etheric body, or aura)—the interface between the physical and the spiritual. It is essentially a veil covering the physical body, which allows impressions from higher realms to filter through
3. The soul body—nested inside the first two bodies, the soul body becomes our main vehicle once the others have been cast off
4. The spirit body—at the heart of the soul body is the spirit body, which remains after the soul body has been shed in preparation for ascending to higher realms of spiritual life

For present purposes, we need not trouble ourselves with the spirit body (stage 4). In the early stages of the dying process—the only stages we're considering now—it is still snugly nestled within the spirit body. So let's limit our discussion to just three entities:

1. the physical body
2. the *intermediate body* that detaches from the physical body
3. the *soul body* that sheds the last vestiges of the physical

The act of shedding the intermediate body, and thus progressing from stage 2 to stage 3, is what Crookall and others have called "the second death." You may recall astral projector William Buhlman's observation that when the initial energy body was shed, a new, more powerful, more vital nonphysical body was unveiled:

> I realized that the first (dense) nonphysical body [= intermediate body, stage 2] is actually an energy duplicate of the physical, while

the second [= soul body, stage 3] possesses a finer vibratory rate, like pure energy, ready to respond to the slightest thought ... Now I understood how limited the first energy-body really is.[5]

Admittedly, this scheme is a bit more complicated than we might like. Its advantage, however, is that it covers a wide variety of disparate phenomena:

- the destructive behavior of poltergeists—ghosts (or, possibly, psychic emanations of disturbed living persons) who throw stones, break glass, etc., and who may be understood as the intermediate body (either temporarily/partially or permanently/wholly separated from the physical body) in a state of violent confusion
- the realism of some apparitions, which are initially mistaken for flesh-and-blood persons—because, as intermediate bodies, they are exact duplicates of the physical body
- the more nebulous quality of other apparitions, especially of persons who have been deceased for some time; these may consist only of the soul body
- the mindless, repetitive actions of the typical haunting spirit—a spirit that may be only the discarded intermediate body, operating by rote
- the varying location of the silver cord, sometimes seen attached to the solar plexus (as a connection to the intermediate body) and at other times attached to the head (as a connection to the soul body)[6]
- the often-repeated statements by communicators speaking through mediums that they must "lower their vibrations" and enter a somewhat confused or befogged condition; this is consistent with the soul body having to take on the intermediate body of the medium in order to operate through the medium's nervous system

We've come a long way at this point, but there's a good distance still to travel. Before we proceed, however, let's pause to consider those cases where all does not go so smoothly.

—Not everyone dies peacefully in bed. In cases of exceptionally sudden and violent demise, the postmortem process can proceed differently in its early stages.

—Suicide can also lead to different initial results.

—Regardless of circumstances, some NDEs, like some OBEs, are unpleasant, even nightmarish.

—In certain cases, the intermediate body is not shed as soon as it should be. For one reason or another, it's retained for days or even years, with unfortunate results for both the deceased and the living.

In Part Two, we'll look at cases of all these kinds.

PART TWO: *The Dark Side*

Oh, how I suffered! I do not see how I could be dead, because when you die you never suffer anymore, and I have suffered.

—spirit of a suicide, addressing psychiatrist Carl Wickland[1]

A talisman of the Demon of the Southwest Wind, "which by its inflamed breath dries up the harvests and consumes men and animals with fever ... He is so ugly that the mere sight of his own image drives him away." (Gaston Maspero, *Life in Ancient Egypt and Assyria*)

CHAPTER NINE:
Death by Violence or Suicide

MOST OF THE CASES we've covered are notable for an absence of pain, fear, or apprehension, and it would be nice to say that every death fits this model. Happily, it appears that most do.

One of Jane Sherwood's communicators, channeled via automatic writing, discusses his peaceful transition:

> Where death comes gradually and naturally like this, one wakes quietly in the new conditions after an interval of a few days. One is fully through, as we say, and although the newcomer has to be cared for and kept quiet until the new rhythms of his body are fully established, he soon becomes strong and vigorous and ready to begin his new life. The transition, like all natural processes, should not be interfered with by violence or haste. Death is a kind of birth and it should proceed with a quiet inevitableness and not be accompanied by pain or distress. Much of the apparent suffering of a death-bed is not consciously felt by the sufferer. His real life is already half retired from the mortal body and neither experiences nor records its pangs. Shakespeare is very near the literal facts when he speaks of "shuffling off this mortal coil."[1]

Hamlet's celebrated metaphor is derived from the act of a snake shedding a coil of skin. Shakespeare and our communicator both seem to be saying that death consists of sloughing off an unneeded part of the body, with the body understood as a compound entity of physical and spiritual forms.

But note the communicator's caveats. All this is true "when death comes gradually and naturally." Moreover, "the transition, like all natural processes, should not be interfered with by violence or haste."

As Hamlet himself would say, "Ay, there's the rub."

Violent death

Robert Crookall devotes a chapter of *The Supreme Adventure* to sudden, violent death, noting, "We are here chiefly concerned with death from a blow (bullet, etc.), from a fall, or from drowning."

He lists several respects in which these deaths are similar to peaceful ones:

- little or no physical pain
- inability to immediately realize one has died
- seeing one's own body
- distress over the grief of living friends

He then goes on to list significant differences. In peaceful deaths, these features are often found:

- sense of peace, security, happiness
- beautiful, clear, brilliant environment
- awareness of a silver cord
- nearly immediate encounters with deceased friends

Violent deaths, on the other hand, are more likely to be characterized by

- confusion or bewilderment
- misty or foggy environment
- no awareness of a silver cord
- delay in meeting deceased friends[2]

In support of these distinctions, Crookall cites communications through mediums. One young man died in the carnage of the battlefield.

> Bewildered, I got to my feet, and looking down, saw my body among many others on the ground. I remembered the battle, but did not realize I had been shot. I was apart from, yet I still seemed held in some way to the body. My condition was one of terrible unrest ... Others of the seeming dead moved. Then many of them stood up and, like me, seemed to emerge from their Physical Bodies, for their old forms still lay upon the field. Soon I found myself among thousands in a similar mental state: none knew just what it happened ... While the passing-out from this old body is without pain, it is a terrible thing to drive a strong spirit from a healthy body, to tear it from its covering. It

is un-natural, and the sensation following re-adjustment is awful ... It was neither night nor day; about us all was gloom. Something like an atmosphere, dark and red, enveloped us all.[3]

Another soldier:

I was one minute in the thick of things and the next minute Lieutenant Wells said, "Our command has crossed: let us go!" I thought he meant to the river and followed him up a hillside that I had not noticed before—a clean spot, not blackened by guns. Lots of our fellows were there, and strange troops. But they looked queer ... I overtook Wells. "What is the matter with me, with us all?" I asked. He said, "Bob, we're dead!" I didn't believe it at first.[4]

Yet another soldier:

As in my case, thousands of soldiers pass over without knowing it. If there be shock, it is not the shock of physical death. Shock comes later when comprehension dawns: "Where is my body? Surely I am not dead?" ... I had been struck by a shell-splinter. There was no pain. It was as if I had been running hard until, hot and breathless, I had thrown my overcoat away. The coat was my body ... After I had recovered from the shock of realizing I was dead, I was above the battlefield. It seemed as if I were floating in a mist that muffled sound and blurred vision. Everything was distant, misty, unreal.[5]

Crookall reserves a separate section for death by explosion. In collecting messages from mediums, he found that deaths of this type were unique in many ways, characterized by a prolonged interval of unconsciousness and a gradual awakening. As one deceased soldier told his brother, "There was a horrible explosion and then I remember no more. By and by I began to wonder why everything was so quiet."[6]

The explanation offered by communicators is that when the physical body is blown apart, the enveloping astral body is also temporarily scattered and must come together again; during this process, the newly deceased person is unconscious. For example, WWI infantryman Raymond Lodge, speaking through a medium, said,

When anybody has been blown to pieces it takes some time for the spirit-body to gather itself all in and to be complete. [The explosion] dissipated a certain amount of the etheric substance which has to be concentrated again ... The spirit is not blown apart, of course, but it has an effect on the spirit.[7]

Suicide

The most comprehensive resource on suicide from a postmortem perspective is *Suicide: What Really Happens in the Afterlife?*, by Pamela Rae Heath and John Klimo. For the rest of the chapter, I'll rely on this book.

The authors draw mainly on channeled material to present a picture of the postmortem consequences of taking one's own life. These mediumistic messages are somewhat inconsistent, with the older ones exhibiting a sterner attitude toward suicide, in line with Christian injunctions against it, while the newer ones take a more sympathetic approach.

Nevertheless, some larger patterns emerge. Heath and Klimo note:

> One of the commonest initial emotions reported by suicides is confusion, which then tends to lead to intense frustration. [Medium] James Van Praagh speaks of a young man who had hanged himself:
> "He can't believe he is dead because he feels so alive. He thinks he screwed something up and is trying very hard to get back into his body through his head. He can't do it, and he's getting very frustrated. He begins to cry!"[8]

Medium Arthur Ford offers a more general observation along the same lines.

> The extreme negative, depressed mental state of the suicide at the time of his self-destructive act carries over into the afterlife, placing him at a great disadvantage in making his adjustment. Many times, upon awakening, he does not realize that he has passed over. He may go into an extreme panic upon discovering that he can no longer control his physical body.[9]

Unsuccessful attempts to regain mastery of the now-defunct physical body may lead the suicide to a temporary manifestation of psychokinetic energy—essentially poltergeist activity—as he tries to influence his physical environment in any way he can.

> The spirit of Jim Pike Junior ... used psychokinesis as a way of getting his father's attention. After a number of events, including clocks stopping and bangs of hair being inexplicably cut, Pike Senior reported:
>
> "March 1, we found books which had been moved, windows open which had been closed, safety pins lying open in several places, clothes misplaced, and a broken Marlboro cigarette (Jim's brand, not smoked by any of the three of us) in front of the nightstand between the twin beds. The culmination of that day came in two episodes.
>
> "As we were examining a number of clothing items in Maren's bedroom which seemed to have been moved without our doing, we witnessed the first and only object in motion. Maren had reached into the closet for something when one of the four tissue-wrapped pieces of a silver dresser set ... began to move toward the edge of the shelf above the pole. As we watched in disbelief, the silver piece slowly slid off the shelf."
>
> These events continue to occur. That this was not a case of either pranksters or psychokinesis from living minds, stressed over the death of a loved one, became clear when the spirit of Jim came through British medium Ena Twigg, to state, "I came to your room, I moved books, I knocked on the door." That the soul was frustrated and trying to communicate seems clear when he later added, "I've been so unhappy because I didn't have a voice and had to find a way to tell you."[10]

Unable to operate his physical body, but still emotionally tied to the physical plane, the suicide may resist shedding the intermediate body which serves as his only remaining link to earth. As a result, he may remain earthbound for some considerable time, confused about his condition and wandering restlessly. Peter Richelieu was told by his spirit guide:

> Because the man suffers so much remorse and because he would give anything to get back into his physical body ... he often refuses to make the effort of will necessary for him to get rid of his etheric body ... He may remain "earthbound" through ignorance, being unable to function properly either in the physical or the astral world, feeling the extreme loneliness that exists under these circumstances.[11]

Depression and confusion can leave the suicide in a temporary (but sometimes long-lasting) state of limbo. Geraldine Cummins conveyed the message that one man's suicide "led to his being plunged into darkness and isolation here for a very long time."[12]

Reflecting on his suicide, a spirit speaking through Anna Wickland said,

> I was so depressed. (Coughing and choking, evidently repeating his death struggle.) I took something. (Committed suicide.) Then I slept for awhile and after that I walked a long time in the twilight. It seemed like the desert.[13]

Margot Gray recounts the NDE of a suicidal person:

> At the last moment I suddenly felt an inner explosion and seemed to be enveloped in a blue flame which felt cold. At this point I found myself floating about six inches above my body. The next thing I remember is being sucked down a vast black vortex like a whirlpool and I found myself in a place that I can only describe as being like Dante's Inferno. I saw a lot of other people who seemed gray and dreary and there was an overwhelming feeling of loneliness about the place.[14]

A common denominator in nearly all accounts, whether stemming from mediumship, NDEs, or hypnotic regression, is regret. Regression therapist Michael Newton says, "When I work with clients who have committed suicide in former lives, the first thing most exclaim right after the moment of death is, 'Oh, my God, how could I have been so stupid!'"[15]

Newton quotes a specific patient who remembered committing suicide in a previous life: "It was a waste to kill myself. I know it now. I think I knew it all along. Right after I died I said to myself, 'God, that was a stupid thing to do, now I'm going to have to do it all over again!'"[16]

Some confirmation of this is found in visitations, impressions, and messages received by people with no history of mediumistic abilities. Such encounters sometimes occur in dreams, as in this case of a young girl dealing with her brother Chet's suicide:

> Maybe six months later, he came to me in a dream and we talked face to face. He was extremely sad because of what he had done to his family.

I remember Chet having a melancholy and confused look on his face. He was very sorry because we were all hurting—because we were all going through this pain. He didn't want to put us through that. He seemed remorseful and bewildered. He hung his head and shook it, like he just couldn't believe what he had done.[17]

Heath and Klimo identify different kinds of regret expressed by suicides:

- regret for the pain and abandonment felt by those left behind
- regret over no longer having a physical body
- regret for their own wasted potential
- regret for karmic backsliding
- regret for their manner of death (an ex-soldier regretted not dying in battle)
- regret for their continued existence when they'd hoped for oblivion[18]

Nor is regret unwarranted. Again and again, the point is made that suicide, in almost all cases, is a serious mistake with significant spiritual repercussions. As Raymond Moody puts it in a discussion of NDEs involving attempted suicide:

Others who experienced this unpleasant "limbo" state have remarked that they had the feeling they would be there for a long time. This was their penalty for "breaking the rules" by trying to release themselves prematurely from what was, in effect, an "assignment"—to fulfill a certain purpose in life.[19]

California medium Johanna Carroll makes a similar point, this time in respect to familial obligations arising from a group soul. Suicide, she says, is

a break in the contract. You know, we have these sacred contracts as individuals and then collectively, based on past life or whatever the intention of the reincarnation is. I mean, we're all part of a whole. And so, we have the family karma contract that collectively we all agree to do our part. The suicide creates what's called a tear in the contract. So that part of it, as the collective energy, needs to be healed.[20]

A communicator calling himself Alexy uses much the same language:

> One of the things with suicide is that we have to pay the price for our faulty deeds. We have broken our agreement.
> We have not been faithful to our word and must be punished, not punished in the way you know punished to be, punished as in feeling and seeing the consequences of our actions and the impact those actions have on those still living.[21]

Michael Newton says simply that "people who killed themselves with a healthy body do have a reckoning."[22] In a hypnosis session Newton talked to a spirit that was ostensibly in the "interlife" or between-lives state:

> *Spirit*: I ... am going to have to make some kind of ... accounting ... of myself. We go through this after all my lives, but this time I'm really in the soup.
> Dr. Newton: Why?
> *Spirit*: Because I killed myself.
> *Dr. Newton*: When a person kills himself on Earth does this mean they will receive some sort of punishment as a spirit?
> *Spirit*: No, no, there is no such thing here as punishment—that's an earth condition. Clodees [the higher self or spirit guide] will be disappointed that I bailed out early and didn't have the courage to face my difficulties. By choosing to die as I did means I have to come back later and deal with the same thing all over again in a different life. I just wasted a lot of time by checking out early.
> *Dr. Newton*: So, no one will condemn you for committing suicide?
> *Spirit*: (reflects for a moment) Well, my friends won't give me any pats on the back either—I feel sadness at what I did.[23]

In short, a physical lifetime is understood as a kind of contract between the incarnational self and the higher self (or group soul or, in some cases, God). A certain span of years is allotted for that lifetime, and the incarnated soul is expected to serve out that life sentence. Suicide may seem like a loophole allowing for early release, but actually it breaks the contract and simply entails more work on the other side and in future incarnations. Joel Whitton and Joe Fisher observe, "People who commit suicide are frequently seized with a feeling of dread in the interlife; they know they must return to cope with the level of difficulty that led to their premature departure from the Earth plane."[24]

Often this is a complicated and slow process, with the spirit held back by emotional baggage. Medium George Anderson describes the spirit of a suicidal man who was not particularly happy in the afterlife:

> Not that it's upsetting him over there, [to the point] where he can't function and be happy, but he admits—right now he holds a grudge ... This is the first time I've heard this, but he says he cannot in his heart and soul over there honestly ask you to forgive them, he says, "Because I haven't."[25]

Summarizing a large number of cases, Heath and Klimo write,

> Contemporary channeled messages make it pretty clear that suicides are not permanently stuck in some unpleasant hell dimension. They may be in limbo for a time, but eventually are able to leave the lower astral plane and advance spiritually—although this may require more help for them to do so than that which is needed by those who have died from other causes. Prayer appears to be a universal method of assistance that can be used by the living or those already in spirit.[26]

Reincarnation is assumed in most of these accounts. While another earthly lifetime gives the spirit a chance to redeem his error, there's still a price to be paid. Heath and Klimo note that "suicide sometimes appears to have a detrimental effect on future lives. Souls may carry with them the habit pattern of wanting to opt out of life."[27] Souls who bail out repeatedly, who tend to quit when the going gets tough, face a difficult and prolonged spiritual progression.

It should be noted that not all cases of suicide are the same. A person who sacrifices his life for others—for instance, by leaping on a hand grenade to save his companions—is not considered a suicide, according to all accounts I've seen. People at the end of their natural life, suffering from extreme pain or an incurable illness, may be treated leniently if they check out via their own volition. And there are accidental suicides, such as cases of asphyxiation during autoerotic play; although these inspire feelings of regret and even shame, they are distinguished from other suicides because of the absence of intention.

Overall, the message from the other side is clear: you're here on Earth because you have a job to do, and you're expected to do it to the best of your ability, even if it's a long, hard slog. There are no shortcuts.

CHAPTER TEN:
Negative Experiences

As we've seen, sometimes death is not peaceful on account of external circumstances. But even a superficially peaceful death can be traumatic if the dying person's state of mind is unsettled. Remember Emperor Augustus crying out in terror on his deathbed as the spirits of forty young men came to carry him off? That story is purely anecdotal, but better documented cases similarly suggest that the first stages of dying, even when the process is entirely natural, can sometimes be an ordeal.

Hellish experiences

There's considerable controversy over how rare "nightmarish" or "hellish" near-death-experiences may be, but some have been reported.

Howard Storm's NDE is probably the most famous example. In a 2012 interview with the *Catholic Herald*,[1] Storm described how his youthful idealism had given way to nihilism, hedonism, and cynicism—until the day in 1985 when he collapsed in a Paris hotel room with a perforated duodenum and underwent an NDE.

> I found myself standing next to my bed, feeling wonderful. My senses were very heightened. The pain was gone. I tried to communicate with my wife. I thought she was ignoring me. I also noticed an occupant in my bed who bore a remarkable resemblance to me. I knew that person was dead.

So far, he could have been any of hundreds of other NDErs. But after this, things began to take a new turn.

> Then I heard people calling me from outside the room, saying: "It's time for you to go. Hurry up. Let's go." They said: "We know all about you. We've been waiting for you." I thought they were from the hospital.

They weren't. When Storm, in his spirit body, left the hotel room, he found himself entering a surreal passageway that was "very dim, grey and fuzzy, like a really bad black-and-white television picture."

> The people led me away, and the hallway subtly became darker and darker and darker over a long period of time. Eventually, I realized that I was in complete darkness, encircled by a crowd of people and overcome with fear. I said to them: "I want to go back." And they started pushing and pulling at me. The more I fought, the better they liked it. They were biting and scratching and tearing at me, all the while yelling and screaming …
>
> I heard a voice say: "Pray to God." I said: "I don't pray. I don't believe in God." Then, it came a second time; and a third: "Pray to God."
>
> So, I tried to think of a prayer. I started to mumble some things. A mention of God came into a few of these phrases. With each mention the people around me became very, very angry, and started screaming at me: "There is no God" and "Nobody can hear you." It angered them so much that they were retreating from me. The mention of God was unbearable to them.

Finally he was left alone. But his NDE was not over. Lying in darkness, he

> had a vivid feeling of being a child and feeling that there was a wonderful God-man named Jesus who was my friend and who loved me. With real sincerity, I called out: "Jesus, please save me." With that, a tiny light appeared in the darkness and it came down over me. Out of this light came two hands. They reached down and touched me, and all the gore and filth that was me just fell away.
>
> In two or three seconds I was healed and filled with an indescribable love. In this world there is no equivalent to that kind of love. These arms picked me up and brought me into this brilliant light. I was held against the body of this man. I knew that he was Jesus. I cried.
>
> We were moving straight up, faster and faster towards the world of light. It dawned on me then that everything I had believed in was wrong, and I was going to where God lived.

A life review—a replay of the meaningful events in his life—followed, after which he was instructed to return to his physical body, a prospect that left him "very upset." Upon recovering, he changed his lifestyle, became a minister, and dedicated himself to converting unbelievers.

Now, with due respect to Howard Storm, I would not interpret his experience in specifically Christian terms. For one thing, I suspect that "Jesus" was Storm's objectification of his own higher self—an idea we'll return to. And while I'm sure Storm would disagree, I doubt that Christian doctrines *per se* had much to do with his rescue. As we will see, other lost souls have been rescued without reference to Jesus or Christianity or any other specific religious ideas. What's necessary is to "raise your vibrations"—to lift yourself up, emotionally and spiritually, so that you can literally *see the light* and allow yourself to be drawn toward it. Storm's remembrance of the simple faith of his childhood was enough to bring about this reorientation.

Storm had never thought about an afterlife. His lack of preparedness, coupled with his mental state (fear and confusion), his agonizing medical crisis, and perhaps some latent guilt over abandoning his ideals, probably account for the hellish nature of his experience. Remember that the *Tibetan Book of the Dead* tells us that our initial postmortem experiences in the bardo will reflect our mood and our subconscious expectations. The same book also advises us to appeal to any deity we know of (it doesn't matter which), in order to elevate our mind and dispel the frightening imagery.

Robert Crookall offers a similar viewpoint:

> When a man is forced to die suddenly in the prime of life [he] is usually awake, alert and active at the time of transition and ... he tends to remain awake for a period. But, since the Soul Body is enveiled by the [intermediate body] ... his consciousness tends to be 'sub-normal' in the sense of being between waking and dreaming. During this waking-dream, the environment of the newly-dead man includes two different kinds of 'objects': the first consists of the 'doubles' ... of physical objects ... The second group of elements in his environment consists of mental images (such as we see nightly in dreams). Thus, the total environment in this, the (abnormal) 'Hades' state, consists of (a) things which are objective and common to everyone in that state (namely, the 'doubles' of physical objects) and (b) 'thought forms,' i.e. mental images (some created collectively but others individually and therefore more or less private to their creators). Just as the substance of the [intermediate body] ... is ideo-plastic, automatically assuming forms that correspond to people's

mental images, so the substance of the 'Hades' environment ... is ideo-plastic ...

This type of environment is clearly the 'Amenta' of the Egyptians, the 'Hades' of the Greeks (and Romans), the 'Sheol' of the Jews, 'Kama Loca' of the Hindus ..., 'Bardo' of the Tibetans, 'Limbo' of the Scholastic theologians and the 'Lower Borderlands,' 'Lower Astral,' 'Plane of Illusion,' 'Greyworlds,' etc., of various communicators.[2]

Tibetan Buddhist teachings are similarly echoed in Jane Sherwood's book *The Country Beyond*. One communicator, who died in a car crash and at first found the postmortem state unpleasant, described

> a long sojourn in what I think of as Hades, the place of the shade, a dim and formless world which I believe is peopled by the miasma of earth emotions and the unconscious projections of its inhabitants.[3]

The subjective nature of these entities is suggested by accounts in which they behave like shape-shifters, morphing from one form to another. Barbara R. Rommer quotes a thirty-year-old woman named Stephanie who, critically ill with a bacterial infection, had a scary NDE:

> Way off in the distance I saw a beautiful woman coming toward me. She was in a flowing robe. I was going toward her. The closer she got to me, her features started to change. Her face became like a bear, then another animal, then another, then at the end her face turned into this, like, boar's face with tusks and slobber, and I started to freak out. Then I was pulled back into my body.[4]

Rommer also quotes the account of a woman named Yolanda, whose initially frightening NDE turned into a wonderful experience after she, like Howard Storm, appealed to a deity:

> I went into this great void where it felt like there was absolutely nothing at all, like I was in outer space. I was floating, but didn't have control and was stuck, trapped, and scared to death. Then came this sound from deep down inside me calling out: "God, God" ...
>
> This is weird, but when I called out to God, a kind of light,

like spiritual lightning, struck my head and went through me, and then something inside me exploded. When this happened I felt like a crackling and tingling in my mind, in my brain, and I felt tingling through my whole body and every cell became energized and alive. It was traumatizing, but it was wonderful. And the light, just like you read about, was just all knowledge, all life, all beauty, and all love.[5]

Jane Sherwood's communicator—the one who died in a car crash—has more to say about his difficult passage.

> I think the experience of death must vary considerably because it is governed by the state of mind in which one passes over. Also, there is a vast difference between a sudden passing and a quiet and prepared one. The shock of an unnatural death sets the invisible being in a mad turmoil and makes adjustment to a new environment impossible for a while. One finds oneself in a fantastic dream world with no continuity of experience. Flashes of vivid awareness burn themselves out into unconsciousness and the chaos of unconnected states of mind have no proper framework of space and time ...
>
> I think I really had the maximum difficulties: an attitude of blank unbelief in any future life, a repressed and powerful emotional state, and the shock of a violent death. So this was not the normal passing but just a difficult and painful personal experience.[6]

By his own account, Howard Storm was hampered by precisely the same difficulties:

- an attitude of blank unbelief in any future life ("I fully expected that to be it: lights out, end of story")
- a repressed and powerful emotional state (at first Storm was "going to create a culture of peace and love," but later he was "going to live for myself")
- the shock of a sudden physical crisis

Partial confirmation of the idea that some spirits begin their sojourn in the afterlife in a bewildered state comes from people who have regular OBEs. Many of them say they've encountered spirits who seemed "confused or lost," and who were apparently either "dreaming or deceased."[7]

Even when the initial transition is relatively easy, it's possible for unresolved issues from one's earthly life to resurface and cause trouble. Alice Stringfellow's 19th-century channeled manuscript includes an account of a spirit who sank into despair some time after passing over:

> He was overjoyed for a time but after a while his past life, like a dark cloud, overshadowed him and he was compelled to retire. He is in solitude and feels that his punishment is just, as he knows how many years he caused H— so much unhappiness and can talk of nothing else and beg her forgiveness. He can see nothing but his past. It is ever before him, so many years of a mis-spent life wasted and gone.
>
> We do all we can to cheer him and only his immediate family see him. He cares to see no one at present. He cannot come to you yet for some time. I will see him every day. He is satisfied about H— and sends his love. He knows he will be all right after a while.[8]

Nightmarish experiences have been reported in other paranormal contexts. Chapter 2 covered the disturbing OBEs of some astral projectors, while in Chapter 6 we looked at so-called alien abductions, which may be misinterpreted OBEs. Abduction cases are generally negative, with the aliens typically characterized by icy indifference or outright hostility. Some abductees remember being used as unwilling experimental subjects. There is often a weird sexual element to the experience. It all sounds quite similar to those negative NDEs and OBEs where the astral body is beset by inhuman creatures.

Psychoactive drugs can also produce frightening and traumatic experiences. With the help of volunteers, Dr. Rick Strassman has performed experiments with the psychotropic chemical N,N-Dimethyltryptamine, or DMT. Some of the resulting experiences have obvious parallels with both alien abductions and unpleasant OBEs.

Such cases sometimes involve human-sized insect creatures. Aaron, a volunteer for the DMT study, reported that

> an insectlike thing got right into my face, hovering over me as the drug was going in ... There is a sinister backdrop, an alien-type, insectoid, not-quite-pleasant side of this, isn't there? ... Like being possessed. During the experience there is sense of someone, or something else, there taking control. It's like you

have to defend yourself against them, whoever they are, but they certainly are there. I'm aware of them and they're aware of me. It's like they have an agenda.[9]

Another volunteer, Rex, remembered a more intense experience.

> When I was first going under there were these insect creatures all around me. They were clearly trying to break through. I was fighting letting go of who I am or was. The more I fought, the more demonic they became, probing into my psyche and being. I finally started letting go of parts of myself, as I could no longer keep so much of me together. As I did, I still clung to the idea that all was God, and that God was love, and I was giving myself up to God and God's love because I was certain I was dying. As I accepted my death and dissolution into God's love, the insectoids began to feed on my heart, devouring the feelings of love and surrender …
>
> As I was holding on to my last thought, that God equals love, they said, "Even here? Even here?" I said, "Yes, of course." They were still there but I was making love to them at the same time. They feasted as they made love to me. I don't know if they were male or female or something else, but it was extremely alien, though not necessarily unpleasant. The thought came to me with certainty that they were manipulating my DNA, changing its structure …
>
> The sheer intensity was almost unbearable. The forms became increasingly sinister the more I fought. I'm going to need therapy after this—sex with insects![10]

Rex adds that the creatures' communication was nonverbal. "It was an empathic communication, a telepathic communication."

In his book *Supernatural*,[11] Graham Hancock argues that cave paintings preserve a record of prehistoric shamans' hallucinatory experiences, initiated by the ingestion of mind-altering plants. He compares cave imagery with the vision quests of contemporary shamans, as well as with Strassman's experiments, and finds that the same imagery often appears in all these cases—notably insects, snakes, and smallish nonhuman creatures with oddly shaped heads, reminiscent of the pint-sized alien "grays" in UFO accounts. A vision quest sometimes subjects the shaman to vivisection, in which the soul body is cut open and unknown objects are inserted, episodes perhaps symbolized in the "wounded man" motifs of cave paintings. Such experiences have much in common with the quasi-medical tortures undergone by abductees and with Rex's nightmarish DMT trip.

Some caveats

Certain researchers, struck by these negative experiences, recommend caution in personal experimentation with the paranormal, such as the deliberate inducement of OBEs or the use of a Ouija board or Tarot deck. NDE researcher Michael Sabom, a committed Christian, draws a sharp distinction between spontaneous and deliberately initiated paranormal experiences. He believes that the former can give us insights into spiritual truths, while the latter are largely the realm of deceptive and malign entities.[12] For the same reason, Roy Abraham Varghese dismisses any consideration of mediumship in his book *There Is Life After Death*, as does Dinesh D'Souza in *Life After Death: The Evidence*. Both books, written from a Christian perspective, limit their presentation to NDEs.

This viewpoint is common in Christian evangelical circles, where great emphasis is placed on hell, demons, and the dangerous influence of the occult. Maurice Rawlings—who, like Sabom, is both an NDE researcher and a Christian—claims to have found an unusually high proportion of hellish NDEs, which he uses as evidence to support his religious beliefs. Other researchers, however, have not been able to reproduce Rawlings's results. When Nancy Evans Bush wrote *Dancing Past the Dark: Distressing Near-Death Experiences*, she could find only a handful of documented cases, and even some of those don't sound particularly hellish (e.g., simply floating in a void).

But concern with the downside of paranormal investigation isn't limited to evangelicals. After collecting hundreds of reports, Robert Crookall advised his readers not to deliberately experiment with OBEs, believing that the hazards outweighed the benefits.

Mediumship can also be problematic. Consider the tragic case of Joe Fisher, whose involvement with a medium led him to believe he'd been targeted by malicious supernatural entities intent on ruining his life. Although the circumstances of his death are ambiguous, it is widely believed that he committed suicide. As we'll see in the next two chapters, there are additional reasons not to invite unknown entities into our lives.[13]

Having acknowledged all this, I think it's only fair to point out that no field of exploration is risk-free. And there are many cases of a deliberately induced altered state of consciousness that yielded consoling evidence of postmortem survival, as well as uplifting spiritual messages. The trance mediumship of Leonora Piper or Gladys Osborne Leonard shows little sign of malign influences.

Shamanic vision quests may be unpleasant, but they can lead to the development of lifelong spiritual powers, which is why the initiate undertakes the quest in the first place.

Even drug experimentation under careful supervision can have profoundly life-affirming consequences. A 2006 Johns Hopkins study[14] of mushrooms containing psilocybin, a psychoactive chemical, found that one-third of participants described their experience as "the single most spiritually significant of their lifetimes," with some comparing it to "the importance of the birth of their first child or the death of a parent." Moreover, after two months, nearly four in five participants reported "increased well-being or life satisfaction" compared with the control group. A follow-up study showed that the beneficial effects lasted more than a year. Some participants did experience fear and anxiety while on the drug, but with no harmful long-term effects.

William James also experimented with a mind-altering substance:

> I myself made some observations on ... nitrous oxide intoxication, and reported them in print. One conclusion was forced upon my mind at that time, and my impression of its truth has ever since remained unshaken. It is that our normal waking consciousness, rational consciousness as we call it, is but one special type of consciousness, whilst all about it, parted from it by the filmiest of screens, there lie potential forms of consciousness entirely different.[15]

His experience played a role in his decision to write *The Varieties of Religious Experience*, today recognized as a classic.

Overall, experimenting with the expansion of consciousness offers both rewards and perils. Given its possible downside, it is best approached with caution. Moreover, the fact that many drug trips and deliberately induced OBEs go badly, while apparently only a trivial percentage of NDEs and deathbed visions are scary, may suggest a fundamental, qualitative difference between experiences that are intentionally sought out versus those that are natural and spontaneous.

It's always tempting to think there's a shortcut to spiritual enlightenment. Maybe there isn't. Maybe we have to practice patience and accept a degree of uncertainty and doubt. And who knows? Patience and the willing acceptance of uncertainty just might be the very spiritual qualities we seek.

CHAPTER ELEVEN:

Lost Souls

IN 2000 BC, a Sumerian priest inscribed a clay tablet with wedge-shaped cuneiform characters, recording the ritual needed to free a ghost after death. As described by Irving Finkel, this is a three-part process. The ghost "is tied at first to the body by the last breath; then is seated in the ghost-chair [near the body]; then is free to go down to the Netherworld."[1]

This tripartite structure is at least superficially similar to the process described by modern clairvoyants and mediums, and in NDEs. In each case the spirit is "tied at first to the body," then separates but remains in the immediate physical area in an invisible bodily form, then makes the transition to the next world.

But what if a given spirit does *not* make that transition? What if it doesn't "see the light" but instead remains on earth for some significant period of time? Then it becomes an "earthbound spirit"— a concept as old as civilization, and probably much older.

The first ghosts

Ancient Mesopotamian priests, like the one mentioned above, were constantly on guard against earthbound spirits and other malevolent forces. Their culture exemplifies what Carl Sagan called "the demon-haunted world." Demons, in the words of archaeologist Georges Contenau,

> might make a traveler conscious of their presence and then dog his footsteps: not only could they enter houses, whistling, muttering and turning everything upside down, but they could also force their way into the stables and there injure or kill the animals or make them bolt: while if they found a man in a state of sin, having put his god away from him, they could take the god's place ... No matter how tightly bolted and barred a house might be, they could make their way in and there do their devils' work, causing families to quarrel and setting their members against each other ... Eventually the sensation of always being compassed by hordes of invisible enemies ... must have become hideously depressing. They compassed [a man] on

every side, lying in wait for him by day and by night ... and though he might fly from his house, the streets would afford him no protection. "The man who hath not god as he walketh in the street, the demon covers him as a garment."[2]

Irving Finkel quotes an ancient spell meant to drive away evil spirits. These include spirits

> who overwhelm constantly like an *alû*-demon
> who constantly pick on victims like a *lilû*-demon
> who constantly enter houses
> who constantly pass over thresholds
> who constantly clamber over roofs ...[3]

A spell from 1800 BC itemizes ghosts who invade our privacy:

> Be it a 'Let-me-enter, let me eat with you'
> Be it a 'Let-me-enter, let me drink with you'
> Be it an 'I am hungry, let me eat with you'
> Be it an 'I am thirsty ...'[4]

The mages of Sumer, Babylon, and Assyria drew a distinction between a demon (*udug*) and a ghost (*etemmu*), but the line of demarcation was unclear, as it sometimes is today. Any ghosts encountered outside of the netherworld were assumed to be restless and up to no good. Among their number, according to an ancient incantation, were

> "he whose body is abandoned on the plain;
> he who is not given burial;
> she who dies a virgin;
> she who dies in childbed;
> she whose baby, that she suckled, is dead;
> he who hath fallen from a palm tree;
> he who hath drowned himself ..."

> and countless others besides, including, for example, all who, for any reason, were not granted honorable burial, and had no friend to bring them funerary offerings. They all nursed some unsatisfied claim, and all joined the company of the *utukku* [demons] in order to torment the living."[5]

In general, troublesome ghosts were either family members unhappy with an interruption of the ritual supply of food and drink to their graves, or ghosts from outside the family—wanderers afflicted by "premature, violent or unresolved death."[6] Some ghosts were described by the phrase "like a living one," which, according to Finkel, "probably means the specter must be clothed, and so, for a minute, could be thought to be a living—but unfamiliar—person."[7] You'll recall that apparitions seen in modern times also sport clothing of one sort or another, and not infrequently are mistaken for living persons. Meanwhile, the "demons" who enter a house, turning everything upside down, sound very much like poltergeists.

Naturally, we have to wonder how much of this angst was purely psychological. I would guess that a great deal of it was. The increasingly detailed and desperate inscriptions, especially in the later kingdoms of Babylon and Assyria, give evidence of what we might call a "social mania," or mass hysteria, perhaps akin to the witch hunts in Europe and North America or the holocausts of sacrificial victims in Mesoamerica. Reading this material, one has the impression that everybody was plagued by ghosts and demons all the time. Some form of neurosis or psychosis was undoubtedly at work.

Nevertheless, there are enough parallels to more recent, well-documented cases to indicate a core of truth in these timeworn cuneiform tablets. Something, after all, had to set off the mania in the first place and periodically restart it. I suggest that earthbound spirits were behind the genuine cases, while aberrant psychology accounts for their unrealistic proliferation.

If all we had to go on were ancient documents, we might chalk up all these accounts to hysteria. But there are more recent cases to consider.

Cases in the modern era

One restless ghost of more recent vintage was a so-called "drop-in communicator"—a spirit who shows up uninvited at a séance. This case, extensively researched by Erlendur Haraldsson and Ian Stevenson,[8] involves Icelandic trance medium Hafsteinn Bjornsson. In 1937 an unknown spirit intruded on one of Hafsteinn's séances, stating, "I am looking for my leg. I want to have my leg ... It is in the sea."

For months, this oddly persistent stranger continued to make regular appearances, continually demanding his leg while refusing to give his name. His personality was distinctly unpleasant. He was rude, sensual, and addicted to physical pleasures like snuff, coffee, and alcohol—character traits that might explain his concern about his physical remains.

About a year and a half after his debut, he finally identified himself as Runolfur Runolfsson, who died at age 52 half a century earlier. "I lived with my wife at Kolga or Klappakot, near Sandgerdi. I was on a journey from Keflavik in the latter part of the day and I was drunk." He stopped at a house, had more to drink, and departed for home in a very inebriated state. On the way, he made the mistake of resting on a rocky outcrop on the shoreline, where he consumed still more alcohol from a bottle and then fell asleep. "The tide came in and carried me away. This happened in October, 1879. I was not found until January, 1880. I was carried in by the tide, but then dogs and ravens came and tore me to pieces." His scattered bones were gathered up and buried, but his thigh bone (the femur) was missing. "It was carried out again to sea, but was later washed up at Sandgerdi. There it was passed around and now it is in Ludvik's house."

Ludvik was Ludvik Gudmundsson, who had joined the séances a short time earlier. Upon Ludvik's arrival, the excited communicator had said that the new sitter knew about his leg and that the leg was now in his house.

Runolfur, who soon became known more familiarly as Runki, added that confirmation of his story could be found "in the church book of Utskalar Church." Some of the sitters found Runki's name, date of birth, and age at death given in that book—all just as he'd stated. Other claims also panned out. Records indicated that Runki was 52 when he died, and that his dismembered remains were buried in January, 1880. The communicator had said he lived with his wife at Klappakot; records showed that he lived with a woman who bore him three children (though she may not have been his legal spouse) and that shortly before his death, he was living in Klappakot. A clergyman's record book said he went missing "on his way home from Keflavik during a storm [and] is believed to have been carried along by the storm down to the beach ... where the sea carried him away." Another local document, discovered years after the séances, accords even more closely with the spirit's account, noting, "People guessed that the sea had taken him when he sat down exhausted."

As for the missing femur, a human bone of that type proved to have been placed inside the wall of a room in Ludvik's house when the building was remodeled, sometime before Ludvik took possession of it. In that era before DNA testing, the recovered bone could not be definitively identified as belonging to Runolfur Runolfsson; even so, it was interred in his name in a religious service. After this, Runki became more cooperative; he even went on to serve as Hafsteinn's main spirit control.

When we remember that one major reason given for the restlessness of ancient Mesopotamian ghosts was the lack of an honorable burial, we may wonder how much things have really changed in four thousand years.

Another message conveyed through a medium purports to tell the story of a lost soul from his own point of view. In 1965, on "a lovely evening in Spring," Dr. Karl Novotny collapsed dead while walking with friends.

> When all the formalities were concluded and my body had been put into a coffin, I realized that I must be dead. But I wouldn't acknowledge the fact; for, like my teacher, Alfred Adler, I did not believe in an after-life. I visited my university colleagues: but they neither saw me nor returned my greeting. I felt most insulted. What should I do? I went up the hill to where Grete lives. She was sitting alone and appeared very unhappy. But she did not seem to hear me either.
>
> It was no use, I had to recognize the truth. When finally I did so, I saw my dear mother coming to meet me with open arms, telling me I had passed into the next world—not in words of course, since these belong only to the earth. Even so, I couldn't credit her statement and thought I must be dreaming. This belief continued for a long time. I fought against the truth and was most unhappy. Eventually, however, I accepted the suggestion of my spirit-guide, who pointed to the glorious realms to which I might aspire, if I gave up my foolish ideas and sought to make progress in the spirit world.
>
> It was not easy for me. It would have been much simpler if I had been convinced of the continuance of life after death; and had trusted to being helped across and joyfully received on the other side. There would then have been no dilemma, nor such a long transition period as those go through who do not trust their spirit-guide and consider earthly life as the most desirable existence. They may continue for many years bound in thought and feeling to the material world, thus slowing up their spiritual progress, although they can neither stop nor prevent it.[9]

Poltergeists

The German word *poltergeist*, coined by Protestant reformer Martin Luther, means "noisy ghost." As Alan Murdie explains, "The term is applied to hauntings that involve strange sounds, the throwing of objects and baffling physical disturbances that suggest an invisible presence prone to playing silly and mindless tricks."[10]

The best short treatment I've seen of this subject is found in

Robert McLuhan's 2010 book *Randi's Prize*. One of the more convincing cases he covers was originally reported by German parapsychologist Hans Bender. McLuhan writes,

> It occurred in 1967 in a lawyers' office in the Bavarian town of Rosenheim. Investigators watched and filmed as decorative plates jumped off the walls, paintings began to swing and drawers opened by themselves. There was rogue electrical activity, too: lights and fuses kept blowing, and the telephones all rang at once, with no one on the line. As many as forty people were said to witness the events, including power technicians, police officers, doctors, journalists and the firm's clients. In this case the disturbances were associated with a nineteen-year-old secretary named Annemarie Schneider. When she walked through the hall, the lamps behind her began to swing and light fixtures exploded, the fragments flying towards her. Scientists from the Max Planck Institute in Munich, called in to help, used monitoring equipment to systematically eliminate every physical cause, including variations in the supply of current, electrostatic charges, static magnetism, loose contacts and faulty equipment. Critically, they also ruled out manual intervention and concluded that the electrical deflections could only be due to some unknown energy that depended in some way on Schneider.[11]

The disturbances ended when the unfortunate Ms. Schneider was dismissed from her job.

Another case involving electrical problems focused on a different teenage girl, Tina Resch. The case is complicated by the undoubted fact that Tina faked at least some of the later phenomena taking place in the household. Nevertheless, it seems impossible to account for all the phenomena in this way. In the early days of the disturbances, Tina's father was sure she was behind it somehow. But, as McLuhan tells us, his skepticism diminished

> after he spent much of that weekend trying to stop the lights and appliances coming on by themselves. An electrician called in to help could trace no fault, and eventually realized that the problems had nothing to do with the circuits—the switches themselves were flipping up and down. The electrician tried to stop this by taping the switches down, but as fast as he could do so the lights came on again. Sometimes the tape simply disappeared, even when Tina was fully in his view.[12]

Let's take a look at one celebrated case in greater detail. Here I'll rely on McLuhan's write-up in the SPR's indispensable *Psi Encyclopedia*.[13] The case of the Miami warehouse took place between December 1966 and January 1967, and seemed to center on a young shipping clerk, Julio Vasquez. During this time, many items stacked on the warehouse shelves fell and broke, even when no one was nearby. By mid-January the situation had reached a critical point. Warehouse owner Alvin Laubheim said,

> From then on, everything started to happen—boxes came down—a box of about a hundred back-scratchers turned over and fell with a terrific clatter over on the other side of the room and then we realized that there was something definitely wrong around here ... And for three days we picked things up off the floor as fast as they would fall down. It was going on all day—quite violently—but not hurting anything, but things would fall to the floor.

Many witnesses observed the phenomena. They insisted that they'd seen objects—one as large as a big cardboard box—move on their own, when no one was within reach. McLuhan writes,

> On Friday 13 January, Laubheim's partner Glen Lewis [witnessed] items that dropped from the shelves immediately after he had placed them there. Tumblers and ashtrays fell off and broke, and leather packages kept falling off even after he had replaced them.
>
> The disturbances reached a peak on Monday 23 January, beginning from the moment the business opened in the morning. A total of 52 separate incidents were logged. Lewis was particularly concerned about a box of tall drinks glasses, and had inserted one side of the cardboard lid into the other so that it could not open. Laubheim says: 'The next thing we knew, there was a terrific crash on the other side of the room and the whole box was lying upside down with all the glasses broken.' The glasses would have to have crossed his line of vision to break where they did, but he saw nothing. The box, weighing fifteen pounds, had moved 24 feet.
>
> William Drucker, the firm's insurance agent, visited on 13 January. He was shown the breakages and examined the shelves to see if they vibrated. However, the shelves were strong, and he could not see how anything but a strong tremor would cause an object to be displaced. Having spent more than an hour in the

warehouse he was on his way out when he heard a 'thud.' He turned and established quickly where everyone in the room had been. He then found two boxes tied together out in the middle of the aisle. There was no sign of floor tremors, the boxes were at least seventeen feet away from Julio, and he had checked the shelves beforehand. He concluded that Julio could not have caused this event.

Reluctantly, Laubheim called in the police, who also witnessed some of the phenomena. In addition, he asked a magician friend, Howard Brooks, to come by. On his first visit, Brooks observed nothing unusual, but upon his return he saw a pair of cartons weighing about two pounds drop on the floor when no one but himself was present.

All of this led up the involvement of parapsychologist William Roll and his colleague Gaither Pratt, both of whom had investigated poltergeist outbreaks before.

During his final two days at the site, Roll logged a total of 28 incidents, in thirteen of which he was present and in a position to be sure that trickery was not the cause. For many of the other fifteen incidents, he interviewed witnesses immediately afterwards, and in ten of these, Julio was said not to be near enough to have been able to cause them ...

Roll confirmed that some objects that fell to the floor had apparently gone round or over other objects standing in their paths. In one instance, Julio was placing an object at floor level when a drinks glass fell from the shelves behind him. (Roll observed Julio from five feet away and saw that he had no contact with the shelf and that both his hands were occupied. No one else was anywhere near to have thrown the glass.) Previously Roll had placed notebooks and other objects in front of the glass. However, these were undisturbed, so the glass would have to have risen into the air at least two inches on its way to the floor.

Julio Vasquez was a troubled young man. In the months prior to the warehouse disturbances, he'd been plagued by bad dreams in which he saw himself killed. Ten days before the first poltergeist incident he was ousted from his family home by his stepmother. In February he was caught shoplifting and sentenced to six months in prison. Once he was no longer around, conditions at the warehouse returned to normal.

Clearly, Julio played some role in the outbreak, but there was no evidence suggesting that he caused the damage deliberately, and, in many cases, items fell when he wasn't even in the room. The simplistic solution that he faked the whole thing won't wash. Even Brooks, a trained magician who was initially skeptical, came to believe that something paranormal was going on.

Such cases are not as rare as you might think. In *Randi's Prize*, McLuhan notes:

> The research literature on poltergeist claims consists of several hundred published cases, of which scores have been the subject of reports by serious investigators. I say "serious" because they have made it their business to seek out such incidents, to interview witnesses and wherever possible to observe the phenomena themselves. Their reports are often quite detailed and correspond to the extent that a clear pattern emerges. In addition, there are a handful of cases such as the Miami warehouse and the Rosenheim office in which experts in different fields are said to concur that they have observed, on many different occasions, some force currently unknown to science …
>
> [Alan Gauld and A.D Cornell] identified 500 cases for which there are published records, and their list would have been much longer, they say, if they had included unsubstantiated media reports.[14]

Moreover, definite patterns among the cases emerge, and these patterns date back hundreds of years to the earliest reasonably well-documented reports, such as the Epworth Rectory case of 1716. Gauld and Cornell found that almost half the cases in their database began with unusual noises—raps, thumps, bangs.[15] The phenomena are often focused on a young person, anywhere from roughly eight to twenty years old. (Tina Resch was fourteen; both Annemarie Schneider and Julio Vasquez were nineteen.) An outbreak is somewhat more likely to center on a girl than a boy.

Because an emotionally overwrought teenager is so frequently the focus of the phenomena, and because the activity can sometimes follow this person from one location to another, parapsychologists often argue that poltergeists are projections of the unconscious mind. But are we *sure* the teenager is generating the phenomena? Correlation is not causation. Moreover, the correlation is not perfect. Murdie points out that Alan Gauld found 76% of poltergeist cases lasted six months or less, with disturbances centering on particular individuals. These suggested human agency with more females than males as the postulated foci. However, 24% of longer term cases (one year or more) seemed unconnected with an individual and appeared to be more place-centered.[16]

Similarly, Ian Stevenson

> wrote an article for the *Journal of the American Society for Psychical Research* titled "Poltergeists: Are they Living or are they Dead?" Stevenson argued that while psychokinesis from a living agent, such as a troubled adolescent, might explain shorter term cases with relatively simple phenomena, there were others that were much more complex and where a discarnate intelligence was suggested, based upon marked differences within cases.[17]

Rather than assuming that a given teenager is subconsciously producing the phenomena, couldn't we argue with equal plausibility that a malicious spirit has latched on to this victim and is following him or her around? Could the turmoil of the young person's emotions serve as a magnet to draw in an unwanted spiritual entity, in much the same way that the Ouija board is said to attract low-level spirits?

A proposal along these lines was made by parapsychologist Maurice Grosse, who investigated the famous Enfield poltergeist. In *Consulting Spirit*, Ian Rubenstein recounts his interview with Grosse.

> "So, what do you think is going on in these poltergeist cases?" I asked him.
>
> Maurice sat back in his chair, his fingers steepled in thought. He paused for a moment, carefully considering his position.
>
> "Some people feel it's all down to spirit influence in these cases; in effect the focus, the person at the center of the disturbance, is a haunted individual. If you like, ghosts haunt places, while poltergeists haunt individuals. Others say it's just down to telekinesis, mind over matter, on the part of the focus, the person around whom these events tend to occur. These people would say that it's all just a manifestation of unexplained mental abilities and would deny the involvement or even the existence of spirits. Of course, other people just blame it all on trickery ...

"My theory, for what it's worth, is that the focus certainly provides energy. In some cases the focus can even use this energy to affect the environment. At the same time, any passing entity can also pick up this energy and play with it, too. Think of a kid kicking around a football in the park. Then a couple of other kids come around and start playing with it as well. It's like a sort of 'energy football.' Think of the emotional energy children generate when they reach puberty. That's why they're so often the focus of such cases."

This made sense to me and seemed to tie in with what I was learning in my psychic development circle. In order to manifest in the physical world, discarnate entities such as spirits required some form of physical energy supplied by a living person.

"So, in this case the girls provided the energy and a spirit came along and used it to move objects and communicate," I summed up. "That's a very interesting theory."[18]

It seems to me that spirit involvement of some kind is necessary to explain many well-documented poltergeist cases, though not necessarily all of them.

Some ghosts are even more intrusive than poltergeists. Like a supernatural virus, they take over a living host.

CHAPTER TWELVE:

Possession

EARTHBOUND SPIRITS NOT ONLY can wreak havoc on your home or place of business, they also can sometimes obsess or possess the living. This idea was prevalent in ancient Assyria and Babylon, as preserved in this ritualistic complaint:

> A ghost smites me again and again; a ghost is making me ill; a ghost afflicts me.
> A ghost continually pursues me; a ghost cannot be loosed from my body.[1]

One such victim groans that "an *utukku*-demon, a *rābiṣu*-demon, a ghost or a *lilû*-demon [has] weighed out paralysis, convulsions, numbness, dizziness, joint-pain and insanity for me: every day they make me howl."[2]

Whether the ghost was merely hanging about as a bad influence (an obsessing spirit) or had actually taken over a person's body (a possessing spirit), the case was likely to require a formal expulsion. Any such procedure was known broadly as *namburbû* (meaning "its release") and consisted of magic words, appeals to powerful gods, and, often, ritualistic actions involving effigies.

For those who opted for a do-it-yourself approach, the victim of possession would recite a spell like this one: "You shall not come near my body again. You are expelled and driven out."[3] At other times, a professional exorcist was needed. The incantation was written with blank spaces for the insertion of the appropriate names in a given case:

> You must take him out of the body of So-and-so, son of So-and-so, and go away ...
> From the body of So-and-so, son of So-and-so are you expelled, are you banished, are you removed, are you driven away![4]

The Watseka Wonder

Of course, we need not rely on cuneiform tablets for possession cases. Plenty of them date from more recent times. In one of the most famous instances, the spirit's intentions were purely benign.

In 1877, thirteen-year-old Mary Lurancy Vennum, known as "Rancy," suffered a seizure with surprising aftereffects. Michael Tymn, an authority on 19th-century spiritualism, tells the tale:

> The next day, while apparently in a trance state, she said she could see spirits of the dead, including her deceased sister and brother. Over the next two months she had a number of similar trance experiences, describing "heaven" and "angels" ...
>
> Two local physicians and the family's Methodist minister all concluded she had become insane and recommended she be sent to an asylum.
>
> Asa Roff, a lawyer, contacted Rancy's parents and persuaded them to first let the girl be examined by a Dr. Stevens from Wisconsin. Roff explained that he had experienced a similar ordeal with his daughter Mary, who had died in July 1865 aged eighteen (when Rancy was just a year old), and that he had regretted having placed her in a sanatorium.[5]

In Stevens's initial examination, Rancy first identified herself as 63-year-old Katrina Hogan and then as another personality, Willie Canning. When Stevens tried to put Rancy in touch with a higher intelligence, she told him

> there were a great many spirits willing to come, and that one "angel" stepped forward giving her name as Mary Roff. Asa Roff immediately identified her as his daughter.
>
> Rancy then declared she would let Mary Roff take over her body for a period of time. Her personality then changed from the wild and ungovernable girl she had been in recent months to become mild, polite, and somewhat timid. She now claimed to know none of the Vennum family and said she wanted to go home.

Rancy/Mary was able to identify many of Mary's family members, neighbors, and friends, all of whom were unknown to Rancy herself. She also passed tests posed by Mary's father, recalling obscure details of Mary's life. In the course of time, the press picked up the story, and the girl was dubbed the Watseka Wonder, after Rancy's hometown of Watseka, Illinois.

In a letter to Dr. Stevens, Asa Roff wrote,

> Mary is perfectly happy; she recognizes everybody and everything that she knew when in her body twelve or more years ago. She knows nobody nor anything whatever that is known to Lurancy.
>
> Mr. Vennum has been to see her, and also her brother, Henry, at different times, but she don't [sic] know anything about them. Mrs. Vennum is still unable to come and see her daughter. She has been nothing but Mary since she has been here, and knows nothing but what Mary knew.

This situation continued for a few months. On May 21, 1878, Asa Roff wrote to Dr. Stevens, saying: "Mary is to leave the body of Rancy today, about eleven o'clock, so she says. She is bidding neighbors and friends good-by ... She tells me to write to Dr. Stevens as follows: 'Tell him I am going to heaven and Rancy is coming home well.'"

The changeover went off on schedule, after which Rancy led a more-or-less normal life, though reportedly the Mary personality did sometimes re-emerge for short periods.

If not for the girl's ability to recognize strangers and recall incidents from Mary's life, the case might be explained as an instance of multiple personality disorder, perhaps influenced by Asa Roff's yearning to be reunited with his daughter. As it is, though, the Watseka Wonder is a strong candidate for spirit possession.

Spirit rescue

Not all invasive ghosts are so obliging as to go away on their own. Exorcism, as we've seen, is one way of ousting the more obstinate squatters. In other cases, the best treatment is therapy—not therapy for the living host, but for the possessing spirit.

One of the pioneers of this approach was psychiatrist Carl A. Wickland, whose 1924 memoir *Thirty Years Among the Dead* recounts his efforts to cure his patients by spiritualist methods. His wife Anna was a medium, and Wickland became convinced that some of the incurable patients institutionalized at his facility were suffering from spirit obsession or possession.

Wickland exposed these patients to static electricity, which was intended to drive the malignant entity out of the patient's "magnetic aura." The entity was then attracted to the entranced Anna Wickland, through whom the spirit spoke. What followed was a therapy session in which the psychiatrist did his best to persuade the deceased to open his "spiritual eyes" and progress to the next stage of development. In many cases these efforts proved successful, and the patient, who had previously resisted all cures, improved markedly and could be de-institutionalized.

One newly enlightened communicator stated,

> All this time, as you have told me, I have been dead. I have been in darkness but, as this gentleman tells me, it was a spiritual darkness. My eyes are open and I can now see.
>
> A beautiful world lies before me.[6]

The Wicklands also participated in "spirit rescue" circles, holding séances that invited random earthbound spirits to drop in and receive counseling. One of these visitors said,

> I know I have been walking a very great deal, and it seems to me I never get anywhere. I saw a lot of people here. I came here with the crowd, and before I knew it, everything was light, and I saw you all sitting around in a circle, singing. I thought it was a prayer meeting, so I stopped, and before I knew anything, I could talk. Before then I thought I must be deaf and dumb and blind, because I could not see anything, and I am so tired.[7]

The ceaseless walking is reminiscent of the fate of one suicide we looked at earlier (also drawn from a Wickland séance): "Then I slept for awhile and after that I walked a long time in the twilight. It seemed like the desert."[8]

Lending credence to these experiments is the fact that many of the communications included evidential details, later verified, which were unknown to the Wicklands at the time. Here's one such case drawn from a rescue circle:

> A spirit who was still following his old occupation without any knowledge of his transition controlled Mrs. Wickland at one of our circles in Chicago …
>
> "I am Hesselroth, from the drug store," he said.
>
> Mr. Hesselroth, the Swedish proprietor of a Chicago drug store, had died the year before in a hospital, but we knew

nothing of this man, his death, or his circumstances; however, on this evening one of his friends, Mr. Eckholm, was in our circle.

The spirit was not aware of his death, claiming that he was still attending to his drug store.

His friend in the circle said he had been informed that the drug store had been sold to the clerk, and so stated to the spirit, but this the latter emphatically denied, saying:

"Abrahamson only manages it for me."

The spirit told of a robbery which had occurred in his house recently, and described the three burglars. He said he had been frightened when they entered, but gaining courage, had gone for his revolver only to find that he was not able to pick it up. He had then struck at one of the burglars, but his hand had gone "right through the fellow," and he could not understand why he could do nothing at all.

After his condition was explained to him he saw many spirit friends appear, who welcomed him to his new home in the spirit world.

Later investigation verified the statement made by the spirit that the drug store had not been sold and also the fact that the house had been burglarized.

It could not be held that the subconscious mind of the psychic played any part in this case, nor could the theory of auto-suggestion be maintained, for Mr. Hesselroth was entirely unknown to every one in the room with the exception of his friend, Mr. Eckholm, and this friend held the opposite idea regarding the sale of the store.[9]

In treating a female patient who suffered from attacks of choking, spells of paralysis, and stomach pain, Wickland found himself in communication with a spirit who

> gave her name as Frances Dickinson and was very despondent. She said she had had severe stomach trouble and when she became paralyzed her husband had left her. Discouraged, desperate and unable to make a living for herself, she had committed suicide by turning on the gas in her room …
>
> The father of the patient was greatly interested in the statements made by the spirit and decided to verify them if possible. Accordingly he made inquiries at the Coroner's office in Los Angeles and looked up records of the Bureau of Vital

Statistics, where he found the following entry:

"Frances Dickinson, age 71, native of Canada, committed suicide by turning on the gas in her room at Number [word missing] South G— Avenue, Los Angeles, June 13, 1922."

Obtaining the address of the undertakers in the case, he found their records showed Frances Dickinson had died from gas, and the body had been cremated June 20, 1922.

Further verification was received from the woman's place of residence and the added information given that she had suffered considerably from stomach trouble.[10]

There were other evidential aspects to Mrs. Wickland's mediumship. At times she exhibited xenoglossy, the ability to speak languages unknown to her—specifically, Eskimo and Russian, both verified by witnesses fluent in those tongues.

The sudden improvement of many of Dr. Wickland's patients can perhaps be explained by the power of suggestion. But how about persons who were treated remotely, remaining unaware of any intervention?

A peculiar case was that of Mr. Mc., a well known man in Chicago, whose family name is one of highest social prominence.

This man suddenly began to act strangely; he shunned the members of his family, and told his wife and relatives that he wished to live on a higher plane and wanted nothing more to do with them. Then one day he packed his trunk and left home, going to live in a small room which he had rented in the lowest section of the city.

We had never seen this gentleman, but a relative of his, who knew of our work, asked us to concentrate for him at our next psychic circle; we did so and a spirit was brought who controlled Mrs. Wickland. After some solicitation she gave her full name, confessing that she had been the first wife of Mr. Mc., and she then told her story. [This spirit, Mr. Mc.'s first wife, had left him, become a morphine addict, and committed suicide.]

After her death she had returned to her husband, and when he married again she felt angrily aggrieved, and at last influenced him to leave his wife and child, to go to quarters where she herself felt more at home.

We convinced her of the great wrong she was doing in controlling her former husband in this manner, and after she had obtained an understanding of the progress awaiting her in the spirit world, she promised to leave, wishing to attain a higher condition.

When next we saw the relative of Mr. Mc., who had asked us to concentrate for him, we told her of the story related by the spirit, and in amazement she admitted it was true in every detail; that the name given was correct and that Mr. Mc. had been married before, but that the unfortunate episode had been regarded by the family as a skeleton in the closet and was never mentioned.

She later reported that Mr. Mc. had returned to his home, normal and sane, and was again living happily with his wife and child.[11]

In another such case, a friend of the Wicklands "complained of the peculiar and erratic actions of a business associate, Mr. P., who had suddenly become extremely irritable and despotic to those in his employ, highly unreasonable, impossible to please, and subject to violent attacks of swearing." Mrs. Wickland was able to channel "an irate spirit," who admitted that while attached to Mr. P., he had "done a lot of swearing," kept him up at night, and tormented him continually.

The angry spirit was eventually persuaded that he had died—an idea he'd resisted because he "had always thought death ended all, and that was all there was to it." He agreed to leave Mr. P. alone. "The following day," Wickland reports, "there was such a remarkable improvement in the conduct of Mr. P., and his behavior was so wholly normal that the entire office force noticed the change, although Mr. P. himself never knew of the experimental effort which had been made in his behalf."[12]

Not all the Wicklands' interventions were successful. Some spirits proved too stubborn or too lost to be helped. Dr. Wickland found the spirits of religious fanatics to be particularly immune to his treatment.

Contemporary cases

A few therapists still use this technique. Among them is Alan Sanderson, a psychiatrist specializing in hypnotherapy, who has become an advocate of spirit release therapy. One of his cases, dating from 1995, involves a patient he calls Clara. He wrote about it at length in the *European Journal of Clinical Hypnosis*.[13]

Clara suffered from depression, anxiety, and panic attacks, and her life had recently started going downhill. While she was under hypnosis, Sanderson inquired, "Subconscious mind, is there anybody with Clara who is not actually part of her?" Clara indicated that there were two such entities, Henrietta and Gladys. Gladys identified herself as Clara's great aunt, who died in 1947. She disapproved of the men in Clara's life, whom she called "brutes," an attitude grounded in her own unhappy marriage.

Sanderson counseled her, "And now, the anger about [your husband], who was impossible, who battered you, and cheated you, and gave you such a difficult time that you didn't at all deserve ... Gladys, you have lived through all that, and now allow yourself to let go of it."

Gladys and Henrietta were eventually persuaded to vacate Clara's body, but two more spirits then turned up, the last of whom, Tony Gizzard, proved somewhat dull-witted.

> *Tony*: Well, er ... I've been asleep.
> *Sanderson*: Oh! You've been asleep, have you? Well, that can happen, that people lose their bodies and they feel that they've been asleep for a long time. But, Tony, you're awake now, aren't you?
> *Tony*: Yeah.
> *Sanderson*: And you see, what's happened is that you actually lost your body and you're a spirit now and you have joined another person, another living person with a body of her own.
> *Tony*: Um.
> *Sanderson*: So you've joined Clara, who is a woman, and you're in a woman's body now. Tony, what year is it for you?
> *Tony*: 1982.
> *Sanderson*: 1982, is it? Well, you may be surprised to hear that it is now 1995.

Sanderson regressed Tony so that he could re-experience his own death. Lying drunk on the floor, he had gone to sleep, or so it seemed. When he'd awakened—or rather, when he'd died and left his body—he had visited a club, where he sat at the bar but inexplicably could not receive a drink. He'd tried chatting up a girl, but the "silly cow" hadn't responded. Now he experienced an alarming revelation.

> *Tony*: Oh, God, I'm in her ... Hm. Ha. (rather embarrassed, amused)
> *Sanderson*: You're in her, are you?
> *Tony*: Yeah, that's where I am.
> *Sanderson*: This is the girl who wouldn't speak to you?

Tony: Yeah.

Sanderson: This is Clara?

Tony: Yeah.

Sanderson: I see, yeah. So that's a surprise. You didn't mean to join her?

Tony: No. Oh ...

Sanderson: So, that explains a lot to you, doesn't it, Tony? You joined her by mistake. You didn't realize you had lost your body!

Tony: Oh no, that's right.

Sanderson: Well, Tony these things can happen.

Tony willingly went into the light, and Clara was finally free of unwanted spirits. She reported:

> Tony ... had died in an alcoholic stupor, and I did wonder about my own excesses with alcohol, which had started at exactly the age that Tony said he joined me ...
>
> Over the next few weeks I noticed many changes in myself. I instantly had so much energy and now have an average 25 per cent less sleep than before my treatment although I am twice as active during the day. I started to feel more and more relaxed about everything in my life as the feeling that someone was looking over my shoulder ready to criticize me at every turn had disappeared ... In the fifteen months since the end of my treatment I no longer have any pains in my head or feel the urge to drink excessive amounts of alcohol. I have lost fifteen kg [33 pounds] excess weight, without dieting, and am down to five cigarettes a day. My moods are much more reliable and I am nothing like so sensitive to people's remarks as I used to be.

Sanderson notes that as of 1998 he had treated more than one hundred patients using the spirit release technique. Sometimes the effects were "strikingly beneficial," as in Clara's case; at other times, the effects were "transitory or absent." He had seen no negative effects. He observes that Clara's case could be interpreted as "the effect of hypnosis on an over-suggestible subject," though he clearly prefers to see it as "an indication of a spiritual reality, which demands exploration."

In a 2014 follow-up, Sanderson adds that when he last spoke to Clara in 2004 (nine years after treatment), she was still "happy and in excellent health."[14]

Carl Wickland used a medium to contact the spirits, while Alan Sanderson uses hypnosis. But the resulting dialogues are strikingly similar. The same is true of another hypnotherapist, Edith Fiore, a psychologist and author of the 1987 book *The Unquiet Dead*. Fiore practices both past-life regressions and what she calls "depossessions"—the removal of harassing spirits.

One of her patients, Peter, had a serious drinking problem that sometimes got him into barroom brawls. Though of upper middle-class background, he frequented "the rougher sorts of establishments" favored by workingmen. A hypnosis session summoned up a spirit who'd been a construction worker. Though asked to leave, the spirit hung on.

> *Fiore*: You're still here. What's your name?
>
> *Patient*: Lou, I think.
>
> *Fiore*: But why are you still here with Peter?
>
> *Patient*: He lets me drink. He can be fun, and I can get him to go to my kind of places.
>
> *Fiore*: What kind of places?
>
> *Patient*: You know, a place that's got real men in it who know how to drink—not a bunch of stuffed shirts.

Further discussion revealed that his last memory of his previous life was an accident in which a Caterpillar tractor rolled over him.

> *Fiore*: You were killed in that accident.
>
> *Patient*: I was?
>
> *Fiore*: What happened after that?
>
> *Patient*: I saw a small boy playing in a backyard. He seemed pleasant enough and friendly. And I felt lonely—and lost. So I went towards him.[15]

Fiore explained to the confused Lou that he had taken possession of Peter at that point. She finally persuaded him to leave. After this session, Peter no longer had problems with alcohol.

Fiore's book also points up a downside of the belief in possession; it can promote a paranoid worldview. Believing that possession can result from almost any moment of weakness, Fiore advises:

> An excellent way to protect yourself is to avoid using "recreational" drugs and alcohol. The amount that weakens the aura varies from person to person and also depends on the energy level. Some of my patients have lowered their resistance with only two glasses of wine. Even getting "stoned" or drunk once can result in a possession that can last a lifetime! …
>
> Possessions can occur after surgery or during hospitalizations …
>
> At funerals, and at all the events associated with them, you need extra protection around yourself …
>
> I believe that most of my patients who were possessed by many spirits, and who frequently picked up new ones in between therapy sessions, were "uncontrolled" mediums or "sensitives." This was especially the case when they had not abused drugs and alcohol. The slightest things weakened their auras: eating a meal with MSG or taking one tablet of pain medication. Even driving by a cemetery or visiting a friend in the hospital resulted in a new possession.[16]

Elsewhere she says that using a Ouija board, attending a séance, visiting a psychic or medium, practicing automatic writing, or trying to get in touch with deceased loved ones or spirit guides can also invite possession. Moreover, children are frequently prone to possession even when they have no obvious risk factors. Apparently a child's aura is often weak enough to allow spirits to get in whenever they wish. She also believes that so-called imaginary friends in childhood are actual spirits, whose close proximity to the child naturally increases the chance of possession.

The only protection against this chronic danger is constantly invoking "white light" as a shield around yourself, and also using it to cleanse your home, which can become a repository for wandering spirits. Fiore says she cleanses every room of her home on a daily basis and practices the white light exercise whenever she feels under stress.

If spirit possession is this common, most people must be possessed, at least some of the time. This is, in fact, Fiore's opinion. Not surprisingly, in her practice she has found countless cases of possession, including cases where a given patient was possessed by dozens of spirits. "Occasional patients," she reports, "were unwitting hosts to as many as fifty or more!"[17]

Either spirit harassment is as prevalent as the ancient Babylonians feared ... or Fiore's own assumptions are being imposed on her patients through the mechanism of hypnosis, which allows direct communication with the highly suggestible subconscious mind. In any event, her hypervigilant attitude hardly seems conducive to inner peace or mental health.

Conclusion

Though it is literally the stuff of ghost stories, the idea of tormenting spirits dates back to the very beginnings of civilization and, in modern times, has been the basis for therapeutic techniques that have had some measure of success. Unless all of the messages received via mediumship and hypnosis are subconscious inventions (and the verifiable details elicited can somehow be explained away), the most likely hypothesis is that some departed souls really do hover close to the earth and attach themselves, wittingly or not, to the living.

Just how widespread is this problem? Robert Crookall takes a typically judicious attitude. He suggests that "a loose vehicle of vitality [= intermediate body], in mediumistic, passive people," may provide an opening for earthbound spirits. "Two features, namely, cold winds and tingles, may indicate that contact has been made." This said, he goes on to remark:

> It is clear that, although 99% of "obsessions" may be psychological, the 1% which are accompanied by these features are nothing of the sort: they are associations—highly undesirable associations—with discarnate Souls who are of low, even of dangerous type: some are definitely hostile.[18]

Fortunately, most spirits go directly into the light, without the need for coaching. In doing so, they make a graceful and uplifting transition from this physical plane to a new manner of being.

In Part Three, we'll look at this transition.

PART THREE: *Transition*

The street rushed up to meet her and she felt its numbing impact ... But she was also aware, from a higher perspective, of her body sprawled across the cobbles ... How inconsequential was this mortal husk now that the blinding light was forcing her attention upwards ... She had walked into the light, like more lustrous and dazzling than the sun yet devoid of any sensation of heat. This absorbing brightness exuded peace and serenity and, utterly relaxed, she basked in its benevolence. There was also the impression of being enclosed in a tunnel or tube or cocoon. Words were quite unequal to the task of describing the magnificent environment to which was drawn at incredible speed.

—past-life regression of Linda Irving, as reported by Joel Whitton[1]

Hieronymus Bosch, *Ascent of the Blessed* (1500-1504)

CHAPTER THIRTEEN:
Beginning the Transition

IN SPIRIT RESCUE, the lost or wandering spirit is told to go into the light. By all accounts this is good advice—quite possibly the very best advice any of us will ever get.

Admittedly, "the light" has become a New Age cliché. It sometimes seems as if every popular book ever written about NDEs has the word *light* in its title. Here's a sample:

- Embraced by the Light
- Closer to the Light
- Saved by the Light
- The Light Beyond
- Lessons from the Light
- Into the Light
- After the Light
- Secrets of the Light
- Transformed by the Light
- The Truth in the Light
- Learning from the Light
- Awakenings from the Light
- The Light after Death
- Beyond the Light
- Light after Death

We can even read *Deceived by the Light* and *Blinded by the Light*, both written from an evangelical Christian perspective to debunk NDEs for being "non-Biblical."

Skeptics understandably make fun of this repetitive trope. Even so, it's possible that the constant reiteration of the term "light" serves a valuable purpose, imprinting the idea in our collective unconscious and making it more likely—whatever our belief system may be—that we'll be open to the light when it appears to us.[1]

To put the light into its full context, let's take a look at a complete NDE. In *Heading Toward Omega*, Kenneth Ring presents the case of Patrick Gallagher, a 46-year-old anthropology professor who suffered a serious auto accident.

> I was floating in the air above the body ... and viewing it down [at] sort of a diagonal angle. This didn't seem to cause any consternation to me at all. I really was completely dead but that didn't cause emotional difficulties.
> Then, after that, I realized that I was able to float quite easily, even though I had no intention of doing that ... Then I very quickly discovered also that not only was I floating and hence free from gravity but free also from any of the other constrictions that inhibit flight ... I could also fly at a terrific rate of speed [and] it seemed to produce a feeling of great joy ...
> Then I noticed that there was a dark area ahead of me and as I approached it, I thought that it was some sort of a tunnel and immediately, without further thought, I entered into it and then flew with an even greater sensation of the joy of flight ...
> I noticed a sort of circular light at a great distance which I assumed to be the end of the tunnel as I was roaring through it ... And the light—the nearest thing I can barely approximate its description to is the setting of the sun at a time under ideal circumstances when one can look at this object without any of the usual problems that staring at the sun causes ...
> And then I went through the tunnel and seemed to be in a different state. I was in different surroundings where everything seemed to be similarly illuminated by that same light and, uh, I saw other things in it, too ... [a] number of people ... I saw my father there, who had been dead for some 25 years ...
> I also felt and saw of course that everyone was in a state of absolute compassion to everything else ... This produced a phenomenal feeling of emotion to me, again, in the free sense that the flight did earlier, because it made me feel that ... there was nothing but love ...
> It seemed nothing like a dream ... It really is a strange sensation to be in, but it does give you a feeling that you are in a kind of eternity.[2]

Bright light is associated with mystical experiences and divine revelations in many cultures. There have even been artistic representations of the departed going into the light, most notably Hieronymus Bosch's *Ascent of the Blessed*, painted sometime around 1500. The painting (included at the start of Part Three) depicts souls floating upward and into a tunnel with a bright light at the end.

The tunnel is what we'll focus on first. It is by no means a part of all NDEs or other messages—in fact, the majority of accounts lack this feature—but it crops up consistently enough to be taken seriously.

The tunnel

In *Light and Death*, Michael Sabom reports various cases of passage through a tunnel or similar space. He quotes a patient named Ted, who suffered a heart attack: "I just blacked out ... I found myself in this little walkway, like a tunnel ... I got about two-thirds of the way down it and a voice—a commanding voice but not a demanding voice—said, 'You can't come in here. Go back.'"

And there's the case of Gene, a physician, whose pupils were "fixed, dilated, and unresponsive" (according to the medical report) after fifteen minutes of CPR and ten or fifteen electrical shocks. He told Sabom,

> What it felt like was that I didn't really have a body. It was like a mind and a soul. From a very far distance I could see a light.
>
> I started approaching this light. Then, as I got closer and closer, it seemed that I was picking up speed. The intensity of the light was like a beam that got brighter and brighter and brighter as I approached it. It was incredible how intense that light was ...
>
> It was a wonderful feeling—ten times better than anything else. This really surprised me. I had never heard of anything like this before. It's not like a dream, either. You forget dreams or remember bits and pieces of them, but this was so vivid. I was so overwhelmingly calm and peaceful. I felt so good that I didn't care which way I went.[3]

Lori had a cardiac arrest while in surgery:

> I went down this dark corridor ...
>
> At the end of the corridor was this bright light. Brighter than any sunlight. Brighter than any star. Brighter than anything you can think of. It permeated everything. Everything was that light. It was so clear.[4]

Arlene received an overdose of anesthesia:

> I had a very fleeting moment of panic and then I just went out. It was the most peaceful feeling I have ever had in my whole life. There is nothing you can even compare it to.
>
> There was something like a moment of blackness and then I found myself walking down a hallway lined with doors. There was a very bright light at the end of the hallway and a voice kept telling me that everything was fine. I felt wonderful and I just kept walking straight towards the light ... I didn't want to come back.[5]

In 1956 a fourteen-year-old boy was on a family trip when the car was trapped in a flash flood:

> I knew I was either dead or going to die. But then something happened. It was so immense, so powerful that I gave up on my life to see what it was. I wanted to venture into this experience, which started as a drifting into what I could only describe as a long tunnel of light. But it wasn't just a light, it was a protective passage of energy with an intense brightness at the end which I wanted to look into, to touch. There were no sounds of any earthly thing. Only the sounds of serenity, of a strange music like I had never heard. A soothing symphony of indescribable beauty blended with the light I was approaching ...
>
> As I reached the source of the light I could see in. I cannot begin to describe in human terms the feeling I had at what I saw. It was a giant infinite world of calm, and love, and energy and beauty. It was as though human life was unimportant compared to this. And yet it urged the importance of life at the same time it solicited death as a means to a better, different life. It was all being, all beauty, all meaning for existence.[6]

Peter Thompson suffered a surgical mishap involving insertion of a cardiac catheter:

> And I was aware I was losing consciousness and of people rushing around me, knocking things over in their efforts to get emergency equipment set up. Then there was nothing—no pain at all. And I was up there on a level with the ceiling—I say "I was there," because that's how it was. It wasn't a dream, it wasn't imagination. It was as real as me sitting here talking to you. I could actually see myself; me, my body, down there on the bed ...

> Then I was floating in what seemed to be a tunnel; dark, but not frightening at all. I could see a light at the end and I felt as though I was being pulled towards it. I had to go—there was no alternative. But still I wasn't frightened. Rather the reverse—I had the most wonderful feeling of peace, more than I've ever felt before, at any time in my life, as though everything that was happening was right. And you know me—this isn't anything like my usual self. The light at the end got brighter and brighter, but it didn't hurt my eyes. Although it was brilliant, it wasn't dazzling. I felt I was being drawn into it and the feeling was, well, the only way I can describe it is pure bliss and love.
>
> There was someone there in the light, waiting for me. And then suddenly I was pulled back, away from it, back, slammed into my body again, back with the pain, and I didn't want to go. I just wanted that peace.[7]

The tunnel is not always perceived in the same way. Sometimes traveling through it is considerably more dramatic:

> I was in a serious car accident in June 1986 ... My car aquaplaned and went into a spin. I was struggling to control it, when suddenly I was not in the car any more.
>
> I was in a black tunnel, or funnel, shooting through it incredibly fast. I was spinning, too, yet it was a different movement from that of the car. I felt I was shooting through this tunnel, head first, spinning round the edges—like water going down the plug, or like a coil. There was a loud roaring—it was very noisy, like the moment of birth ...
>
> The tunnel ... was completely black to begin with but seemed to be getting less dark and less clearly defined further on ... [She heard a debate going on around her, many different voices discussing whether or not she should go back. She took no part in the debate.]
>
> Then I opened my eyes; I was astonished because I was in my body, in the car, and I hadn't expected to be. I thought, "Oh, they've put be back!" and I think I was a little disappointed.[8]

Mrs. S.A.P. Thirlwall, eight years old at the time of her NDE, reported another thrilling ride:

> I started zooming down this really black tunnel at what seemed like 100 mph. Then I saw this enormous brilliant light at the end

which seemed to take on the shape of an angel. When I reached the light I heard a voice saying, "Go back, go back," and seeming to will me to make the return journey. I then came back along this tunnel, but very slowly.[9]

At other times the tunnel is visualized in surprisingly mundane terms. Jenny McMillan, hospitalized for a threatened miscarriage, had a serious blood pressure drop:

> After that I faded out and found myself up at the top left-hand corner of the room against the ceiling, looking down in quite a detached way at all the people fussing about round my body. I realized that I must be dying and the odd thing was that I didn't mind in the least. I remember being very interested in the experience in a very unemotional academic way and feeling that it was quite an adventure—no regrets at all ...
>
> There was a big sash window below me which was open at the top and through which the blazing light of that hot summer was coming in and I was vaguely surprised to discover that that was not the way out. Against the ceiling beside me was a wide-bore pipe or narrow tunnel through which I was obviously meant to make my exit and in the distance at the end of that it seemed to be even brighter. Bright light was nothing exceptional that summer, but this did seem to be actually like the sun itself up there. The pipe itself was corrugated or ridged in some way, rather like the sort of tube that you can attach to a tumble-drier to let the damp air out of a window.[10]

She did not go through the tunnel or pipe, but instead found herself back in her body.

Another person who perceived the tunnel in surprisingly physical terms was Jane Dyson, who had an NDE while on life support after a car accident:

> I had the incredible experience of knowing I was dying and going through a bright shining tunnel towards dazzling light at the end. I felt quite calm, apart from feeling surprised that the tunnel was made of polished metal, jointed and held together with something like rivets. Although I was not aware of the [NDE] phenomenon before my own experience, I felt it should have been more ethereal somehow.[11]

During a week of Vipassana meditation in 1967, Dorothy Bailey had an OBE that included a very material tunnel—in fact, it was a chimney!

> I was floating in the air and could see landscape below, and wanted to get to another place. The knowledge was given to me that if I dived down through one of the factory chimneys that were standing around, that was the route. I looked down and there was the black opening in front of my feet. I was standing on the rim of the chimney. Remembering my diving training I took up the classic position on the rim with my toes curling over the edge and then dived through.
>
> The body felt weightless but I was conscious of a gradual acceleration. I was in this dark tunnel (not falling but traveling horizontally) with the walls beginning to flow by at some speed. [A "golden disc" of light appeared at the end of the tunnel and grew brighter and larger.] The disc was now filling half the total scene. The light from it made the brick walls rushing by visible, and I was amazed and a little afraid of the speed.[12]

So here we have the opening to a chimney with (presumably sooty) brick walls inside. I think of such cases as examples of analytic overlay, as we discussed in connection with OBEs. The person who has the sense of going down a passageway of some sort, and who jumps to the conclusion that it's a smokestack or a concrete tunnel, is unwittingly guilty of this kind of interpretive error. From *perceptions* of forward motion and an enclosure, she imagines a definite *thing*: smokestack, tunnel. Having reached this conclusion, she will probably continue to perceive her environment as a smokestack or a tunnel.

Maurice James encountered a more colorful and exotic version of the tunnel while suffering cardiac arrest in intensive care:

> The sensation was of being weightless and falling down or into a kaleidoscope of ever-changing colors. The colors were pleasant and I was not in the least bit frightened, but I sensed that I did not want to go at the moment. I fell down the kaleidoscope tunnel many times, sometimes going deeper than others.
>
> I felt I was on a yo-yo but that the force which brought me back was mine to control. I also had the feeling that as I gained confidence I was able to descend deeper. Several times I went beyond the end of the kaleidoscope tunnel and was able to see

the world beyond ... The land beyond the entrance was beautiful and like a grassy meadow in a valley bounded by low hills. It was very green and pleasant and warm and filled with a golden sunlight—I could feel the warmth from where I stood at the entrance. A faceless figure who was alone kept asking me—"Come, come"—and he would reassure me constantly. He seemed to have human form but his face was indistinct.[13]

Some people see no tunnel at all, but only a light. One of them was David Verdegaal, who lay in a coma for two weeks: "Then I saw a light that seemed to grow brighter and brighter until its brilliance had completely encircled me, as if my very soul had been transformed and enveloped in love."[14]

Other reports describe the tunnel not as dark, but as very bright or even made of light.

- Hazel Graham: "I felt 'floaty' and then I was in the tunnel of light."
- Audrey Organ: "Here I was in the tunnel of glorious golden light."
- Jean Giacomozzi: "I recall floating in a very bright tunnel. Everything seemed so calm and peaceful."
- H.N. Smith: "There was an intense white light all around, so bright that I could not see any colors."
- Henry Foster suffered a catastrophic collapse of blood pressure. "I experienced a feeling of utter peace and was conscious that I was smiling. Around me was an overall brightness (not brilliance) and there was a distant bright light to which I was drawn. I was moving through a tunnel of beautiful light ... Something inward told me 'not yet,' and the light began to recede. I came round to find myself lying back in the chair."
- Elizabeth Rogers had a heart attack at age 59. "Then everything became warm and bright and light and beautiful. The iron band [of pressure around the chest] was gone and I was traveling along a tunnel. It was light, light, light. I didn't move my feet, I just 'floated' I suppose. But it was calm and peaceful and just lovely."[15]

There are similarities and differences among these accounts, but the basic idea of being drawn to a bright light, often through a passageway of some kind, is consistent.

It is sometimes argued that the tunnel experience merely reflects the effect of oxygen deprivation on the brain—specifically the shutdown of the visual cortex, which leads to a kind of "tunnel vision." But how about a patient blind from birth who has never received any visual impressions in his life? Brad Barrow, whose case was covered earlier, is such a person, and during his NDE he had the typical tunnel experience: "He found himself in a tunnel and emerged from it to find himself in an immense field illuminated by a tremendous, all-encompassing light."[16] Besides, not every patient whose NDE includes the tunnel exhibited oxygen deprivation.

Many more instances of the tunnel experience could be cited, but the sheer ubiquity of such reports raises a problem of its own. Could the tunnel and the bright light at the end have become a kind of pop-culture meme, and could this meme be influencing recent accounts of NDEs?

To guard against this, we would need to find a group of NDErs who are highly unlikely to have been influenced by New Age literature or by TV and movie depictions of dying. As it happens, there is such a group: small children.

Tunnel reports by children

Katie, whom we met earlier—she's the seven-year-old girl who survived drowning in a swimming pool—told Melvin Morse that

> the first memory she had of her near-drowning was "being in the water." She stated, "I was dead. Then I was in the tunnel. It was dark and I was scared. I couldn't walk." A woman named Elizabeth appeared, and the tunnel became bright. The woman was tall, with bright yellow hair. Together they walked to heaven. She stated that "heaven was fun. It was bright and there were lots of flowers." She said that there was a border around heaven that she could not see past. She said that she met many people including her dead grandparents, her dead maternal aunt, and Heather and Melissa, two adults waiting to be reborn. She then met the "Heavenly Father and Jesus," who asked her if she wanted to return to earth. She replied "no." Elizabeth then asked her if she wanted to see her mother. She said yes and woke up in the hospital. Finally, she claimed to remember seeing me in the emergency room, but could not supply any other details of the three-day period during which she was comatose.[17]

A nine-year-old girl identified as Nina had an NDE during appendicitis surgery:

> I heard them say my heart had stopped but I was up at the ceiling watching. I could see everything from up there. I was floating close to the ceiling, so when I saw my body I didn't know it was me. Then I knew because I recognized it. I went out in the hall and I saw my mother crying. I asked her why she was crying but she couldn't hear me. The doctors thought I was dead.
>
> Then a pretty lady came up and helped me because she knew I was scared. We went through a tunnel and went into heaven. There are beautiful flowers there …
>
> The tunnel I went through was long and very dark. I went through it real fast. There was light at the end. When we saw the light I was very happy. I wanted to go back for a long time. I still want to go back to the light when I die … The light was very bright.[18]

Raymond Moody quotes the case of eleven-year-old Jason, hit by a car:

> I don't remember getting hit but suddenly I was looking down at myself I saw my body under the bike and my leg was broken and bleeding. I remember looking and seeing my eyes closed. I was above.
>
> I was floating about five feet above my body and there were people all around …
>
> The ambulance drove off and I tried to follow it. I was above the ambulance following it. I thought I was dead. I looked around and then I was in the tunnel with a bright light at the end. The tunnel seemed to go up and up. I came out on the other side of the tunnel.
>
> There were a lot of people in the light but I didn't know any of them. I told them about the accident and they said I had to go back …
>
> I was in the light for a long time. It seemed like a long time. I felt everyone loved to be there. Everyone was happy … When I was in the light I didn't want to go back. I almost forgot about my body.
>
> When I was going up in the tunnel two people were helping me. I saw them as they got out into the light. They were with me the whole way.

> Then they told me I had to go back. I went back through the tunnel where I ended up back in the hospital where two doctors were working on me.

In response to questions, Jason elaborated, "As soon as I knew I was dead this tunnel opened up and I saw the light at the end. When I went in there was this 'swoosh.' It was fun being there."[19]

Kenneth Ring cites a case written up in *Critical Care Medicine* involving a girl who was only six months old at the time of her NDE. The infant suffered renal and circulatory failure and barely survived. Pediatrician David B. Herzog wrote,

> Some months after her discharge, she had a panic reaction when encouraged by some siblings to crawl through a tunnel at a local store. The cause of this reaction was not obvious but the "tunnel panic" was seen again on a number of occasions. According to her mother, during these episodes the patient would talk very fast, be unduly frightened and overwhelmed, and would seem as if she knew the tunnel quite well. At the age of three and a half, when her mother was explaining the impending death of her grandmother, the child replied, "Will Grandma have to go through the tunnel to get to see God?"[20]

Tunnel reports prior to 1975

But isn't it theoretically possible that even very young children were somehow influenced by pop culture? Who knows what a child may have seen on TV?

Fortunately, we don't have to rest our case here. We can look at studies carried out before 1975—that is, prior to the publication of *Life after Life* and therefore prior to the popularization of the tunnel experience.

The Supreme Adventure, by Robert Crookall, was published in 1961, predating general knowledge of NDEs by fourteen years. Nevertheless, it includes many tunnel reports. Crookall writes,

> A common symbol used in describing the act of shedding ... the Physical Body is that of passing through a "tunnel" (or a "door," "passage," "tube," "shaft," "hole," "funnel," etc.): this is clearly related to the "momentary coma" [experienced upon separating from the body], though lasting somewhat longer and, perhaps, with some dim consciousness, of existence if not of environment.

There are many considerations which strongly suggest that in this symbol a genuine experience of a surviving soul is indicated.[21]

He lists statements by people who had OBEs or, in some cases, what we would now call NDEs. Where possible, I give the date of the account.

- "I seemed to float in a long tunnel. It appeared very narrow at first but gradually expanded into unlimited space." (1952)
- "Suddenly there appeared an opening, like a tunnel, and, at the far end, a light. I moved nearer to it and was drawn up the passage." (1950)
- "I was falling … down a dark, narrow tunnel or shaft … Sometimes the speed is so tremendous that one gets the effect of tumbling through a hole into a new sphere."
- "I find myself going down a long dim tunnel … At the far end is a tiny speck of light which grows, as I approach, into a large square, and I am there!"
- "In one of my own experiences I seemed to pass through a tunnel in a dream-like state and emerged through the opening at the end into a scene of bright sunlight." (1956)
- "I was hurried off at great speed. Have you ever looked through a very long tunnel and seen the tiny speck of light at the far end? … Well, I found myself … hurrying along just such a tunnel or passage." (1935 NDE)

Crookall also includes a 1946 mystical experience:

I closed my eyes and watched a silver glow which shaped itself into a circle with a central focus brighter than the rest. The circle became a tunnel of light proceeding from some distance on in the heart of the Self. Swiftly and smoothly I was borne through the tunnel.

He gives a number of statements from people who had an OBE under anesthesia:

- "I was in a long tunnel with a light at the end … I knew that if I could only get to the light at the end I should understand everything." (1935)

- "I seemed to float down a dark tunnel, moving towards a half-moon of light that was miles away."
- "On being given ether I was moving, at a terrific rate, through what seemed to be a tunnel."
- "I found myself in an avenue of trees, slowly moving farther and farther from my body ... I continue to advance along the avenue towards a brilliant light at the end of it." (1955)
- "I found myself proceeding along a straight black tube with hardly any room to move." (1894)

Crookall observes that the tunnel symbol can be "used for describing the experience of reentering the Physical Body ... This also is felt as a brief coma, 'blackout', or passage through a 'tunnel' (depending on the duration of the experience)."

One NDEr said, "I turned away from the bright light ... and entered a gloomy tunnel. I fought my way back to a tiny light in the distance ... When I got back to the light, I found myself back in bed."

Crookall even quotes an account given by Plutarch in A.D. 79, in which a certain Aridaeus suffered a severe fall and was momentarily startled out of his body. Surviving the fall, he felt himself reenter his physical shell. "Then, as though he were suddenly sucked through a tube ... he lit [i.e. alit] in his body."[22]

> In *The Unanswered Question*, Kurt Leland summarizes a Hopi Indian's NDE, which was first written down in 1932.
>
>> During the winter of 1907, at the age of seventeen, Don Talayesva was attending an Indian school in Riverside, California, far from his family on the Hopi Reservation. While grieving the death of a beloved older sister who had died in childbirth, Don caught a cold that lasted for weeks and turned into pneumonia. Toward the end of December, he apparently went into a coma [and] saw a spiritual being standing by his bedside. The being was dressed as a Hopi Kachina and carried a blue

feather to indicate that he'd come from the Land of the Dead. The being announced that he was Don's guardian spirit and had been watching over Don for all his life.

After the spiritual being appeared, Don reports: "A cold numbness crept up my body; and I knew I was dying." …

Don then found himself out of his body. The pain in his lungs that had caused him to spit blood disappeared. As Don reports, "Something lifted me and pushed me along through the air, causing me to move through the door, down the hall, and out upon the campus in broad daylight. I was swept along northeastward by a gust of wind, like flying" …

While out of body, Don moved through a landscape he identifies as the San Bernardino Mountains. He eventually came to a "hole like a tunnel, dimly lighted." A voice invited him to enter. As Don reports: "Stepping in through a fog and past the little lights, I moved along swiftly."[23]

In contrast to most other accounts, the tunnel in this case led to an earthly environment—namely, Don's own reservation, where he observed his family members but could not communicate with them.

Tunnel reports from the deceased

Crookall notes that the reports he collected agree with communications via mediums. All these accounts preceded the popularization of NDEs by many years.

- A spirit speaking through a medium said, "I remember a curious opening, as if one had passed through subterranean passages and found oneself near the mouth of the cave … The light was much stronger outside."

- In another séance, the communicator said that in helping people make the transition, he tried "to make this passage through the tunnel as happy as possible." (1931)
- Another communicator said he traveled through a "dark tunnel" while leaving his body.
- Yet another spoke of "traveling down a tunnel."
- A 1926 communicator said: "I saw in front of me a dark tunnel. I stepped out of the tunnel into a new world."

Messages delivered through mediums seem to agree that returning to the physical body can also require going through a tunnel. This is true even if the spirit is trying to temporarily enter the body of a medium. The deceased George Pellew, communicating through Leonora Piper, told an investigator: "Do not look at me too critically: to try to transmit through the organism of a medium is like trying to crawl through a hollow log." Another discarnate compared entering a medium's body to getting into "a sort of funnel" (1948).

One would-be communicator failed to get through. The medium's spirit control informed the sitters: "He was able to see the light in the darkness of a long funnel. But he doubted so much that it went out. He was frightened for fear he would never find his way back." (1936)[24]

A tunnel report from a past life?

So we have tunnel experiences reported in OBEs, NDEs, mystical states, and messages conveyed by mediums from those who've actually died. That would seem to exhaust the options—but not quite. How about a memory apparently preserved from a previous incarnation?

In *Lessons from the Light*, Kenneth Ring reports on a letter he received from a mother regarding her son, Steven, who had an unusual conversation with her when he was only two years and two months old. She wrote,

> I was framing a picture of my grandmother and grandfather, who have been dead since before Steven was born. Steven was sitting nearby playing with a toy, and asked me what I was doing. I told him and explained that it was a picture of his grandma and grandpa, who were now dead. No one had ever discussed death with Steven before …

> I began by saying that they were no longer here with us and that they had gone to be with God ... Before I could say more, he said in a very matter-of-fact way: "When you die, it's a tunnel."...
>
> I asked if there was anything in the tunnel. He replied that there was light in the tunnel. I asked what color the Light was, and he replied, "White." I asked if, when you die, you go through the tunnel. He answered affirmatively. I asked what you do when you come to the end of the tunnel. He said, "You go to the Light." He also volunteered that grandpa (pointing to the picture) was there with "a light on his head."

In her letter, the mother added,

> I thought it was significant that several of your NDErs mentioned a feeling of homecoming, a familiarity, a feeling that they had always known everything they experienced. Is it possible that very young children retain some memory of having been there? Is it possible that by the time most of them have adequate verbal skills to express it, the memory is gone?[25]

Shared tunnel experiences

Can other people participate in the dying process of their loved one? Sometimes, yes. These unusual events, dubbed "shared death experiences," involve one or more persons close to the patient clairvoyantly perceiving what the patient sees.

> I was with my sister who was thirty years old and dying of cancer. She was twisting her hands and her knuckles were almost white. I knew she was terrified of dying, she said so many times while she was ill. She was trying to tell me what she could see. So I said I could see something as well and I would tell her what I could see and she could say yes or no. I could see this beautiful gold light at the end of a tunnel; she agreed, so I held her hand and down we went together. She was afraid but I told her it was all right, I was with her and I wasn't afraid. It seemed as though we were almost floating but the main thing was the light at the end of the tunnel was getting bigger and brighter.[26]

The experience ended when the narrator, Barbara Sherriff, was forced back by something "almost like a gust of wind." Her sister died that night.

Not all such experiences end with the death of the loved one. Helen Springfield's mother survived a brush with death, making this experience a shared NDE:

> My mother entered hospital in 1986 for major heart surgery. Unfortunately, complications set in and she was returned to theater. I was later informed that following the second bout of surgery her heart was very weak and tired, and it was only medication and the heart and lung machine that was keeping her going. I found myself watching my mother for the rest of the day and I saw her mother and father (long since passed over) around her ... I stayed at home, but was still able to watch my mother clearly. I could see her parents and other long-dead members of her family. I could see rays of orange, purple and gold around her. I watched my mother with her parents on either side of her walk down a tunnel, surrounded by a silver light. She turned and looked at me and I felt compelled to look at the time. It was 4 p.m. and just as a mother is attached to a baby by the umbilical cord, I could see a shaft of gold light with orange running between my mother and myself, and as she turned she called to me—it was so loud she could have been standing in front of me—and she reached out her hand to me. I could see myself take her hand and I saw her walk back through the tunnel towards me. Later in the day I spoke to my father on the phone and asked what had happened at 4 p.m. and he told me that mother's condition had started to change and stabilize and that at 4 p.m. my father and the rest of the family went into the hospital's chapel and lit a candle in prayer.[27]

Conclusion

Common denominators in the above material are pretty obvious. Though some details vary, the basic experience seems remarkably consistent, whether reported by young children or adults; whether reported before or after 1975; and whether reported by survivors or via mediums.

The transitional phase of the dying process involves a passage, often apprehended as a tunnel, to a nonphysical plane of existence.

CHAPTER FOURTEEN:
Encounter

EVEN THOSE WHO MAKE no mention of the tunnel or any other passageway often talk about going into the light. Moreover, the light is sometimes personified as an intelligent presence radiating love and sympathetic kindness.

But as all such accounts make clear, words are not adequate to describe this encounter. After psychologist Carl Jung had a near-death experience, he wrote to a friend, "What happens after death is so unspeakably glorious that our imagination and our feelings do not suffice to form even an approximate conception of it."[1]

Encounters with the light

Doreen Dhingles spoke of her husband's NDE:

> At 11:30 p.m. he stirred and said he had died. I asked what it was like; he replied, "Ecstasy." He described the tunnel and light, then said they had sent him back to me as his work wasn't finished ... A couple of days later I asked if he remembered what had happened and he repeated everything word for word, adding, "If anyone asks if there is a God I shall say yes, I have seen him." He went into hospital for the last days of his life and the nuns from the local convent went in relays to be with him up until his death. They all said he walked with God.[2]

Jayne Smith's difficult childbirth in 1952 gave rise to an NDE:

> I was standing in a mist and I knew immediately that I had died and I was so happy that I had died but I was still alive. And I cannot tell you how I felt. It was, "Oh, God, I'm dead, but I'm here! I'm me!" And I started pouring out these enormous feelings of gratitude ...
>
> The mist started being infiltrated with enormous light and the light just got brighter and brighter and brighter and, it is so bright but it doesn't hurt your eyes, but it's brighter than anything you've ever encountered in your whole life. At that

point, I had no consciousness anymore of having a body. It was just pure consciousness. And this enormously bright light seemed almost to cradle me. I just seemed to exist in it and be part of it and be nurtured by it and the feeling just became more and more and more ecstatic and glorious and perfect. And everything about it was—if you took the one thousand best things that ever happened to you in your life and multiplied by one million, maybe you could get close to this feeling, I don't know. But you're just engulfed by it. Then you begin to know a lot of things.

I remember I knew that everything, everywhere in the universe was okay, that the plan was perfect. That whatever was happening—the wars, famine, whatever—was okay. Everything was perfect. Somehow it was all a part of the perfection, that we didn't have to be concerned about it at all. And the whole time I was in this state, it seemed infinite. It was timeless. I was just an infinite being in perfection. And love and safety and security and knowing that nothing could happen to you and you're home forever. That you're safe forever. And that everyone else was.[3]

Channeling a small child named Kakie who died of an illness, Leonora Piper said, "I saw the light and followed it to this pretty lady." This 1893 sitting is noteworthy for the remarkably evidential material Piper produced, speaking in the child's vocabulary and idiom and making specific references to unusual toys she'd owned.[4]

Brian Weiss's regressed patient Catherine sometimes recalled going into the light after the death of one of her previous personalities. Her remarks under hypnosis indicate the presence of higher-level beings there.

"I am aware of a bright light. It's wonderful; you get energy from this light." She was resting, after death, in between lifetimes. Minutes passed in silence. Suddenly she spoke, but not in the slow whisper she had always used previously. Her voice was now husky and loud, without hesitation.

"Our task is to learn, to become God-like through knowledge. We know so little. You are here to be my teacher. I have so much to learn. By knowledge we approach God, and then we can rest. Then we come back to teach and help others" ...

Catherine had never read the studies of Dr. Elizabeth Kübler-Ross or Dr. Raymond Moody, who have both written about near-death experiences. She had never heard of the *Tibetan Book of the Dead*. Yet she was relating similar experiences to those described in these writings.[5]

Not everybody, however, feels ready to face the light. This may be especially true of people who encounter it when they are not near death.

Dorothy Bailey had a spontaneous OBE while meditating. Her passage through a "chimney" (tunnel) was quoted earlier. Here is a later part of her experience:

> Then, when [I was] traveling fairly fast, a small pinpoint of golden light appeared in the distance. With the speed of travel the point expanded until I saw it was a disc, expanding at an ever-increasing rate as I accelerated and accelerated towards it. Suddenly I realized it was the end of the tunnel and the beautiful other place was to be found through it. I mentally glimpsed it. Yet the golden disc seemed to be on its own and vibrant with light. It grew at an ever-increasing rate and I knew I was traveling too fast. It was inevitable and imperative that I entered and immersed myself in this living light to get to the desired place, the beautiful land outside, but I felt I was traveling too fast to hit it at the right time. It was important to reduce the rate of my approach. The disc was now filling half the total scene. The light from it made the brick walls [of the "chimney"] rushing by visible, and I was amazed and a little afraid of the speed. "I must reduce speed, it will have danger in it to hit the light at this moment (I am impure, things to clean up). Later on, yes, most definitely, but not yet."
>
> So I pressed my heels and elbows out sideways to act as brakes and pressed them hard against the walls. The light filled all my vision to 180 degrees, warm, living. Then I "woke up" (though it was not a dream), whole-minded and peaceful.[6]

Descriptions of going into the light are not limited to NDEs. They crop up pretty frequently in mediumistic communications. Of course, one might object that recent messages via mediums are influenced by the popularization of NDEs and "the light." But this objection carries less force in the case of older communications.

Allan Kardec's *Heaven and Hell*, published in 1865, includes a message from the "Widow Foulon" in a séance held earlier that year.

> After my last breath, I passed through a sort of syncope … Afterward, as if I were emerging from a long fainting spell, I awoke little by little and found I was surrounded by friends

> whom I did not recognize. They lavished care and attention on me. They showed me a shining star and said, "You are going there with us, for you no longer belong to the earth" ... We formed a graceful group rushing toward realms unknown. With the certainty of finding happiness, we rose and rose and the star grew bigger and bigger in front of us.[7]

Another of Kardec's communicators was Maurice Gontran, who died of lung disease at age eighteen. Through a medium he said,

> An unknown force carried me through space. A brilliant light surrounded me but did not fatigue my sight! I saw my grandfather, who was no longer emaciated or feeble, but youthful and fresh. He held out his arms to me and gathered me close to his heart.[8]

In this case, admittedly, we do not precisely have a passage toward a bright light, but rather the sense of being surrounded by light. Still, there is the impression of being carried through space and the apprehension of a light that, while incredibly brilliant, "did not fatigue my sight."

Cosmic consciousness

We saw in Jayne Smith's account that immersion in the light made her feel that she began "to know a lot of things." Indeed, a sense of universal knowledge is often reported—an omniscient perspective in which the veil is lifted and ultimate truths are clearly perceived. This experience is by no means limited to nearly—or actually—dying. Many people have reported episodes that can be classified as "peak experiences" (psychologist Abraham Maslow's term) or "kundalini experiences" (from Hindu tradition).

One of them was Fyodor Dostoevsky, who described just such an experience in his youth. He had stopped to look at the Neva River in St. Petersburg in the evening when suddenly a strange new perspective swept over him.

> It seemed, in the end, that all this world, with all its inhabitants, both the strong and the weak, with all their habitations, whether beggars' shelters or gilded palaces, at this hour of twilight resembled a fantastic, enchanted vision, a dream which in its turn would instantly vanish and waste away

as vapor into the dark blue heaven. Suddenly a certain strange thought began to stir inside me. I started and my heart was as if flooded in that instant by a hot jet of blood which had suddenly boiled up from the influx of a mighty sensation which until now had been unknown to me. In that moment, as it were, I understood something which up to that time had only stirred in me, but had not as yet been fully comprehended. I saw clearly, as it were, into something new, a completely new world, unfamiliar to me and known only through some obscure hearsay, through a certain mysterious sign. I think that in those precise minutes, my real existence began …

I began to look about intently and suddenly I noticed some strange people. They were all strange, extraordinary figures, completely prosaic …, rather down to earth titular councilors [low-level bureaucrats] and yet at the same time, as it were, sort of fantastic titular councilors. Someone was grimacing in front of me, having hidden himself behind all this fantastic crowd, and he was fidgeting some thread, some springs through [*sic*], and these little dolls moved, and he laughed and laughed away.[9]

Richard Maurice Bucke included many similar accounts in his influential 1901 book *Cosmic Consciousness*. One of them was provided by a woman identified only as C.M.C. After years of inner struggle and spiritual yearning, she experienced what she called "the supreme event of my life." (The following excerpt has been heavily abridged.)

The tension deep in the core of my being was so great that I felt as might some creature which had outgrown its shell, and yet could not escape. It was a great yearning—for freedom, for larger life, for deeper love. There seemed to be no response in nature to that infinite need. Nothing remained but submission.

At last, I let go of myself! In a short time, to my surprise, I began to feel a sense of physical comfort, of rest, as if some strain or tension was removed. Never before had I experienced such a feeling of perfect health. And how bright and beautiful the day! I looked out at the sky, the hills and the river, amazed that I had never before realized how divinely beautiful the world was! The sense of lightness and expansion kept increasing, the wrinkles smoothed out of everything, there was nothing in all the world that seemed out of place.

The light and color glowed, the atmosphere seemed to quiver and vibrate around and within me. Perfect rest and peace and joy were everywhere, and, more strange than all, there came to me a sense of some serene, magnetic presence—grand and all pervading. Retiring early that I might be alone, soon all objective phenomena were shut out. I was seeing and comprehending the sublime meaning of things, the great truth that life is a spiritual evolution, that this life is but a passing phase in the soul's progression. I felt myself going, losing myself, my identity. Now came a period of rapture, so intense that the universe stood still. And with the rapture came the insight. I saw with intense inward vision the atoms or molecules, of which seemingly the universe is composed—I know not whether material or spiritual—rearranging themselves, as the cosmos passes from order to order. What joy when I saw there was no break in the chain—not a link left out—everything in its place and time. Worlds, systems, all blended in one harmonious whole. Universal life, synonymous with universal love!

In the morning I awoke with the spiritual sense so strong that what we call the actual, material things surrounding me seemed shadowy and unreal. This shadowy unreality of external things did not last many days. Every longing of the heart was satisfied, every question answered, the "pent-up, aching rivers" had reached the ocean—I loved infinitely and was infinitely loved!

Out of this experience was born an unfaltering trust. Deep in the soul, below pain, below all the distraction of life, is a silence vast and grand—an infinite ocean of calm, which nothing can disturb; Nature's own exceeding peace, which "passes understanding."[10]

Jane Roberts became famous for channeling the wisdom of an entity called Seth, but before those sessions began, she had a spontaneous experience of cosmic consciousness (not her term) in which she perceived the physical world as

> really tissue-paper thin, hiding infinite dimensions of reality, and I was suddenly flung through the tissue paper with a huge ripping sound ... to find a whole universe open up ...
>
> During that experience I knew that we formed physical matter, not the other way around; that our senses showed us only one three-dimensional reality out of an infinite number that we couldn't ordinarily perceive; that we could trust our senses only so far and only so long as we did not ask questions that were beyond their limited scope of knowledge.
>
> But more: I just didn't know, for example, that everything

place. He said it was all an illusion. I thought he was just confused. But he was not confused. He wasn't visiting heaven, not the way we think of heaven. He described it as a vastness that you can't even imagine. It was a place where the past, present, and future were happening all at once.[17]

Cosmic consciousness in NDEs

All these accounts mirror the reports of people caught up in the light of an NDE. One such person is Audrey Organ, who found herself rising into the light during her NDE:

> I was going upwards and had great mental awareness, a sense of great excitement. All around me were the answers to everything, no puzzles because I had been given the key to understanding everything. What was so thrilling was that the perfect, logical simplicity convinced me that only the Creator could have made it so ... Enlightenment is the wonder, and here I understood the luniverse.[18]

In an interview, Eben Alexander discusses the ideas he was led to by his deep and extended NDE:

> At the core, it's all One and at the deepest Core it's all divine—all One with God. Even the materialists—the scientists, cosmologists, those who do string theory and quantum gravity; they're all basically converging to say that pure information is the core of all that exists. Everything we see as space, time, mass, energy ... can be essentialized into vibrating strings of energy and higher dimensional space-time. And at the very deepest level, everything is entangled into one. Sir James Jeans said long ago, "The Universe begins to look much more like a great thought than a great machine." That's a crucial understanding of what this all really is. And if you're able to go far enough, [you'll see] ... that this whole material world is a very cleverly wrought illusion, that time and space are all illusion. You have to know that Consciousness is not this epiphenomenon of the brain, but is, in fact, a far richer thing that completely precedes and is outside of (and supporting) all of the material realm and this apparent reality.[19]

Cosmic consciousness is also described by a contributor to the online database of NDEs maintained by the Near-Death Experience Research Foundation at NDERF.org. To date, more than 5,200 such submissions have been collected, though it's worth noting that few have been independently investigated. The contributor writes,

> White light is what I remember and the simplest way I can explain the moment is to say, "I saw God." This is what I ultimately came to understand as a mystical experience but at the time, I had never heard of such a thing. This is what Siddhartha Gautama, Jesus Christ, Meher Baba and many others were talking about. This is what Meister Eckhart wrote about only I didn't know about Eckhart at the time. It is what I have referred to as a non-experiential experience and there is nothing to be remembered. The moment is eternally now and memory serves no function. I am, however, left with impressions. I sense that in some way I was exposed to pure information at a rate that far overloads the capacity of any physical entity. It was all that is all at once and it is Love.[20]

Dr. Tony Cicoria, an orthopedic surgeon, had a near-death experience in 1994 when he was struck by lightning. He reports that during his experience "time did not exist ... I did not have any sense of time." He recalls being "immersed in a bluish white light that had a shimmering appearance as if I were swimming underwater in a crystal clear stream. The sunlight was penetrating through it. The visual was accompanied by a feeling of absolute love and peace." He goes on,

> What does the term 'absolute love and peace' mean? For example, scientists use the term absolute zero to describe a temperature at which no molecular motion exists; a singular and pure state. That was what I felt; I had fallen into a pure positive flow of energy. I could see the flow of this energy. I could see it flow through the fabric of everything. I reasoned that this energy was quantifiable. It was something measurable and palpable. As I flowed in the current of this stream, which seemed to have both velocity and direction, I saw some of the high points and low points in my life pass by, but nothing in depth. I became ecstatic at the possibility of where I was going. I was aware of every moment of this experience, conscious of every millisecond, even though I could feel that time did not exist. I remember thinking, "This is the greatest thing that can ever happen to anyone."
>
> Suddenly, I was back in my body. It was so painful.[21]

What makes this case especially interesting is its aftermath, as covered by Oliver Sacks in his 2007 book *Musicophilia*. Following his NDE, Cicoria developed a newfound appreciation for music, which included the ability to write complex musical notations without apparent effort. He says these compositions are simply "downloaded" into his brain.

At first he found himself with "this insatiable desire to listen to piano music," something that had never particularly appealed to him before. He began buying classical music albums, obtained a piano, and taught himself to play. "And then," Sacks writes,

> on the heels of this sudden desire for piano music, Cicoria started to hear music in his head ... The music was there, deep inside him—or somewhere—and all he had to do was let it come to him. "It's like a frequency, a radio band. If I open myself up, it comes. I want to say, 'It comes from heaven,' as Mozart said."
>
> His music is ceaseless. "It never runs dry," he continued. "If anything, I have to turn it off."
>
> Now he had to wrestle not just with learning to play the Chopin, but to give form to the music continually running in his head, to try it out on the piano, to get it on manuscript paper. "It was a terrible struggle," he said. "I would get up at four in the morning and play till I went to work, and when I got home from work I was at the piano all evening. My wife was not really pleased. I was possessed." ...
>
> Some years passed, and Cicoria's new life, his inspiration, never deserted him for a moment. He continued to work full-time as a surgeon, but his heart and mind now centered on music.[22]

Oliver Sacks did not see Cicoria's newfound talents as paranormal, regarding them as purely accidental byproducts of his cerebral trauma.

Timelessness

A sense of timelessness is common to both cosmic consciousness and immersion in the light of an NDE.

- Jayne Smith called her experience "timeless."
- Jane Roberts "knew that time wasn't a series of moments one before the other ... but that all experience existed in some kind of eternal now."
- The lawyer who corresponded with Eben Alexander saw "past, present, future."
- Roger Ebert, in his wife's interpretation, saw heaven as "a place where the past, present, and future were happening all at once."
- The NDERF contributor wrote, "The moment is eternally now."
- Dr. Cicoria said, "I could feel that time did not exist."

In the NDERF database, a contributor named "Peter N" describes his NDE in similar terms:

> I had no sense of time there. The time frame if there is one at all is utterly different from here. This to the extent that to me it makes no sense to talk of time there. Something is happening there that nullifies time in any sense of the way that we understand it, or feel it, or believe it to be.[23]

Reviewing the lessons from her NDE, Anita Moorjani writes,

> Neither do I believe anymore that we live out all our lives sequentially in linear time, which is the framework that many people have for their ideas about karma. It's what I was brought up to think as well.
>
> In the NDE state, however, I realized that every moment in all our lives—past, present, future, unknown, unknown, and unknowable—exist[s] simultaneously, as though outside of what we know as time. I became aware that I already was everything I was trying to attain, and I believe that's true for everyone.[24]

Notice how similar this is to Jane Roberts' insight that time is not "a series of moments one before the other ... but that all experience exist[s] in some kind of eternal now." But Moorjani had an NDE, while Roberts' experience happened when she was perfectly healthy. This underlines the point that the basic experience of inner illumination is the same whether it takes place in everyday life or on the threshold of death.

In *Changes of Mind*, Jenny Wade charts the development of consciousness from birth to death (and before and after!). The early post-birth stages are relatively simple mindsets culminating in "Achievement/Affiliative consciousness," which prioritizes accomplishments or relationships as the case may be. After this come the higher levels. "Authentic consciousness" is characterized by minimal ego-based distortion, nonconformity, and a calm acceptance of life's ever-changing challenges. At a still higher level is "Transcendent consciousness," characterized by the pursuit of "ego death" (transcendence of the personal self) in the search for unity with the ground of being. Finally, there is "Unity consciousness," in which this goal has been met.

Wade's Unity consciousness is essentially Bucke's cosmic consciousnesses, and both sound very much like full immersion in the light. For Wade, a sense of total unity is achieved, marked by boundless empathy and compassion for all beings, which are apprehended as "multiplicities of the One" in a state of constant creative flux. Fear and other negative feelings are banished. Death, in the sense of personal extinction, is no longer an issue. Everything exists as part of everything else, forever.[25]

How much is remembered?

Immersion in a timeless matrix of universal knowledge is undoubtedly an overpowering experience. Unfortunately, in NDEs, most of that knowledge is lost when the person returns to the physical body. Audrey Organ, quoted earlier as having "been given the key to understanding everything," acknowledged that she did not retain this understanding after being revived. "I kept the sense of having had a wonderful experience, a revelation. Unfortunately, the magic key to understanding pure logic had been taken from me. I still see through a glass darkly."[26]

Some NDErs do claim to recall the details of what they learned while in the light, but their statements don't always hold up.

In 1978, when he was 33, Tom Sawyer (his real name) was partially crushed when a truck he was repairing collapsed on him. He came back from his NDE a changed man. At a later point, he began to warn people about the dangers of the ozone hole:

> I do see a strong probability toward a double-fold acceleration of the melting of the South Pole. Now that's going to be contingent on the ozone layer down there …
>
> As our springtime comes, and with it the onset of the larger and actually harmful absence of the ozone layer around the Arctic, there is the extreme possibility for large segments of that hole to break off and go northerly. If it goes over populated areas we're going to have much more than hundredfold numbers of skin cancers, some blindness, things of that nature … In other words it will be the residual effect of additional ultraviolet rays affecting the animals, the crops, and the whole atmosphere. I don't see this is world-wide just yet, but it's becoming probable that such areas will move far enough north to really affect land masses.[27]

Needless to say, this scenario did not pan out. Nor do we hear about the ozone hole in more recent NDEs, undoubtedly because the issue is no longer in the news. It seems likely that the ozone hole, first detected in 1985 and a hot topic in 1993 when Sawyer's warnings were published, was a concern at the back of Tom Sawyer's mind, and that he got his subconscious concerns mixed up with whatever he might have learned in the light.

After his NDE, Dannion Brinkley became well-known for predicting a series of disturbing events in the near future, but his predictions have not come true, even though some of the dates he specified have long since passed. Peter and Elizabeth Fenwick take note of this inaccuracy in their book *The Truth in the Light*:

> As [Brinkley's] book was published in 1994 it is difficult to comment on predictions reported in about events which happened before this date, events such as the Chernobyl nuclear disaster and the Gulf War. The dates of these events—1986 and 1990—and many other pre-publication happenings came into Dannion's head with pinpoint accuracy as he saw them on his spiritual tele-screen. But, as tends to be the way with prophecies, those events due to take place after 1994 are foretold with less precision: a world in "horrible turmoil by the turn of the century," two horrendous earthquakes in America "by the end of the century," Armageddon somewhere around 2004. Dannion is also able to hedge his bets; he was told that "the years between 1994 and 1996 are critical ones."[28]

The Fenwicks published their book in 1997. From the perspective of 2023, we can assess the later prophecies with greater clarity. Needless to say, there were no horrendous earthquakes in America at the end of the 20th century; the years between 1994 and 1996 were not noticeably more important than any other two-year period; and happily, the 2004 Armageddon was postponed. As for a world being in "horrible turmoil," this can mean almost anything. There's always turmoil somewhere.

Moreover, as the Fenwicks gently point out, it's impossible to judge whether or not Brinkley accurately predicted events in 1986 and 1990, given that he didn't put his predictions in print until 1994. Anyone can predict something that's already happened. The most generous explanation is, again, analytic overlay. It appears that Brinkley, sensing generalized strife and tumult, interpreted these perceptions with his analytic mind and came up with the kinds of predictions that can be found in any tabloid newspaper.

While the "universal knowledge" imparted in some NDEs may leave only ambiguous traces and is open to reasonable doubt, there's another respect in which NDEs have provable, lasting effects.

Transformed lives

Most NDE researchers have been impressed with how often patients who report an NDE make radical changes in their values and lives. Nor can these changes be attributed solely to their brush with death. People who have survived heart attacks and other medical crises without undergoing an NDE don't generally exhibit the same change in outlook and quality of life.

> In the largest prospective study of cardiac arrest survivors, which included follow-up evaluations two and eight years after the event, Van Lommel et al. (2001) found that all survivors of a cardiac arrest at follow-up were more self-assured, socially aware, and religious than before the event; but that those survivors who had reported NDEs, unlike the other survivors, also showed increased empathy and intuition, greater interest in spirituality, and less fear of death.[29]

Surbhi Khanna and Bruce Greyson conducted a study of 251 people who had come close to death, 90% of whom reported having an NDE. The NDErs were compared with the 10% who did not remember any such experience. The researchers report:

> Although both experiencers and non-experiencers fell within

the normative range of posttraumatic growth, the NDErs scored significantly higher on the PTGI [Posttraumatic Growth Inventory]; and among the NDErs, posttraumatic growth was positively correlated with depth of NDE.

The data from this study suggest therefore that NDEs are associated with increased posttraumatic growth and that the "deeper" the NDE, the more profound is the posttraumatic growth reported. This association held for the full-scale PTGI and for each of the five component factors. These findings are consistent with the model of posttraumatic growth that hypothesizes challenges to the assumptive worldview as a major stimulus to posttraumatic growth.[30]

What kind of personal growth are we talking about? Let's look at some examples from Bruce Greyson's memoir *After*.

Steve Price was a 24-year-old marine serving in Vietnam who had an NDE after being struck by shrapnel. Afterward

> I led my unit. I did all the things I was supposed to, but I couldn't shoot my gun. All I ever wanted was to be a Marine, but I realized I could no longer do my job. The NDE had an incredible effect on my life. The matter how hard I tried, I couldn't fire my rifle. Eventually, I left the Marines and now I work as a lab technician ... I'm now mild-mannered, thoughtful, and a lot different from the hard-charging, macho marine I once was. I've become so sensitive that when other people hurt I can feel it.[31]

Joe Geraci, a 36-year-old policeman:

> I was a no-nonsense, hard-nosed cop. My NDE changed all that. I left the hospital a completely different man. After being a cop used to bloodshed, I found I could not watch TV because it was too violent. After endangering myself and my partner on patrol because I couldn't fire my gun, I quit the police force and retrained as a teacher.[32]

Then there's Mickey. He was a mobbed-up guy who shook down people for money—until he had an NDE. Afterward he could no longer do his job and was allowed to leave the syndicate. His girlfriend left him because he was no longer concerned with material goods. He started a new career helping delinquent children and victims of spousal abuse.

> After the NDE, my whole outlook changed. I could feel when people are in pain. Before, sometimes I had to cause people pain. I couldn't do that anymore …
>
> The experience made me more sensitive to and aware of others' pain. I still get very teary about others who are in pain. People I know can't understand that.[33]

Dan Williams suffered a cardiac arrest while withdrawing from drugs. He had a history of addiction and drug- and alcohol-related criminal charges. He asks,

> How does a guy go from a hopeless drug addict, nearly homeless and broke, stealing drugs to support my habit, to owning senior living communities, often sitting and comforting the dying? I still cannot fathom the amazing transformative power of my NDE …
>
> [During the NDE] I was able to see my addiction for what it was and confront, or I will say fight it. It represented the worst of me and I was pissed. I was ashamed of what I had become. For the first time in my life I felt rage, and for the first time in my life I had the upper hand on my addiction. In my NDE, I fought and won and now the addiction was over. I've never desired taking a drug or drink since that happened sixteen years ago … Instead of taking from my fellow man, I am of service to my fellow man … I am not lost anymore.[34]

Not all NDErs enjoy fairytale endings, as Greyson goes on to point out. Cecelia, a 61-year-old teacher, had difficulty coming back from her NDE:

> I regretted I had not died. The magnificent peace that I had experienced was something I could not shake. I went through weeks of depression. Everything became such an effort: dressing myself, tying shoes, chewing food, swallowing, driving a car, turning the wheel, walking up stairs, turning doorknobs, walking, walking—everything, even talking! Carrying around the physical body just seemed like too much effort …
>
> I did not know how to climb out of this hole … I bought myself a notebook to keep a journal of how I was to get through this. My first entry was written to God in anger. I asked, "Why am I alive?"[35]

Lynn was involved in a bicycle accident that resulted in an NDE:

> I didn't want to be back ... I was so depressed that all I wanted to do was die ... All I could think about was how much I hated it here, and that I wanted to go back to that place ... That place was so wonderful, and I wanted to go back so badly.[36]

Other NDErs face the frustration of being unable to explain their experience or to have it taken seriously. After three nurses told 38-year-old Edith that her experience was only a hallucination, with the last one telling her "in a cold, matter-of-fact manner that if [she] continued to talk that way a psychiatrist would be called in," she became afraid to share her story with anyone else.[37]

Changes in personality and lifestyle prompted by the NDE can put great strain on family relationships, even leading to divorce. Some NDErs have attempted suicide in a misguided desire to return to the light.

Still, the majority of people who've had an NDE seem to be transformed for the better. As Dee Wells said of her friend, the philosopher A.J. Ayer, "He became so much nicer after he died."[38]

Conclusion

In many ways, being "in the light" of an NDE appears to be identical to the experience of cosmic consciousness when it occurs outside the context of a medical crisis.

There is a difference, however. While episodes of cosmic consciousness do sometimes hint at the presence of a superhuman intelligence, like Dostoevsky's laughing puppeteer, contact with this intelligence seems far more intimate and extended in the NDE (or between-lives) state.

It is here that we seem most likely to encounter a presence in the light.

CHAPTER FIFTEEN:
A Presence in the Light

> I was moving through a tunnel of bright light toward something which I can only describe as a presence (either the light or something beyond the light). I had no sensation of being called or beckoned, the presence was simply waiting for me.
>
> —Henry Foster's NDE[1]

IMMERSION IN THE LIGHT is sometimes accompanied by more than a sense of total knowledge. There is also awareness of a divine presence. The same "Peter N" who was quoted in the previous chapter went into far more detail about his NDE:

> Suddenly, almost instantaneously, on this light exploding, coming into being around me, my sense of expansion of self rocketed to unbelievable proportions, it was as if I had just suddenly exploded outwards in all directions; I could not identify where my 'self' was ... It was in this state that I first became aware of wave upon wave upon wave of love moving into and through me from every spatial direction imaginable ... Then I became aware of the presence of a being of a power, magnitude and intelligence that was utterly indescribable and that was this light that I now knew to be here ...
>
> Then it came upon me that I knew I was inside this being and it inside me. We were merged so that there was no separation—and yet I also knew that I existed, as did it, as a discrete entity.[2]

Then there's Philip, who suffered an asthma attack so severe that he was expected to die:

> I went away.
> When I left, I felt my spirit when I left my body and went into the presence of God. While in the presence of God ... I didn't want to come back. It was unspeakable joy. I can't even

explain it. I was in harmony with wherever I was. I was very alert about everything. Once I came into his presence, I felt I had come to the ultimate point in my life.[3]

The following account is from *Heading Toward Omega*, by Kenneth Ring. Tom Sawyer, whom we met in the last chapter, went into the now-familiar tunnel.

> Then all this time, the speed is increasing ... It might possibly be the speed of light or possibly even faster than the speed of light. You do realize that you're going just so fast, and you're covering vast, vast distances in just hundredths of a second ...
>
> And then gradually you realize that *way*, way off in the distance—again, unmeasurable distance—it appears that it might be the end of the tunnel. And all you can see is a white light ...
>
> You then realize that you are coming to the end of this tunnel and that this light is not just a brilliance from whatever is at the end of the tunnel—it's an extremely brilliant light. It's pure white. It's just so brilliant ...
>
> The next sensation is this wonderful, wonderful feeling of this light ... It's almost like a person. It is not a person, but it is a being of some kind. It is a mass of energy. It doesn't have a character like you would describe another person, but it has a character in that it is more than just a thing ...
>
> Then the light immediately communicates to you ... This communication is what you might call telepathic. It's absolutely instant, absolutely clear ...
>
> The first thing you're told is, "Relax, everything is beautiful, everything is OK." ... You're immediately put at absolute ease. It's the most comfortable feeling that you could ever imagine. You have a feeling of absolute, pure love. It's the warmest feeling ... And it's so absolutely vivid and clear.
>
> Then the thing is, the light communicates to you and for the first time in your life [there] is a feeling of true, pure love ...
>
> The second most magnificent experience ... is that you realize that you are suddenly in communications with absolute, total knowledge. It's hard to describe ... You can think of a question ... and immediately know the answer to it ...
>
> Upon entering that light ... the atmosphere, the energy, it's total pure energy, it's total knowledge, it's total love, pure love ...
>
> As a result of that [experience], I have very little apprehension

about dying my natural death ... Because if death is anything, anything at all like what I experienced, it's gotta be the most wonderful thing to look forward to, absolutely the most wonderful thing.[4]

Once again, we see the experiencer reporting an immersion in "absolute, total knowledge."

What does it mean?

While such accounts often characterize the presence in the light as God, Jesus, or Krishna, these interpretations appear to be mainly an attempt to find a word for the ineffable. At least one NDEr makes it explicitly clear that the being of light was unidentifiable.

> I was with an angel or God or somebody that I had total harmony with but with total communication without saying anything ... I was with a spirit or angel or I don't know. Somebody else will have to name my companion.[5]

So just what is this mysterious presence that communes with us in the light? No definitive answer is possible, but in my opinion, the best guess is offered by Kenneth Ring in *Life at Death*. After giving many examples of a godlike presence or voice perceived in the light of an NDE, he writes,

> I submit that this presence/voice is actually—oneself! It is not merely a projection of one's personality, however, but one's total self, or what in some traditions is called the higher self. In this view, the individual personality is but a split-off fragment of the total self with which it is reunited at the point of death. During ordinary life, the individual personality functions in a seemingly autonomous way, as though it were a separate entity. In fact, however, it is invisibly tied to the larger self structure of which it is a part ...
>
> This higher self is so awesome, so overwhelming, so loving, and unconditionally accepting ... and so foreign to one's individualized consciousness that one perceives it as separate from oneself, as unmistakably other. It manifests itself as a brilliant golden light, but it is actually oneself, in a higher form, that one is seeing ...
>
> The higher self, furthermore, has total knowledge of the

individual personality, both past and future. That is why, when it is experienced as a voice, it seems to be an "all-knowing" one (to use the phrase of one respondent). That is why it can initiate a life review and, in addition, provide a preview of an individual's life and events.[6]

Though we have yet to cover the life review, we've already seen that immersion in the light is usually accompanied by a sense of timelessness, the perception that past, present, and future are all happening at once. Moreover, the intense intimacy that so many people feel upon coming into contact with the being of light suggests a deep personal connection.

At least one NDEr, Mellen-Thomas Benedict, apparently understood the light as his higher self while he was still undergoing the experience. In 1982, while on hospice care, Benedict found himself outside his body.

> Suddenly I was fully aware that I was standing up, but my body was in the bed. There was this darkness around me.
>
> Being out of my body was even more vivid than ordinary experience. It was so vivid that I could see every room in the house, I could see the top of the house, I could see around the house, I could see under the house.

After this, he entered into the light.

> I had some conversations with the light. The light kept changing into different figures, like Jesus, Buddha, Krishna, mandalas, archetypal images and signs ….
>
> I cannot really say the exact words, because it was sort of telepathy. The light responded. The information transferred to me was that your beliefs shape the kind of feedback you are getting before the light. If you were a Buddhist or Catholic or Fundamentalist, you get a feedback loop of your own stuff. You have a chance to look at it and examine it, but most people do not.
>
> As the light revealed itself to me, I became aware that what I was really seeing was our Higher Self matrix …
>
> And it became very clear to me that all the Higher Selves are connected as one being, all humans are connected as one being, we are actually the same being, different aspects of the same being …

The different questions that each of us has are very, very important. This is how Godhead is exploring God's Self—through you. So ask your questions, do your searching. You will find your Self and you will find God in that Self, because it is only the Self.[7]

Note especially that "the light kept changing into different figures, like Jesus, Buddha, Krishna." In considering a broad range of NDEs, Gregory Shushan observes:

> What is being described cross-culturally is a being that radiates light. Interestingly, this is explicitly supported in the Bardo Thödol [*Tibetan Book of the Dead*], which states that a "Clear Light" will appear in whatever form is most beneficial to the individual: as the Buddha to a Buddhist, as Vishnu to a Vaishnava Hindu, as Jesus to a Christian, or as Mohammed to a Muslim ... The description of dying in the Bardo Thödol, in fact, so closely corresponds to the NDE that it can effectively be seen as verification that the book genuinely is what it purports to be—a preparation for what happens at death.[8]

The implication, both in the Bardo Thödol and in Benedict's NDE, is that all these religious figures are symbolic images generated by what Benedict calls "our Higher Self matrix."

Not everyone agrees with this interpretation, of course. Michael Sabom, a pioneer in the study of NDEs and one of the most important contributors to the field, has been critical of such conclusions. As a conservative Christian, he believes that "without the Word of God, we are without a roadmap to determine good from evil, and Satan and his demons are free to deceive 'even the elect' (Matthew 24:24)."[9]

For this reason, Sabom is inclined to interpret the being of light as the Christian God. And to be fair, this is exactly how many NDErs themselves interpret the experience. This being so, who am I to challenge their interpretation? After all, they're the ones who went "to the other side," so to speak, while I'm just an armchair critic.

There is some force in this objection, but there are also problems with it. Most obviously, it fails to address the fact that people in non-Christian cultures usually do not encounter Jesus or the Christian God. Sabom relies on a study he conducted in his home state of Georgia, in which most of the respondents found their Christian faith confirmed by their NDEs.[10] Given their pre-existing religious beliefs, this is not surprising.

In cultures different from that of the American South, different results have been obtained. Hindus typically encounter Hindu deities; Native Americans encounter Native American deities. Respondents surveyed by the International Association of Near-Death Studies (IANDS) were more inclined to interpret their experience in terms of what might be called New Age beliefs, which probably reflected their own spiritual backgrounds (or the reading they'd done since their NDE).

In short, it seems tendentious to privilege the reports of American Christians over reports of people from different religious traditions.

The higher self

When I made this point about the higher self on my blog, one outraged reader responded, "So you're saying YOU are God!?!" I hope it's clear that this is a misunderstanding. The "me" that correlates with my ego is, in this view, only a minuscule part of a much larger identity.

The higher self is what F.W.H. Myers[11] called the subliminal self, a term that encompasses both the subconscious (the basement of the mind) and the superconscious (the penthouse). Both the subconscious and the superconscious are only intermittently and partially available to us during our physical incarnation, but upon separating from the physical world, we achieve a new unity. It is as if a receiver narrowly focused on only the middle frequency bands suddenly obtained the ability to tune in to the total spectrum. The resulting flood of information would be dazzling, overwhelming—just like the bright light. And yet all of those frequencies had existed all along; we just hadn't been picking them up.

Once, while in a meditative state, I focused on the image of a diamond as a metaphor for this higher self. The image was not original with me, having shown up in channeled literature (notably in the writings of Maurice Barbanell, attributed to a spirit teacher called Silver Birch), but my experience was emotionally powerful all the same. Shortly afterward, I wrote about a blog post about it.

> I was shown an image of a diamond, brilliant and multifaceted. But this was no ordinary diamond. It was alive. The facets, which were far more luminous than any real-life diamond's, were in constant motion. They were constantly shifting positions like the pieces of a mosaic, creating patterns that were intricate and harmonious. It did not appear that there was anything random about these patterns; rather, they seemed to involve the working-out of some larger scheme, much in the way that notes of music can be used to work out the themes and melodies of a musical composition.
>
> I was told that this diamond was my true soul, and that the individual facets were merely contributing elements. The real me, the eternal me, was the diamond as a whole, even though I wasn't aware of it in everyday life.
>
> These living and moving facets each represented some persona that my larger soul had adopted—presumably in some previous (or perhaps future) earthly incarnation. The sum total of all these facets made up the diamond itself.
>
> Let me expand on this a little. The diamond could be seen as the so-called "group soul" often discussed by metaphysical writers. But I was given to understand that the "group soul" is something of a misnomer, because actually we are talking only about a group of personae; the diamond/soul itself is our own personal soul in its purest and highest form. To think of it as a group soul is to imagine that our individual self is just one of the facets of the diamond, when in fact our soul consists of all the facets and more, because it includes the core of the diamond as well. Thus we are much greater, much more all-encompassing, than we might think.
>
> What was most strongly impressed on me was the sheer beauty of the soul. It seemed to me that this soul was the most beautiful and precious thing in the world. Of course, I'm not just talking about my own soul, but about any human soul. The

impression I had—and this is where the emotional impact came in—was that if we could only grasp the magnificence and perfection of our own souls, we would have a whole new perspective on life, and negative things ... would pale into insignificance.

Again, while I cannot really convey the feeling I got, I came away with an extraordinarily strong impression that our soul—mine, or yours, or anyone's—is an object of exquisite beauty, unfathomable complexity, and ultimate perfection. Even the flaws that we perceive in ourselves are not really flaws, but elements necessary to a larger harmonious whole.

There are many wonderful things in our physical reality, including stars and galaxies, but the impression I got was that each of us, inasmuch as we represent this diamond-like perfection of the soul, is a far more wondrous and valuable thing than any physical object.[12]

In discussing the ecstatic unions (or reunions) that occur in some OBEs, William Buhlman writes, "After decades of examination, I believe that many of these experiences are an internal reunification of our multidimensional nature."[13] This comment is in line with the channeled teachings of Jane Roberts' Seth, the between-lives hypnotic regressions of Michael Newton, and, for what it's worth, my own meditative experience.

Conclusion

Immersion in the light initiates a powerful emotional and spiritual transformation. But this is only the beginning of the changes in store for the newly discarnate soul.

CHAPTER SIXTEEN:
Beings of Light

MANY VARIATIONS ON THE EXPERIENCE in the light have been reported. Although nearly everyone agrees on overwhelming feelings of tranquility and joy, the specifics can differ markedly. These variations raise questions of their own.

Unknown human figures

In 1970, Joseph F. Dippong nearly suffocated. He lost consciousness and reportedly showed no signs of life.

> Then another consciousness slowly began to unfold. It could have happened in seconds, in minutes, in years, or even in an eternity ...
>
> Everything that occurred to me while I was in this state of consciousness was vastly beyond anything I have ever experienced and yet at the same time it was familiar—as if I had always known of its existence ...
>
> As my senses expanded I became aware of colors that were far beyond the spectrum of the rainbow known to the human eye. My awareness stretched out in all 360 degrees. It was as if I was in the center of a lotus flower which was unfolding its beauty around me in every direction. I became aware of being in the middle of a tunnel. I was speeding closer and closer to a light at the other end. In the far distance I saw what I can only describe in the limited language available to me now, as two circles.
>
> In the middle of one circle was the most beautiful being. It was neither a man nor a woman, but it was both ... An immense, radiant love poured from it ... The light radiated outward. It was a brilliant white superimposed with what I can only describe as a golden hue. I was filled with an intense feeling of joy and all. I was consumed with an absolutely inexpressible amount of love ...
>
> The second circle surrounded the first. In it I became aware of six shimmering mother-of-pearl-like impressions which unfolded and opened up in the way the petals of a freshly

created flower open up to the sun. They were living beings. Their beauty, charm, splendid emanating colors, and the closeness I felt to them were breathtaking ... I became aware that it [the light] was part of all living things and that at the same time all living things were part of it ... My only desire was to have more and more of it and to bathe in it forever.[1]

Here we have a new wrinkle—multiple presences in the light, at least one of which is humanlike in appearance. In other cases, such beings assume a more readily recognizable human form.

Michael Sabom reports on a woman, Jamie, who suffered several heart attacks and had total of three NDEs. In one of them a "meditating guide" whom she had visualized in her meditations since she was fourteen years old was there to meet her.

> He looked at me most sincerely and most lovingly. It was like ... all the emotions and vibrations you can gather. He said to me, "You are going back." ...
>
> He said, "There are five things I want you to do. I'll be with you." ...
>
> The first thing he wanted me to do was to live life to its fullest the best way I could and that I would be taken care of. The second thing he told me to do was to laugh every day and at every little thing. The third thing he told me to do was to lift up my brothers and my sisters and humankind—cats and dogs and possums and puppies. The fourth thing he told me to do was to help people to learn and to enlighten them, to be an example and teach what I had learned and to pass it on to those who come to me. And that I would know who they were. And the fifth thing he told me was to love unconditionally.
>
> Then he said, "You must go back now."[2]

Sabom also summarizes the results of a study of 47 near-death experiencers. Spiritual beings were encountered by thirty of them.

> In each encounter, the spiritual entity was recognized as an *authority in control*. Most commonly, this authority commanded the dying person to return to life and/or prevented the person from crossing a barrier and proceeding into death ... Darrell was told to "go" back by the "Lord"; Pam was "pushed" back by her "uncle"; Gene was turned back by his "mother"; Laurie was stopped by "angels"; and so on.

Less frequently, the near-death experiencer was given a choice to live or die. For example, Brent ... discussed his fate with a "voice" during his NDE:

Brent: "What's going on? Am I dead?"
Voice: "Yes, right now you are."
Brent: "What are they [the resuscitation team] trying to do?"
Voice: "They are trying to save you."
Brent: "Will they succeed?"
Voice: "That's up to you."
Brent: "Well, I really wanted to stay a little longer. I would like to spend more time with my family. I would like to see my children through college."
Voice: "Well, it's your decision."[3]

In an article for the *Journal of Near-Death Studies*, Richard J. Bonenfant relates a 1981 experience in which a woman nearly drowned. She

> found herself slowly drifting upwards in a dark environment. Although still disoriented and confused, she no longer felt the fear, distress, and panic of drowning. She was now comfortable and fully alert in her new surroundings. The subject reported that she felt herself gently rising at an oblique angle, as if she were riding an invisible escalator ...
>
> The subject then became aware of a distant light located slightly above and ahead of her. The light appeared small and distant at first but grew in brightness and size as she progressed toward it. While moving towards the light, the subject felt that she was passing through a dark tunnel, slowly at first, but later with great acceleration. As she moved within the light she was filled with awe, peace, and love.
>
> The subject discerned, framed within the light, the figure of "a beautiful woman" with hands outstretched to receive her. This woman was described as being clothed in a white dress, and having long, dark-blonde hair and blue eyes. The angelic being radiated a sense of "motherly love" to the subject. The subject remarked that her only desire was to reach the safety of those outstretched hands. But when she was nearly within reach, the figure withdrew her hands and told the subject, through her eyes, that is was not yet her time and that she would have to return.
>
> Almost immediately, the subject found herself back in her physical body gasping for breath on the deck of the swimming pool.

Note the details of rising upward, travel through a tunnel, telepathic communication, and a harsh return to the physical world—all common features of NDEs.

This account has an interesting follow-up. Fifteen years later, the woman's eleven-year-old daughter was undergoing a series of operations. One night in the hospital, the mother was cradling her daughter in bed when

> suddenly, a subdued light appeared behind the subject's left shoulder. She immediately turned her head about to determine the source of the illumination. There was no evident explanation for the light, but when she returned her gaze toward her daughter, she saw the identical "beautiful woman" who had appeared to her during her NDE. The angel-like figure was only a couple of feet away. Her head was resting on her arms at the edge of the bed. Gazing at both mother and daughter, the angel communicated telepathically to the mother that she was not to worry because her daughter would be all right. The subject was awestruck by the encounter and briefly closed her eyes to refocus them upon the being, but when she reopened her eyes the figure was gone.
>
> When questioned about the identity of this female entity, the subject was absolutely sure that it was the same angel-like being that she had observed during her earlier NDE. There was only one minor difference. In the visitation, the angel's hair was "up" about her head rather than falling down below her shoulders. The second appearance was very brief, lasting only several seconds, and the subject observed only the head, shoulders and arms of the angelic figure. As a result of the visitation, the subject was not only comforted that her daughter would recover, but became convinced that "a personal relationship" existed between herself and the lady-in-white. To the subject, this being was her own special "guardian angel."[4]

In *Many Lives, Many Masters*, Brian Weiss's hypnotically regressed patient Catherine recalls heavenly intervals between incarnations. In one of them, she floated out of her body and saw

> a wonderful light ... There are people coming to me. They are coming to help me. Wonderful people. They are not afraid ... The soul finds peace here. You leave all the bodily pains behind you. Your soul is peaceful and serene. It's a wonderful feeling ... wonderful, like the sun is always shining on you. The light is so

brilliant! Everything comes from the light! Energy comes from this light. Our soul *immediately* goes there. It's almost like a magnetic force that we're attracted to. It's wonderful. It's like a power source. It knows how to heal ... [Asked if the light has a color, she replies:] It's many colors.[5]

In the light, Catherine channeled spiritual entities whom Weiss dubbed the Masters. They communicated esoteric wisdom that was allegedly beyond Catherine's normal knowledge.

Groups of three are surprisingly common in these encounters.

- Nita McCallum: "At the time of my NDE I was a practicing Roman Catholic. Had I died I would most certainly have expected that any visions I had would have related to my faith ... As it was, when I suddenly found myself in this gentle glowing light and standing a little below the three beings above me, they appeared as young Indian men, and, though they were dressed alike in high-necked silver-colored tunics with silver turbans on their heads, I felt they were young Indian princes, or rajas. Two were facing each other and the third facing me. And from a jewel in the center of each forehead or turban three 'laser' beams emitted, meeting in the center. My whole lifestyle was changed as a result—much reading about various religions and philosophies."
- Audrey Quinn, after major abdominal surgery in 1980: "I was floating in total blackness when far ahead of me I saw a wrought-iron gate—a tall church window-shaped gate—which was open. Through the gate I saw a group of three figures, apparently male, all dressed in Arab-type flowing gowns with hoods which looked to be made from a type of chain-mail. The figures were standing on a platform, much like the Olympic type of stands, the middle one higher than the two side ones. The figures and the gate seemed to be lit from within—not quite fluorescent, but their surroundings were still totally black."
- Hazel Graham, seriously ill with the flu: "I felt 'floaty' and then I was in a tunnel of light. At the end I seemed to be standing in front of three old Chinese men who all had long white beards, and who also wore white robes. They looked pleasant but rather puzzled. One said to me, 'You should not be here, it is not the Year of the Seventh Horse.'"[6]

Peter and Elizabeth Fenwick, whose book *The Truth in the Light* is the source of the above three cases, write,

> Figures in monk-like habits or long flowing robes are a recurrent theme in near-death experiences. Ella Silver saw people in "long garments, white, with a cord around their waist." S. Woodham felt she herself was wearing a "long, long, long night dress." Mr. G. Thomas saw a figure with hair down to his shoulders and dressed in a robe with wide sleeves which reached down to the floor. D. J. R. Cook saw a person white clothing, Alf Rose a woman in a white robe, and Hazel Graham's three old Chinese men all had long white beards and white robes.[7]

> Very rarely, the encounter with the being of light is seemingly confirmed by a third party, as in this case reported by Brian Weiss:
>
>> I have had several patients with near-death experiences. The most interesting account was that of a successful South American businessman who was seen by me for several sessions of conventional psychotherapy ... Jacob had been run over and knocked unconscious by a motorcycle in Holland in 1975, when he was in his early thirties. He remembers floating above his body and looking down at the scene of the accident, taking note of the ambulance, the doctor attending his injuries, and the growing crowd of onlookers. He became aware of a golden light in the distance, and as he approached it, he saw a monk wearing a brown robe. The monk told Jacob that this was not his time to pass over, that he had to return to his body. Jacob felt the wisdom and power of the monk, who also related several future events in Jacob's life, all of which later occurred. Jacob was whooshed back into his body, now in a hospital bed ...

> In 1980, while traveling in Israel, Jacob, who is Jewish, visited the Cave of the Patriarchs at Hebron, which is a holy site to both Jews and Muslims. After his experience in Holland, he had become more religious and had begun to pray more often. He saw the nearby mosque and sat down to pray with the Muslims there. After a while, he rose to leave. An old Muslim man came up to him and said, "You are different from the others. They very rarely sit down to pray with us." The old man paused for a moment, looking closely at Jacob before continuing. "You have met the monk. Do not forget what he has told you."[8]

Known human figures

Meeting loved ones in the afterlife is extremely common, according to the more extended NDEs and, of course, mediumship. Usually such meetings take place after one has passed through the light into another world. Occasionally, however, people report meeting recognizable loved ones while still hovering over their body or while in the tunnel approaching the light.

A 52-year-old man suffering cardiac arrest experienced leaving his body:

> I was sitting up there somewhere and I could look down ... [With me was] my older brother, who had been dead since I was a young fella. I couldn't see, but I knew he was right by me, even patting me on the shoulder, saying, "It's entirely up to you—you can do anything you want to do. If you want to stay and you don't want to go back, in your body, and you see how bad shape it's in, you can stay and I'll be right by your side and everything is going to be fine."[9]

Heart attack victim Elizabeth Rogers remembers traveling in a tunnel toward a brilliant light which she expected to enter. But then ...

> I saw a group of people between me and the light. I knew them;

my brother, who had died a few years before, was gesticulating delightedly as I approached. Their faces were so happy and welcoming. Then somehow my mother became detached from the group. She shook her head and waved her hand (rather like a windscreen wiper) and I stopped, and I heard the doctor say, "She's coming round," and I was in my bed and the doctor and my husband were there. My first words to the doctor were "Why did you bring me back?"[10]

An account cited by Chris Carter combines elements of the NDE with "peak in Darien" deathbed visions.

I began bleeding badly after the birth of my daughter and I was instantly surrounded by medical staff who started working on me. I was in great pain. Then suddenly the pain was gone and I was looking down on them working on me. I heard one doctor say he couldn't find a pulse. Next I was traveling down a tunnel toward a bright light. But I never reached the end of the tunnel. A gentle voice told me I had to go back. Then I met a dear friend, a neighbor from a town that we had left. He also told me to go back. I hit the hospital bed with an electrifying jerk and the pain was back ... It was three weeks later that my husband decided I was well enough to be told that my dear friend in another town had died in an accident on the day my daughter was born.[11]

In such cases, the people encountered seem real enough. But what are we to make of what followed after a pedestrian was struck by a speeding car?

I went through this period of darkness ... There was this light, like someone holding a flashlight, and I started going towards that. And then the whole thing brightened up and the next thing I remember was I was floating ... We were going through this shaft of light ... The light kept getting brighter and brighter ... It was so bright, and the closer we got, the brighter it got, and it was blinding ... I had angels around me ... But the angels around me were all my children. My oldest son was seventeen at the time but yet he was in the lead and I couldn't get over it because he was like around six years old. All my children were at my side, three on one side, three on another side, and my son was in front of me ... They were all almost the same age ... I think it has something to do with the most favorite time I have had with my children in my life ... There was no communication between them and myself.[12]

This man perceived his children in a tunnel of light, at a time when all of his children were still very much alive. Moreover, he perceived them as all being the same age, when in reality they were different ages. It seems obvious that his perception was, in some sense, nonobjective—perhaps an instance of our old friend analytical overlay, or perhaps an example of the thought-forms that the *Tibetan Book of the Dead* warns us we will see in the first stage of our postmortem adventure.

But if this is true, how can we be sure that *any* of the loved ones we encounter out of body or in the tunnel or, for that matter, in the afterlife environment beyond the light, are real? Couldn't all of them be mistaken perceptions or thought-forms? Could the entire afterlife experience be a kind of extended hallucination in which all the beings we meet, even our dearest companions, are merely figments of our own mind?

It's a tricky question. I think the key point is that this part of the process is still transitional. The approach to the light, or even the entry into the light, is not the final stage. All available information tells us that, if the dying process continues to completion, the person goes through the light and into another world, which will serve as a dwelling place, at least for a time. Conditions beyond the light appear to be quite distinct from conditions near or even in the light.

Encounters in the tunnel or in the light appear to exist on a continuum. Some of the loved ones, such as the seven children, must be symbolic imagery. In other cases, such as monks and habits or "angels" in white robes, the figure may or may not be purely symbolic. When it comes to recognizable deceased loved ones behaving in appropriate ways, it's probably simplest to assume they are who they appear to be.

It's also worth noting that the more obviously symbolic figures generally don't interact with the experiencer in the way that the more realistic figures do. "There was no communication between them and myself," reported the man who saw his seven children. Recall also the "young Indian princes, or rajas" with jewels and their turbans emitting laserlike beams, or the "figures ... standing on a platform, much like the Olympic type of stands," none of whom directly interacted with the experiencer. And there are fairly frequent perceptions of a beautiful female (or androgynous) figure radiating light and love but communicating no particular message.

These experiences contrast pretty clearly with unambiguously recognizable figures of deceased loved ones who do communicate (usually telepathically): the older brother who "was right by me, even patting me on the shoulder, saying, 'It's entirely up to you—you can do anything you want to do,'" the relatives "gesticulating delightedly as I approached" until one of them—the mother—put the kibosh on the celebration, the former neighbor who "told me to go back."

Occupying a middle ground are possibly symbolic encounters like Jamie's meditating guide or Brent's disembodied voice.

Moreover, as the Tibetan Buddhists knew, it's possible to see through such illusions. In our study of negative experiences, we saw examples of shape-shifting imagery, and of imagery that vanished altogether in conjunction with a change in the level of consciousness. Conversely, deceased loved ones encountered in the post-light phase of the afterlife seldom, if ever, shape-shift or vanish; typically, the more we see of them, the more real to us they are.

Similarities and differences

The differences among these examples are obvious. Some experiencers are in touch with a faceless presence; others perceive unknown human or human-like figures radiating compassion and wisdom; still others perceive particular individuals known to them from earthly life.

These variations shouldn't blind us to the commonalities of the experience. One recurring theme in cases of all types is unconditional love.

- wave upon wave upon wave of love (Peter N)
- an immense, radiant love poured from it (Dippong)
- he looked at me most sincerely and most lovingly (Jamie)
- the angelic being radiated a sense of "motherly love" (Bonenfant)

Also common is an awareness of vast intelligence and knowledge that is not entirely impersonal but has at least some of the qualities of a sentient being.

- The presence of a being of a power, magnitude and intelligence that was utterly indescribable (Peter N)
- The presence of God (Philip)
- It's almost like a person. It is not a person, but it is a being of some kind (Sawyer)

People remember a deep sense of intimacy, harmony, and connectedness with this being.

- I was inside this being and it inside me. We were merged so that there was no separation—and yet I also knew that I existed, as did it, as a discrete entity (Peter N)
- I was in harmony with wherever I was (Philip)

Direct mental communication is possible between the experiencer and this being.

- The light immediately communicates to you ... This communication is what you might call telepathic (Sawyer)
- It was sort of telepathy. The light responded (Benedict)

Individuals figures are often clad in attire conventionally associated with spirituality.

- the figure of "a beautiful woman" with hands outstretched ... clothed in a white dress (Bonenfant)
- They appeared as young Indian men ... young Indian princes or rajas ... dressed alike in high-necked silver-colored tunics with silver turbans (McCallum)
- Three figures, apparently male, all dressed in Arab-type flowing gowns with hoods (Quinn)
- Three old Chinese men who all had long white beards, and who also wore white robes (Graham)
- figures in monk-like habits or long flowing robes (Fenwick)
- people in "long garments, white, with the cord around their waist" (Silver)
- A monk wearing a brown robe (Weiss)

The being or beings prevent NDErs from proceeding, either by direct order or by persuasion.

- Darrell was told to "go" back by the "Lord" (Sabom)
- Laurie was stopped by "angels" (Sabom)
- Brent ... discussed his fate with a "voice" (Sabom)
- The monk told Jacob that this was not his time to pass over (Weiss)
- A gentle voice told me I had to go back. Then I met a dear friend, a neighbor ... He also told me to go back (Carter)

- My mother ... shook her head and waved her hand ... and I stopped (Rogers)

Conclusion

Entering the light is a profound, multifaceted experience that is probably a bit different for everyone. But for all us, it's a joyful, indeed ecstatic reunion with a higher power, however we wish to interpret it. In some ways it marks the culmination of our earthly life.

But we aren't through learning yet. In fact, the really personal lessons are yet to come.

CHAPTER SEVENTEEN:
The Life Review

THROUGHOUT HISTORY, WE FIND a persistent belief that dying can be accompanied by a whirlwind review of our earthly experiences. Our entire life is said to "pass before our eyes." This is well-known. What's less commonly recognized is that there are two different forms of the so-called "life review."

The first form, and the one that seems to be more widely reported, is a relatively unemotional overview that merely recapitulates a person's history—a kind of summing-up. Memories are observed with detachment, even indifference, and whatever conclusions they may inspire are purely intellectual.

The superficial life review

In Thomas De Quincey's *Confessions of an English Opium-Eater*, published in 1822, we find this early historical anecdote:

> I was once told by a near relative of mine that, having in her childhood fallen into a river, and being on the very verge of death but for the assistance which reached her at the last critical moment, she saw in a moment her whole life, clothed in its forgotten incidents, arrayed before her as in a mirror, not successively, but simultaneously; and she had a faculty developed as suddenly for comprehending the whole and every part.[1]

Robert Crookall unearths an account originally published in 1851:

> Dying is really not such a terrifying experience. I speak as one who has died and come back ... Suddenly my whole life began to unroll before me and I saw the purpose of it. All bitterness was wiped out for I knew the meaning of every event and I saw its place in the pattern. I seemed to view it all impersonally.[2]

Carol Zaleski summarizes the case of Admiral Beaufort of the

British Navy, who nearly drowned in 1791 when he was a young boy: "As soon as Beaufort stopped struggling, a feeling of contentment swept over him; his mind became calm but at the same time alert and invigorated, and he found himself reviewing his life in reverse chronological order."

She quotes Beaufort's own account, as given by Dr. William Munk in 1887 :

> The whole period of my existence seemed to be placed before me in a kind of panoramic review, and each act of it seemed to be accompanied by a consciousness of right or wrong, or by some reflection on its cause or its consequences; indeed, many trifling events which had been long forgotten, then crowded into my imagination, and with the character of recent familiarity.[3]

Greg Taylor reports on a similar case involving a different admiral, Richard Byrd, which was

> described by Byrd himself in his book, *Alone*, published in 1938. It occurred as a result of carbon monoxide poisoning that Byrd suffered during his well-known Antarctic expedition. He recalled that "I saw my whole life pass in review," and also that he "realized how wrong my sense of value had been and how I had failed to see that the simple, homely, unpretentious things of life are the most important" ... Byrd told how the struggle "went on interminably in a half-lighted borderland divided by a great wall. Several times I was nearly across the wall into a field flooded with a golden light but each time I slipped back into a spinning darkness."[4]

In other, more recent cases, nothing seems to have changed. Kenneth Ring quotes a victim of near-drowning in his 1980 book *Life at Death*.

> It was amazing. I could see in the back of my head an array, just (an) innumerable array of thoughts, memories, things I had dreamt, just in general thoughts and recollections of the past, just raced in front of me, in less than thirty seconds. All these things about my mother and grandmother and my brothers and these dreams I've had. I felt like this frame, millions of frames, just flashed through ... It was thoughts and images of people. And a lot of thoughts just raced (snaps his fingers several times)

in split seconds ... Silly things—just nitpicking things I thought I'd forgotten ... It was like I was going through this memory, and ... like my whole memory was re-taping. I was in reverse. And everything was backtracking so I could go over it again like a tape recorder.[5]

The earliest systematic investigator of the life-review phenomenon was Albert Heim, a mountain climber whose interest in the subject began when he survived a serious fall. In 1892 he described his experience as he hurtled downward:

> I saw my whole past life take place in many images, as though on a stage at some distance from me. I saw myself as the chief character in the performance. Everything was transfigured as though by a heavenly light and everything was beautiful without grief, without anxiety, and without pain ...
>
> I acted out my life, as though I were an actor on a stage upon which I looked down from practically the highest gallery in the theatre. Both hero and onlooker, I was as though doubled.[6]

Heim went on to interview other climbers who'd had the same experience. In a report presented to the Swiss Alpine Club, he found many commonalities in accidental falls.

> There was no anxiety, no trace of despair, no pain; but rather calm seriousness, profound acceptance, and a dominant mental quickness and sense of surety. Mental activity became enormous, rising to a hundred-fold velocity or intensity ... No confusion entered at all. Time became greatly expanded ... In many cases there followed a sudden review of the individual's entire past; and finally the person falling often heard beautiful music and fell in a superbly blue heaven containing roseate cloudlets. Then consciousness was painlessly extinguished, usually at the moment of impact, and the impact was, at the most, heard but never painfully felt.[7]

Some years earlier, in 1862, another mountain climber, Edward Whymper, fell while climbing the Matterhorn:

> Like persons who have been rescued from drowning, I remember that the recollection of a multitude of things rushed through my head, many of them trivialities or absurdities, which

had been forgotten long before; and, more remarkable, this bounding through space did not feel disagreeable.[8]

Falling off the Matterhorn is bad enough, but consider this more recent account of a parachutist who survived a plunge of 3,500 feet after his chute failed to open.

> It's like a picture runs in front of your eyes, like from the time you can remember up to the [present moment] ... It seems like pictures of your life just flow in front of your eyes, the things you used to do when you were small and stuff: stupid things. Like, you see your parents' faces—it was everything. And things that I didn't remember that I did. Things that I couldn't remember now, but I remember two years ago or something. It all came back to me, like it refreshed my mind of everything I used to do when I was little ... It was clear as day, clear as day. It was very fast and you can see everything.[9]

In *Lessons from the Light*, Kenneth Ring presents a list of excerpts highlighting common features of these experiences.

- The life review was absolutely, positively, everything for the first 33 years of my life ... from the first breath of life right through the accident.
- It proceeded to show me every single event in my 22 years of life, in a kind of instant three-dimensional panoramic review ... The brightness showed me every second of all those years, in exquisite detail, in what seemed only an instant of time.
- My whole life was there, every instant of it ... Everyone and everything I had ever seen and everything that ever happened was there.
- Then I was seeing my whole life from beginning to end, even all those little things you forget along the way.
- I had a total, complete clear knowledge of everything that ever happened in my life—even little minute things that I had forgotten.
- My life passed before me ... even things I had forgotten all about. Every single emotion, all the happy times, the sad times, the angry times, the love, the reconciliation—everything was there. Nothing was left out.[10]

There are even literary precedents. The titular hero of Leo Tolstoy's last novel, *Hadji Murad*, faces death in the same way.

> This wound in his side was mortal and he felt that he was dying. One after another images and memories flashed through his mind. Now he saw the mighty Abununtsal Khan clasping to his face his severed, hanging cheek and rushing at his enemies with dagger drawn; he saw Vorontsov, old, feeble and pale with his sly, white face and heard his soft voice; he saw his son Yusuf, Sofiat his wife, and the pale face, red beard and screwed up eyes of his enemy Shamil.
>
> And these memories running through his mind evoked no feelings in him, no pity, ill-will or desire of any kind. It all seemed so insignificant compared to what was now beginning and had already begun for him.[11]

The in-depth life review

Our story grows more complicated when we turn to the second type of life review. This one is neither indifferent nor purely intellectual; it is an intense, emotional, deeply affecting experience that feels much more like a judgment than a mere recapitulation.

Certain life reviews have features of each type. One woman remembered, "Some [images] I watched in a very detached way ... But some of the things I got emotionally caught up in."[12] Another woman recalled a dual perspective:

> Like, if you were going to have a life review, and we were going to have a play of it, I would be in the play, but I'd also be watching the play from the audience. And I would feel all the emotions, pain and suffering of all of the characters around me in the play. And I'd feel it as an actor in the play, and I'd also experience it as the viewer of the play. So I'd have both perspectives.[13]

But usually, the second type of life review is easily distinguishable from the first type. Not only does it have a much higher level of emotional intensity, but it often requires the person to experience the thoughts and feelings, even the physical pain, of other people.

It also normally takes place at a different point in the overall experience and under different circumstances—usually after having progressed all the way through the light and into a new, more earthlike environment. For that reason, its placement here is somewhat out of sequence. But for purposes of comparison and contrast, I think it makes sense to treat both life reviews back to back.

One of the more famous cases of the in-depth type involves the same Tom Sawyer we've met before. In part of his life review, he relived a fight with a pedestrian who had crossed in front of his car:

> He yelled some four-letter words at me and reached through the window and slapped me across the face with an open hand.
>
> Well, at age nineteen, that instantly gave me license to annihilate this man because it was totally justifiable—he hit me first, it's self-defense. I pulled the keys out of the ignition, stepped out of the truck and I beat that man up. I hit him many times …
>
> Now it's life-review time! I can follow the adrenalin rush from the center of me outwardly, can feel the tingling sensation in my hands and experience the warmth of my face getting red. I can feel the rage that this jerk had violated my calm pursuit of happiness. My vindication and justification were experienced now in very slow motion …
>
> I never knew that man afterwards, never heard anything about him. But after the life review I came to know his chronological age—he was 46 years old. I know that he was in a drunken state and that the rationale behind his desire to drink to oblivion was that he was in a severe state of bereavement for his deceased wife …
>
> I came to know the second stool in the bar where that man had his drinks …
>
> I also experienced seeing Tom Sawyer's fist come directly into my face. And I felt the indignation, the rage, the embarrassment, the frustration, the physical pain … I felt my teeth going through my lower lip—in other words, I was in that man's eyes. I was in that man's body.[14]

Another NDEr recalled that the life review "showed me not only what I had done, but *even how what I had done had affected other people* … because I could feel those things."[15]

Still another remembered "one particular instance … when, as a child, I yanked my little sister's Easter basket away from her, because there was a toy in it that I wanted. Yet in the review, I felt her feelings of disappointment and loss and rejection."[16]

A contributor to an NDE newsletter writes that even unkind thoughts can have consequences:

> It was a three-dimensional, panoramic view of my life, every aspect of my life. Everything I had ever said or done, or even thought, was right there ... I rethought every thought, I re-experienced every feeling, as it happened, in an instant. And I also felt how my actions, or even just my *thoughts*, had affected others. When I had passed judgment on someone else, I would experience myself doing that. Then I would change places in perspective, and experience what that judgment had felt like for them to receive from me.[17]

I'm not so sure I like the idea that stray thoughts can have devastating repercussions. Who wants to be constantly on guard against every untoward thought? It seems like a recipe for repression and anxiety. Moreover, it means I've severely wronged many of my fellow drivers on America's roads. But perhaps the lesson is simply to try to elevate one's thinking and avoid rash judgments.

One of the most detailed life reviews of this type was recounted by a man who, as a small boy, put his younger brother into a shopping cart and impulsively pushed the cart down a hill. The cart crashed, and the younger brother was injured. The incident came up in his NDE life review, in which he relived the frightening experience from multiple points of view, most of which he had not even considered at the time.

> And I could feel in my brother, at first it was excitement. You know, "I'm goin' so quick, I'm movin' real fast," you know, a real thrill for him. And then, when he saw this upcoming wall he couldn't avoid, it turned into panic and fear and distress. And it's not like I watched him panic. I *felt* him panic. And I felt me, at the top of the hill, realizing what I did ...
>
> And not until my brother realized he was bleeding from his head did he become terrified inside. And I felt this intense fear and pain that he [was feeling] ...
>
> And I run inside [a nearby synagogue], and there was an elderly lady ... And she saw—and I felt from her, like a, "Oh, my God, what just happened," and like a fear. That is, in the *life review* I felt it. When it happened I barely paid attention to it ...
>
> [The congregation became alarmed.] And in the life review, it's like I felt all the chaos. And I felt everyone. It's like it was a bombardment of feelings, concerns, emotions, anger ... Like, if

> you're in a crowd, and everyone is running toward you, and you're feeling entrapped. Well, in the review, not only were they running toward me, they were throwing all these emotions at me, all these feelings. And they were all hitting me, and I was feeling them.
>
> But at the time this was actually happening, I only knew that I was causing a commotion, but I was blinded to what everyone was feeling.[18]

Rarely, a life review offers three separate perspectives—the viewpoints belonging to oneself, to those affected by one's actions, and to one's higher self.

> I wasn't just watching the events; I was actually reliving them again, while at the same time I was also re-experiencing the actions from other people's points of view. I was them. I was reliving the experience from their point of view and at the same time (and I don't know how this works) I was also experiencing it from a higher reality; the truth of the matter. So what I saw was my own lies and my own self-deception to myself, which I had used to convince me that doing certain things was okay because people had deserved it. Then I was experiencing the emotional impact it had on other people. I felt their pain. I felt the shock on them ... [But] the judgment came all from myself. It was not from an outside source, but then this being that was with me was also sending me comforting messages—thank goodness!—and one of them was that it was alright as I was only human.[19]

The life review in religious traditions and mediumship

The idea of a comprehensive final judgment on one's life is at least as old as organized religion. In *First Ghosts*, Irving Finkel tells us that the ancient Mesopotamian sun god, known variously as Utu and Shamash, decided each "ghost's individual case" in a judgment known as "the day of the lot of mankind."[20] Those who somehow evaded judgment were doomed to wander the earth and harass the living. One Mesopotamian document identifies "a ghost who frightens people in dreams [and] who works evil against men from a place of murder" as one "whose judgement has not been passed, whose case has not been decided."[21]

Final judgment was equally important to the ancient Egyptians, whose jackal-god Anubis would weigh the deceased's heart on a scale balanced by a feather. If the heart outweighed the feather, it signaled a life of irredeemable sinfulness, and the unfortunate defendant was delivered to the less-than-tender mercies of Ammit, Eater of Souls. Not surprisingly, believers expected to approach this final judgment in fear and trembling. Some took the trouble to memorize complicated religious formulas deemed necessary to pass the test.

Although such traditions are clearly overlaid with mythological embellishments, the basic idea of an emotionally charged and personally decisive life review lies at the bottom.

In the modern world, channeled literature also speaks of this type of life review. F.W.H. Myers, channeled by Geraldine Cummins, observed that "the cruel man" begins his afterlife experience in a state of confusion, a kind of mental and existential fog, until he

> faces up to his own misery, to his vice; and then the great change comes. He is put in touch with a portion of the Great Memory ... the Book of Life. He becomes aware of all the emotions aroused in his victims by his acts ... No pain, no anguish he has caused has perished. All has been registered, has a kind of existence that makes him sensible of it once he has drifted into touch with the web of memory that clothed his life and the lives of those who came into contact with him on earth.[22]

Note that Myers does not say merely that the cruel man sees the events of his life flash by, but that he experiences the pain that he has caused others.

In *The Country Beyond*, Jane Sherwood channels a communicator calling himself "E.K."

> Soon after shedding the etheric [= intermediate] body and waking fully on the astral plane ... one's thoughts begin to be much concerned with the life of earth which has been left behind. The clear-cut memory has been lost with the etheric body, and yet as one begins to use the astral [= soul] body and it grows in strength, the scenes and events of the past life begin to come vividly back ... The impressions of people, events and acts which now come crowding back are far more real and comprehensive than when they were actually experienced. The difference in this presentment of the past is that included in it now is the reaction of other people. I find this difficult to explain. Everything that happens to you affects others as well as yourself and every event has therefore has as many aspects in

reality as there are consciousnesses affected by it. Each of these others concerned in these events had their emotional life altered thereby even though you were quite unconscious of what was being brought about by your agency. Now, in this process of recollection, as an incident comes back to one's mind it brings with it the actual feelings, not of oneself alone but of the others who were affected by the event. All their feelings have now to be experienced in oneself as though they were one's own. This means that the effects of deeds on the lives of others must be experienced as intimately as though to do and to suffer the deed were one. Where sorrow and wrong have been inflicted, sorrow and wrong must be *felt*, not merely known to exist.

Most of our deeds on earth are performed in ignorance of their real bearing on the lives of others. There may be an uneasy sense that others are involved in suffering because of us but we often choose to ignore this. We have understood a situation with our mere intellect and have kept back sympathy which is the beginning of knowing in oneself what this suffering is ... Where sorrow and wrong have been inflicted, as I said, they must be felt. We have to face the reliving of our whole earth experience in this way.[23]

Cummins's book was published in 1932; Sherwood's, in 1944. To me, it's striking that an observation made by so many NDErs—people with no known interest in spiritualism, occultism, or automatic writing—should have been foreshadowed so precisely by communications channeled decades before NDEs were widely reported.

Seth, communicating through Jane Roberts, offers a similar picture of postmortem life review.

> You examine the fabric of the existence you have left, and you learn to understand how your experiences were the result of your own thoughts and emotions and how these affected others ...
>
> Until this examination is through, you are not yet aware of the larger portions of your own identity. When you realize the significance and meaning of the life you have just left, then you are ready for conscious knowledge of your other existences.
>
> You become aware, then, of an expanded awareness. What you are begins to include what you have been in other lives, and you begin to make plans for your next physical existence, if you decide upon one. You can instead enter another level of reality, and then return to a physical existence if you choose.[24]

The nature of the judgment

One important difference between ancient traditions about postmortem judgment and the more modern accounts delivered by near-death survivors and mediums is that, in modern cases, the judgment is almost invariably passed by the individual himself.

An Australian man remembering an NDE he had at age fourteen says,

> I told the Light that I thought there was a judgment on many people and that I expected him to judge me rather sternly. He said, "Oh, no, that doesn't happen at all." However, at my request, they then played back over the events that occurred in my life ... And I was the judge.[25]

This remains true even when spiritual authorities apparently oversee and assess the review. Allan Pring, a former RAF pilot who had an NDE during surgery, says,

> I experienced the review of my life which extended from early childhood and included many occurrences that I had completely forgotten. My life passed before me in a momentary flash but it was entire, even my thoughts were included. Some of the contents caused me to be ashamed but there were one or two I had forgotten about of which I felt quite pleased. All in all, I knew that I could have lived a much better life but it could have been a lot worse. Be that as it may, I knew that it was all over now and there was no going back. There was one most peculiar feature of this life review and it is very difficult to describe, let alone explain. Although it took but a moment to complete, literally a flash, there was still time to stop and wonder over separate incidents ...
>
> After the life review I spent some time resting and considering the implications of what had happened. I did not feel that I had been judged except by myself ...
>
> [Later] I was in a room, without windows or doors, but having four corners in each of which "sat" a "person." "They" began to question me in a friendly way, rather like being debriefed after a wartime operational flight. At first the questions were simple to answer but the next questions followed on logically and became progressively more difficult. However, I knew the answers. Eventually the questions were becoming impossible to answer; they concerned existence, the meaning and purpose of life and the universe itself. I could not possibly

know the answers but I did! The questions came faster and faster and I knew with the most intense feeling of joy that no matter what "they" asked me I would know the answer.[26]

Observe that, despite the "debriefing," Pring explicitly states, "I did not feel that I had been judged except by myself."

The second death

We have, then, two kinds of life review. The first kind is quick, largely unemotional, and nonjudgmental, while the second is extended, deeply emotional, and tied in with soul-searching personal judgment. How can we make sense of this apparent inconsistency?

Various sources attest that we undergo not one death, but two. Here's Jane Sherwood's "E.K." again:

> Comparison of various accounts of the death-change make it clear that there are at least two stages, separated by intervals of unconsciousness. Actual death is followed by a period of unconsciousness which lasts for some time; this gives way to a kind of awareness but not a consciousness of one's environment. The new senses have not yet begun to function so there is nothing, or at best a misty, unreal setting, fantastic and dreamlike. During this interval, the memory appears to be stimulated so that one lives through a resumé of a lifetime just past. Then one sinks into a second period of unconsciousness which should give place to a full awakening in the new world. We might with justice speak of a first and second death because not only the physical body has to be shed but the next body also.[27]

This ties in closely with Crookall's idea of separating first from the physical body and later from the intermediate body (his "vehicle of vitality"), with its distorting and veiling influence.[28] It's as if blinders have been taken off.

Crookall interprets the first life review—the one that is unemotional and largely without moral significance—as the intermediate body imprinting itself on the soul body, or, in more modern terms, information being downloaded in a kind of "data dump." The second life review, coming after the intermediate body has been discarded, occurs when the soul (now in touch with the higher self) is able to survey the panorama of its earthly life and form mature judgments about it. To distinguish it from the first life review, Crookall calls this one the Judgment.

Crookall acknowledges that a few people have experienced the Judgment at a surprisingly early point in the dying process. Even in his day, before the term "near-death experience" had been coined, there were scattered reports of people who had nearly died and who reported a life review complete with moral judgment. Such reports, he found, pertained only to a minority of cases, an observation that still appears to be true.

In his hypothesis, NDErs who undergo the Judgment are those whose intermediate body is unusually "loose" to begin with—usually mediums, psychics, seers, and people of elevated spiritual awareness. Whether or not this explanation accounts for the discrepancy is impossible to say.

In any case, the typical sequence of events appears to be as follows:

1. Partial separation of the intermediate body from the physical body
2. A whirlwind review of one's lifetime (the "data dump")
3. Final separation of the intermediate body; the physical body is cast off
4. Progression into the light
5. Separation of the soul body from the intermediate body, which is cast off
6. An in-depth review of one's lifetime, including moral lessons

Conclusion

An initial, usually unemotional life review is followed by an in-depth, emotionally affecting review that allows the departed to judge his own life. The second life review is concurrent with greatly expanded awareness.

By now, the personality that survived death has undergone a significant change in consciousness, having communed with the light, experienced total knowledge and unconditional love, and reviewed an entire earthly history.

This change in consciousness is soon matched by a change in "location," as the soul moves into a new, idealized environment.

Transition is coming to an end; it's almost time for arrival. But we're not quite there yet. We have a short detour to make.

CHAPTER EIGHTEEN:
Mediumship

BECAUSE MEDIUMSHIP PLAYS such a large role in our upcoming accounts, it's time to pause and consider its validity as evidence, as well as its strengths and weaknesses in general.

Reality of the communicators

Some people hold that messages coming through a medium actually originate in the minds of the sitters and are obtained via telepathy. Unfortunately for this explanation, ESP as tested in the laboratory has not proven nearly so robust; telepathic or clairvoyant impressions are typically intermittent, sometimes puzzling, and never completely reliable. No known psychic can read minds effortlessly enough to construct a believable persona of a loved one in real time, while carrying on a conversation laced with that person's characteristic turns of phrase, mannerisms, and facial expressions; yet trance mediums like Gladys Osborne Leonard, Leonora Piper, and Eileen Garrett accomplished all of this routinely.

In cases where the sitter doesn't even know the loved one in question, the ESP hypothesis must be further stretched to include telepathic interaction with the minds of geographically distant persons and even clairvoyant visions of documents long filed away and forgotten—which have been mentioned in some séances and subsequently tracked down.[1]

This rather strained hypothesis is usually known as super-ESP (or super-psi, or living-agent psi). Super-ESP is imagined to be a wide-roving amalgam of telepathy, clairvoyance, retrocognition, and precognition, a combination so all-inclusive as to approximate omniscience. Because super-ESP is hypothetically capable of acquiring information from any source anywhere at a moment's notice, it can explain pretty much anything. But again, there is no real-world evidence that ESP can operate in this way, and the hypothesis is so infinitely elastic that it seems incapable of falsification even in principle.

SPR researcher Richard Hodgson, who specialized in mediumship, was initially partial to the ESP hypothesis. His viewpoint changed after he subjected his extensive sittings with Boston medium Leonora Piper to a rigorous analysis. His approach was to focus on the alleged communicating personalities themselves, in order to determine if their patterns of behavior were consistent with ESP or with spirit control.

He noted that recently deceased communicators typically had trouble getting a message across, unless assisted by a more experienced spirit. With practice, however, communicators developed greater skill. Moreover, those who had suffered a debilitating illness prior to death were likely to be confused and disoriented in their first communications, but often improved later.

If the messages were obtained by telepathy from the sitters, he wondered, why would it matter when or how the communicator had passed over? On the other hand, if the messages did indeed originate with the departed, it would make sense if those who'd crossed over recently were less experienced and competent at coming through, while those who had been on the other side longer would be more expert.

Further, Hodgson found that different communicators would often come through with varying levels of clarity in a single session. Since neither the medium nor the sitter had changed, the only variable would seem to be the varying abilities of the communicators themselves.

Finally, he noted that communicators frequently showed an active interest in people and events that had been important to them in life, but which were of no special importance to the medium or, in some cases, even the sitter.

All of these patterns, he concluded,

> present a definite relation to the personalities alleged to be communicating, and are exactly what we should expect if they are actually communicating under the conditions of Mrs. Piper's trance manifestations. The results fit the claim.
>
> On the other hand these are not the results which we should expect on the hypothesis of telepathy from the living.[2]

Mrs. Barrett and Mrs. Leonard

Florence Barrett's 1937 book *Personality Survives Death* is an especially useful resource because it serves as a compendium of various issues in mediumship. Most of the séances it presents involve the famous British medium Gladys Osborne Leonard. Tested extensively by the Society for Psychical Research, Mrs. Leonard was responsible for some of the most compelling evidence for the validity of mediumship, including the celebrated Bobbie Newlove case.³

Mrs. Barrett's efforts were predominantly focused on contacting her late husband, William Barrett. Though she didn't set out to test Mrs. Leonard, the many sittings provided opportunities to do so.

On a couple of occasions a so-called "book test" was attempted. The object of these tests was to demonstrate that the communicator was clairvoyantly aware of obscure facts unknown to the sitter or the medium—specifically, a particular passage in a random book.

One such test recorded by Mrs. Barrett was only partially successful, but the other was a definite hit. William directed his wife to a room in their London house.

> If you were going to walk round right from the door to a window, take the third shelf from the bottom, count the books from the door end. Take the fourth book from the door end: you open it at page 132. Will you see if on that page there is something to do with eyes or eyesight? And something which would apply to me, to my character, activities and endeavors when on Earth. "Eyesight" has nothing to do with me, but a reference to eyesight or *vision* is given there.⁴

Mrs. Barrett notes that the word "vision" was spoken in direct voice, a subject we'll return to.

When she got home, she followed the instructions, which led her to a book titled *A Short Sketch of English Literature*. On page 132 was a paragraph on "The Vision of Piers Plowman." The content of the paragraph related to "the teaching of abstract principles by illustration drawn from the familiar things in life" (Mrs. Barrett's words), which she felt applied very well to her husband's earthly activities.

Another sitting provided an item of evidence similar to a book test, when William spontaneously mentioned an umbrella.

> *William*: Umbrella—I saw it the other day. You were near it, mine. You were standing near it in the corner of the hall.
> *Florence*: Is it there still?
> *William*: Yes, it should be. It *was* there. I used it a long time ago. One point is wrong in the umbrella: it's all right but for that, and the gumming stuff is unstuck from the inside.
> *Florence*: I'll try to find it.
> *William*: It has been in the hall corner behind the door. A little test—something you do not know and would not remember.

Mrs. Barrett comments, "I had no idea an umbrella of his existed, but I looked for it on my return and found it where he said, and one point had come unsewn and the material stuck on the inside top had come away in places."[5]

One common objection to mediumship is that the medium is merely verbalizing ideas already present in her subconscious. A particular incident in one of the Barrett-Leonard séances argues against this theory.

> *William*: You mustn't sign that paper of hers—the woman's.
> *Florence*: Do you mean the medium's?
> *William*: Yes, you mustn't sign the papers she has on the table for you. I have certain things and work I want to do with you, and it will prevent my doing those more important things if you put your name to such a paper ...
>
> [Mrs. Barrett writes:] At the end, when Mrs. Leonard came out of trance she took a paper from the table and said, "This is the forward [to her new book] Sir Oliver has written; I am sure you will be willing to sign this." I felt the only course was to tell her just what had been said in the sitting.
>
> She looked very disappointed, but after a few moments' silence she said, "Well, I know I should not do anything myself if I had such a message from the other side, so I cannot ask you to do it; but I *am* sorry."[6]

The instructions delivered through Mrs. Leonard while in trance, which directly contradicted her hopes about signing the paper, seem unlikely to have come from her subconscious.

In an effort to safeguard against fraud, anonymous sitters have sometimes been brought to a séance without an appointment. This meant the medium would have no chance of researching them. By chance, one of Mrs. Barrett's sittings worked out just this way, when a certain Mrs. W. ended up attending a session at the last minute.

Through unforeseen circumstances, Mrs. W. ended up staying with Florence Barrett on a weekend when Florence was scheduled to sit with Mrs. Leonard. The sitting, originally set for Saturday afternoon, was changed at the last moment to Saturday morning; too late, Florence realized that Mrs. W., who did not want to attend, would unavoidably be with her at that time. Even so, the two women had arranged that Mrs. W. would stay in the "open car" (one with no roof) while Florence went inside. Just as they arrived, however, it began to rain. At this point, Mrs. W. gave up her objections and decided to participate. In short, her attendance could not have been anticipated by the medium.

During the séance, William Barrett, speaking through Mrs. Leonard, said, "I have someone with me; George, because George wanted to speak to someone, not you [meaning Florence]; he is not very interested in you—another lady." George was Mrs. W.'s late husband.

After William's introduction, George himself spoke through Mrs. Leonard. Among other things, he said, "A place with which I used to be connected and lived in is going to be occupied by someone else." Florence Barrett later confirmed that his house, which had been vacant, had just been leased by a former student.

George yielded the spotlight to William, who provided more information:

> *William*: An elderly lady is with him—medium height, gray hair parted in the middle. She has a nice-shaped face, oval, with well-cut features. She is dressed rather old-fashioned looking. She passed over before him.
> *Mrs. W.*: This well describes his mother.
> *William*: And a younger lady also looked after him. There is an elderly gentleman with him too—taller than me, heavier built; he is gray and has rather a clever face and head; he has a Roman nose. He has a rather distinguished face—a dignified looking gentleman. He was in the spirit world before George … He was a man for whom [George] had great respect and often talked about him. He had a portrait of him in his house, a good one: he was very pleased to meet him.
> *Mrs. W.*: G.W. on leaving College was secretary for several years to an elderly and distinguished politician, and a life-long friendship was formed. No other man ever took his place or influenced him so much. He had been dead for six or seven years. His portrait—a reproduction of a painting—was the only one that ever hung in our house.
> *William*: Annie—you keep saying Annie—there is a lady—passed over many years ago.
> *Mrs. W.*: Annie, his only sister, died in 1917.[7]

Mrs. Leonard could not have researched Mr. W.'s life and personal connections, inasmuch as his widow's visit was spontaneous and unannounced.

But couldn't the medium have been engaged in "cold reading"—the mentalist technique of making leading statements and reacting to a sitter's responses? To rule out this possibility, serious investigators have conducted "proxy settings," in which the person whose loved ones are being contacted is not even present. In such a case, the medium cannot use cold reading, because the proxy sitter knows none of the details and can exhibit no meaningful reactions.

This type of sitting, too, is recorded in Mrs. Barrett's book, though again it was unplanned. She had been asked by a friend, Archdeacon Talbot, to arrange his appointment with Mrs. Leonard in order to contact his son Michael. Prior to the scheduled Talbot séance, Florence Barrett had a sitting of her own, and the subject came up, introduced by William Barrett, who said,

> You know the younger one that passed over lately, the one that A. was a friend to—he went over rather quickly ... He did not know he was going, but had to have help to get over the sense of surprise and shock ... There is someone else who has helped him very much who had passed over. Someone who came to meet the young man when he passed over. A woman, rather dark in color, who would have been about 65 to 70 when she passed over; her hair had turned gray, but she still had dark eyebrows, smooth hair parted in the center, a face more long than round, thin a little in the cheeks, rather good features, nose is rather straight, showing the bridge just a little. She is related to the one who has just come over lately. You would not know her, but the other people would, the two elderly people [previously mentioned], they would know her; she is connected with them.

This description matched Michael's aunt, Miss Talbot, who was related to the two elderly people already recognized as Michael's parents.

Other details were provided. Florence Barrett wrote them all down, though they meant nothing to her. Afterward, she "read them to Archdeacon Talbot, who recognized them one by one."[8]

Here we might wonder if Mrs. Leonard had researched Talbot's family after the appointment was set up and had taken advantage of the séance with Mrs. Barrett to disclose some of what she'd learned. Arguing against this is the fact that, throughout decades of investigation, Mrs. Leonard was never caught in any instance of fraud. In any case, there was another séance in which this explanation is ruled out.

On this occasion, Mrs. Barrett, while at home, privately directed a question at her husband. She asked if he could locate the spirit of a friend's recently deceased child. At a séance the next day, she followed up on this issue, which had never been raised in Mrs. Leonard's presence.

> *Florence*: Have you heard anything of the child I spoke of?
> *William*: I have been interested in a child, not on earth, one who passed over. This is a child passed over rather lately and I have taken care of it at its passing—I received the child.

He went on to connect the child with people bearing the initials B and M and the name Nanny. He gave the child's name as Vi and said that in passing over she felt "chokey. Something made it feel difficult in breathing ... Before she passed over there was something the matter with one arm or hand; she couldn't move it ... The end came rather quickly—she seemed better, then was ill again." She had been thinking of a birthday when she passed.

Mrs. Barrett did not know the details of the girl's death, but later learned that a case of measles had developed into pneumonia and encephalitis, with symptoms that included difficulty breathing and paralysis of an arm and leg. The little girl's name was Violet, but she was usually called Vi. Her nurse was Nanny, while M was the initial of her favorite schoolteacher and B represented Ben, "a great friend whose letter telling about his birthday was read to her shortly before she became unconscious."[9]

In this case there is no possibility of cold reading, since Mrs. Barrett knew none of these facts except, presumably, the girl's name. Nor could the medium, Mrs. Leonard, have done any research, since Mrs. Barrett's interest in the child had not been expressed on any previous occasion.

At another sitting, the appeal for help was directed to William by a third party, and Mrs. Barrett knew nothing about it until later. During the séance William unexpectedly said,

> Let P.W. find her own way. Let her do what she wants to do, and be sure it is what she wants to do ... She must choose whatever it is she thinks best for herself.

Mrs. Barrett explains:

> Unknown to me, a friend of mine, P.W., had prayed the day before that a message might be sent to her through [William] to

let her know if it was right for her to do the thing she wished to do. She asked me if I would read to her the notes of my sitting, but it was only after reading this script to her that she told me of her prayer.[10]

Clearly, no form of cold reading or advance research can explain this.

When Mrs. Barrett sat with a different medium, William raised the subject of a spirit who had known his wife.

> Anna is someone who serves you. She tells me she has come to serve you and send love from the world of spirit. She is medium height and build, with browny dark hair—plain. She's fair, round and fresh-looking. Eyes blue-gray, homely looking. Did she have pains in her chest?

Mrs. Barrett comments:

> This is an accurate description of a maid we called Julia: the description exactly fit Julia, but the name was wrong. On returning home I asked a senior maid if Julia had another name, Anna. She said, "We used to tease her by calling her Anna because her name was really Juliana." She died in 1929 of sarcoma of the chest.[11]

As before, the explanation of cold reading can't apply because Mrs. Barrett herself didn't know that Julia was sometimes called Anna. Nor is it likely that the medium—Kathleen Barkel, whom Florence rarely visited—knew anything about a household servant who had died a year earlier.

> In addition to mental mediumship, there is such a thing as physical or materialization mediumship, in which the medium—almost always operating in a dimly lit or pitch black environment—apparently causes objects to move or to appear out of nowhere and sometimes brings forth physical manifestations of spirits. This type of séance was extremely popular in the heyday of spiritualism, until

exposés conducted by escape artist Harry Houdini, various newspaper editors, and the Society for Psychical Research combined to discredit it.

The tricks employed by fake mediums of this sort are legion. The medium can use a folding or telescopic pointer to manipulate distant objects. (Remember that the séance may take place in complete darkness.) Phosphorus can simulate "spirit lights." A stuffed glove at the end of a rod can simulate a spirit hand touching the sitter. A cool breeze can be produced simply by blowing on a sitter's face. Even if the medium's hands are held by the sitters on either side, she can use her knees to raise the table, making it "levitate." Moreover, the medium can often free one hand without being noticed. As Houdini proved on countless occasions, ropes, handcuffs, and other restraints are no obstacle to the fake medium who is also a skillful escape artist.

If the medium retreats into a cabinet (a small compartment in the séance room) to "gather her energies," she may use the opportunity to retrieve items previously hidden there or concealed on her own person. A surprisingly large quantity of cheesecloth or muslin, both of which are materials of gossamer thinness, can be compacted into a ball not much bigger than a large vitamin pill and swallowed; under cover of hymns or inspirational songs sung by the sitters, sometimes at the direction of the medium's accomplice, the medium can cough up this wad of fabric and unravel it, then wear it to create a vague diaphanous appearance in the dark.

There have even been cases where accomplices have joined the proceedings via a secret entrance to pose as materialized spirits. In one notorious instance, medium Edith Stillwell foolishly permitted Andrija Puharich and Tom O'Neill to film one of her séances using infrared photography; the footage clearly showed a parade of imposters traipsing about the séance room.[12]

In short, this type of mediumship is fraught with opportunities for fraud and seems to attract some of the most unscrupulous charlatans. The Society for Psychical Research discredited so many physical and materialization mediums that their investigations into this category of mediumship were eventually discontinued.

That said, I will add that, in a few cases, I think physical mediums have produced authentic results. Two who come to mind are Daniel Dunglas Home and Eusapia Palladino. Home was never caught cheating and did not require darkness for his séances. Late in his career, he was successfully tested by physicist William Crookes in dim ambient light and in the presence of witnesses. Among other things, he produced music from an accordion while it was secured in a wire cage that made it impossible for his fingers to touch the keys. The explanation offered by skeptic James Randi—that Home concealed a harmonica behind his "very full 'soup-strainer' style mustache"—doesn't hold up. For one thing, one of Crookes's colleagues shined a lantern on the accordion and saw the keys moving without human contact. For another, Home's modest mustache could not have concealed a harmonica.[13]

Palladino, by contrast, certainly did cheat—in fact, she openly admitted it. At times she would interrupt a séance to announce that she felt the urge to cheat coming on! Nevertheless, when properly controlled by the sitters, she was capable of producing effects that seem to have no non-paranormal explanation. Howard Thurston, the leading stage magician of his era, stated, "I witnessed in person the table levitations of Madame Eusapia Palladino ... and am thoroughly convinced that the phenomena I saw were not due to fraud and were not performed by the aid of her feet, knees, or hands."[14]

Overall, most physical mediumship strikes me as too dubious to rely on, especially since the majority of the phenomena, even if genuine, can plausibly be attributed to psychokinesis rather than spirit action.

Bosh

It would be a mistake to think that even the best séance is an unbroken succession of evidential "hits." In almost all cases, a great deal of material constitutes what William James derisively termed "bosh"—claims that cannot be tested or that later prove to be false.

Florence Barrett's book records many such instances, though she herself, at the time of publication, was not in a position to evaluate most of them. For instance, William asserted that cancer is caused by contamination of the intestines; he recommended fasting and cleansing as a preventive measure. This claim hasn't gained much traction in the past ninety years, though some researchers do think changes in gut microbiota are responsible for high cholesterol, depression, autism, and other conditions.

In another dubious medical disquisition, William claimed that bacteria in themselves are not harmful; instead, the harm they do is caused by some sort of gas associated with them.

He said he'd been working with deceased astronomer Camille Flammarion, and that the two of them had used a telescope to explore the other planets in our solar system. One of his astronomical predictions proved accurate. On January 11, 1930, he said that a new planet would soon be found. Two months later, on March 15, astronomers at Lowell University reported the discovery of Pluto (then classified as a planet). Undercutting this success somewhat is that he was supposedly observing not just one but "three ... planets soon to be discovered in the orbit of the sun." Further, he had "proved" the existence of life on other planets by visiting them, finding "giant flora and fauna" on the moon as well as "Martian humanity [which was] closest akin to earthly ... Mars has two suns, and consequently there is less change of climate; it is clear and warm." Mars, of course, has only one sun (our own), but conceivably this was a mistaken reference to its two moons; in any event the planet is not warm, but bitterly cold, and, like our moon, shows no signs of life.[15]

In addition to visiting other planets, William claimed to have visited various historical locations—including, dubiously, Atlantis.

> You know how I should like you to be with me, so that we could go together to see interesting places which did exist and are apparently lost—Ancient Egypt. Do you remember my speaking to you about Atlantis? I can visit those places now as they were.[16]

Another questionable claim involved meeting Jesus Christ. "I have seen Him, have spoken to Him, and I'm going to see Him this Easter, when I know you will be thinking of Him and me."[17]

Prophesying future events, William declared in 1932, "There will be further developments toward the East which will involve England."

Florence asked, "Will there be wars?"

He replied, "Not a great war. I think we shall keep out, but there'll be great anxiety; warfare of a kind without meaning war for England."[18] Sadly, this prediction proved far too optimistic.

In a 1935 sitting, his predictions had darkened somewhat but still missed the mark.

> *William*: There is a temporary lull in war conditions, but it is not ended; there is bound to be trouble, not only with Italy but with Germany.
> *Florence*: Do you mean war?
> *William*: I do not think England will be seriously involved, or not so much as other countries, but a very difficult position is facing England and I do not know quite what will happen, or how she will come out of it.[19]

But why?

Investigators have long puzzled over these lapses. In a séance that provides valid information, often not known to the medium and sometimes not even known to the sitter, there will also be flatly wrong, sometimes far-fetched, even nonsensical claims. Skeptics tend to focus on the latter category of messages, having fun with accounts of lunar fauna, Martian humanoids, and seemingly casual visits with Jesus ("I'm going to see Him this Easter"), while believers highlight the evidential statements that defy easy explanation.

What, then, can we make of this mixture of evidential details and "bosh"? A possible lead to an answer is provided by William Barrett in another séance, when he discusses the difficulties inherent in communication:

> Sometimes I lose some memory of things from coming here; I know it in my own state but not here.
>
> In dreams you do not know everything, you only get parts of the dream. A sitting is similar; when I go back to the spirit world after a sitting like this I know I have not got everything through that I wanted to say.
>
> That is due to my mind separating again, the consciousness separating again. In the Earth body we have the separation of subconscious and conscious. Consciousness only holds a certain number of memories at a time. When we pass over they join,—make a complete mind that knows and remembers everything, but when one comes here to a sitting the limitation of the physical sphere affects one's mind, and only a portion of one's mind can function for the time being. When I withdraw from this condition [my] whole mind becomes again both subconscious and conscious; my subconscious mind encloses my conscious one and I become whole again mentally. I think that accounts for many people getting the idea (and it is wrong in one way and right in another) that it is bad for them to try to communicate, because certain people have sensed that there is limitation in communicating with another plane of existence and they have exaggerated it. I cannot come with and as my whole self, I cannot …
>
> I have a fourth dimensional self which cannot make its fourth dimension exactly the same as the third. The fourth dimension is an extension—that is not the right way of saying it, but the only way I can say it. It is like measuring a third dimension by its square feet instead of by its cubic feet; that is very much the difference between third and fourth dimension; and there is no doubt about it I have left something of myself outside which rejoins me directly I put myself into the condition in which I readjust myself.[20]

In terms of the trifold system we discussed in Chapter 8—physical body, intermediate body, and soul body—we could say that, in order to possess the medium and speak through her, the spiritual communicator must assume control of the medium's intermediate body. In so doing, he takes on all the limitations of such a body, including some degree of mental fog.

Barrett's description dovetails with a famous quote channeled by automatic writer Alice Fleming (Rudyard Kipling's sister, who used the pseudonym "Mrs. Holland"), purportedly originating with F.W.H. Myers:

> The nearest simile I can find to express the difficulties of sending a message—is that I appear to be standing behind a sheet of frosted glass—which blurs sight and deadens sound—dictating feebly—to a reluctant and very obtuse secretary. A feeling of terrible impotence burdens me—I am so powerless to tell what means so much—I cannot get into communications with those who would understand and believe me.[21]

The "sheet of frosted glass ... which blurs sight and deadens sound" may be the enveloping intermediate body with its frustrating limitations, which the soul body must put on in order to interact with the physical world.

Specific words seem especially difficult to get across. In one séance William could not recall the name of someone he'd known in life. He explained:

> When I am in my own sphere I am told a name and think I shall remember it; when I come into the conditions of the sitting I then know that I can only carry with me—contain in me—a small portion of my consciousness. The easiest things to lay hold of are what we may call ideas; a detached word, a proper name, has no link with the train of thought except in the detached sense; that is far more difficult than any other feat of memory or association of ideas ...
>
> If I want to say "I am Will," I find that is much more difficult than giving you a long, comprehensive study of my personality. "I am Will" sounds so simple, but you understand that in this case the word "Will" becomes a detached word.[22]

> A specific example of communication difficulties is found in Florence Barrett's comparatively rare sittings with Mrs. Barkel, whose séances were marked by occasional "direct voice" mediumship. This unusual phenomenon involves hearing a

voice distinct from the medium's, which seems to come out of thin air. In Mrs. Barkel's sittings, direct voice phenomena typically consisted of only a few words now and then.

At one point, speaking in the persona of William Barrett, the entranced medium said, "Apart from this medium it was the best sitting I've had—only the power didn't last. I was afraid of dragging it out because that's where mistakes occur."

At that moment the direct voice spoke: "It was an Indian control."

The medium, in the persona of her spirit control: "He [i.e., William] says an Eastern was in command."

Florence Barrett, addressing William: "I heard your voice say, 'It was an Indian control.'"

The medium, speaking as William: "You hear my voice, the medium gets my thoughts."

Direct voice: "Indian is correct."[23]

The idea William wanted to get across was that the other medium used a control (a spirit gatekeeper) of Indian origin—meaning the Indian subcontinent. This was undoubtedly a reference to Mrs. Leonard, whose control was an Indian girl named Feda. The idea was communicated to the medium as "an Eastern[er]," while William's own "direct" voice more accurately used the term "Indian."

Even in this brief back-and-forth, you can see a three-way process, with William sometimes speaking through the medium, at other times relaying his thoughts through the spirit control, and at still other times speaking in direct voice. You can also see that the spirit control gets only the gist of what William is trying to say, phrasing it differently ("an Eastern[er]"), while William, speaking in direct voice, puts it in his own words ("an Indian").

The idea that the spirit must assume an intermediate body and temporarily restrict his consciousness implies that the communicating personality is only a fraction of the total personality. Conversing with the spirit through a medium may be like holding a conversation with someone who's talking in his sleep. The sleeper may keep up his end of the dialogue in some ways, while completely losing the plot at other times. Hence, the confused, foggy, sometimes childish quality of much mediumistic communication, especially when less experienced communicators are trying to get through.

Parapsychologists have long theorized that the sometimes exotic "spirit controls" claimed by trance mediums are subpersonalities of the mediums. While this is possible, I suspect that both the controls and the loved ones speaking through trance mediums are subpersonalities not of the *mediums*, but of the *spirits*.

The communicators themselves, after all, often claim they must "lower their vibrations" to operate on the earthly level, and while the meaning of this phrase is hard to pin down, it suggests a diminution of the communicator's mental acuity and range. As William himself observed, only part of the communicator can get through. Thus communication is inevitably compromised to a greater or lesser extent, depending on the skill of the communicator, the talent of the medium, and the atmosphere of the sitting, among other things.

If communicating spirits (whether controls or friends and family members) are only offshoots or fragments of their total minds, it may explain how they can confabulate, make inaccurate predictions, prove unduly suggestible, and yet, in the very same sitting, produce strong evidence of identity.[24]

Reliability of the messages

However we choose to explain these imperfect communications, the fact remains that we can't fully trust any message received through a medium unless it can be independently verified. And when it comes to accounts of the world inhabited by departed souls, such verification is hard to come by. The best we can do is try to match up such accounts with NDEs, accounts of intervals between past lives, and long-standing spiritual and religious traditions. Needless to say, any conclusions we draw must fall well short of certainty.

Nor should this be surprising. The deeper we get into the postmortem experience, the harder it is to validate what we're told, and the more challenging it becomes to translate an alien environment into familiar terms. As William Barrett explained through Mrs. Leonard, people who have passed on exist in a "four-dimensional" state that those of us with three-dimensional minds cannot conceive of.

One person who had an NDE states this idea explicitly:

> Now, there is a real problem for me as I'm trying to tell you this, because all the words I know are three-dimensional. As I was going through this, I kept thinking, well, when I was taking geometry, they always told me there were only three dimensions, and I always accepted that. But they were wrong. There are more. And of course, our world—the one we're living in now—*is* three-dimensional, but the next one definitely isn't. And that's why it's so hard to tell you this. I have to describe it to you in words that are three-dimensional. That's as close as I can get to it, but it's not really adequate. I can't really give you a complete picture.[25]

Anyone who's read the 19th-century satire *Flatland*[26] will remember how the Flatlanders—triangles, rectangles, and circles inhabiting a sheet of paper—are unable to imagine a three-dimensional reality. In the same way, those of us who inhabit a three-dimensional spatial universe (with the additional dimension of time) cannot really grasp a four-dimensional spatial universe (with a qualitatively different temporal dimension).

In short, we can accept these accounts as a partial glimpse of a larger reality without taking them too literally. Reader beware: Some of what follows in Part Four is surely bosh.

PART FOUR: *Arrival*

I was in a country where I'd never been before.
It was very big there, and so beautiful. I'd like to go back there again.
I can still taste the sweet water that I drank there. For there was a fountain there and I drank out of it.
I saw flowers that were three times as big as ours. They smelled sweeter than the prettiest flowers we have here at the height of summer.
I saw a lot of people a great distance away. When I started to run towards them, they moved away from me just as fast ...
How heavy my arms and legs are now ... In that other land where I was, everything was light as a feather.

—NDE quoted by Jean-Baptiste Delacour[1]

C.K. Van Nortwick, *The Dawn of Day* (1930)

CHAPTER NINETEEN:
Otherwith
Otherwhere

> The worlds above are not general, not vague. They are deeply, piercingly alive, and about as abstract as a bucket of fried chicken, the glint off the hood of a Trans Am, or your first crush. That's why the descriptions of heaven brought back by people like Swedenborg can sound so absolutely crazy. I know perfectly well how crazy my own account sounds, and I sympathize with those who have difficulty with it. Like a lot of things in life it sounds pretty far-fetched till you see it yourself.[1]

THOSE ARE THE WORDS of Dr. Eben Alexander, the neurosurgeon whose book *Proof of Heaven* became a bestseller. I've quoted them here because what follows in this chapter probably will sound "absolutely crazy" to many readers.

Even if your personal boggle threshold (the point at which you automatically reject a claim) was not reached by the previous material, you may hit it here. After all, it's one thing to talk about separating from the body, moving into a bright light, communing with your higher self, and reliving past events. It's another thing to talk about finding yourself in an idealized environment of houses and cities, gardens and trees. It sounds not only too good to be true, but also too much like a fairytale—a child's conception of the hereafter. That's why even people who accept much of the evidence for life after death often balk at such descriptions.

And yet there's a long history of reporting on the afterlife in exactly these terms. In fact, its pedigree dates all the way back to ancient Egypt.

The Field of Reeds

Most early conceptions of the afterlife are distinctly depressing. The Hebrew Sheol, the Greek Hades, and the Sumerian Kur are dark, misty realms populated by confused, almost mindless wraiths. Quite possibly, this picture of the hereafter originated in mediumistic communications from spirits in the earliest stage of postmortem existence, still enshrouded by the intermediate body and unable to clearly perceive their environment or understand their condition.

The far different Egyptian picture may suggest a more elevated level of mediumship—something that would not be surprising, given Egypt's reputation in the ancient world for advanced esoteric knowledge. While other traditions envisioned the soul body as a dim phantom (Israel and Greece) or a birdlike gargoyle subsisting on dust (Mesopotamia), an Egyptian hoped to be reborn as an *akh*, "a glorified being … a sort of light-filled, eternal spirit." These were "the most elevated spirit-forms of the dead … 'the luminous ones,' associated with dazzling light."[2] And unlike the shadowy realms pictured by its neighbors, Egypt's afterlife was vibrant and glowing, an idealized representation of the physical world known as the Field of Reeds (A'aru). In an article for an online encyclopedia, Joshua J. Mark tells us that in A'aru

> one would find those loved ones who had passed on before, one's favorite dogs or cats, gazelles or monkeys, or whatever cherished pet one had lost. One's home would be there, right down to the lawn the way it had been left, one's favorite tree, even the stream that ran behind the house.[3]

He quotes author Margaret Bunson (first paragraph) and historian Clare Gibson (second paragraph):

> Eternity itself was not some vague concept. The Egyptians, pragmatic and determined to have all things explained in concrete terms, believed that they would dwell in paradise in areas graced by lakes and gardens. There they would eat the "cakes of Osiris" and float on the Lake of Flowers. The eternal kingdoms varied according to era and cultic belief, but all were located beside flowing water and blessed with breezes, an attribute deemed necessary for comfort …
>
> The Field of Reeds was an almost unimaginably ideal version of Egypt where cultivated crops grew to extraordinary heights, trees bore succulent fruit, and where transfigured souls (who all appeared physically perfect and in the prime of life) wanted for nothing in the way of sustenance, luxuries, and even love.[4]

Those who preferred not to cultivate fields or perform other labor in the next life could employ shabti dolls—small carved figures entombed with the dead—as their slaves.

Once the shabti went off to work, the soul could then go back to relaxing beneath a favorite tree with a good book or walk by a pleasant stream with one's dog. The Egyptian afterlife was perfect because the soul was given back everything which had been lost. One's best friend, husband, wife, mother, father, son, daughter, cherished cat or most dearly loved dog were there upon one's arrival or, at least, would be eventually; and there the souls of the dead would live forever in paradise and never have to part again. In all of the ancient world there was never a more comforting afterlife imagined by any other culture.[5]

But *was* it merely imagined? The Egyptian afterlife matches up remarkably well with some modern NDEs and a great deal of mediumship.

One of the earliest and most important of those mediums was Emanuel Swedenborg, active in the 18th century and still influential today.

The Swedish seer

Swedenborg, a Swedish scholar and polymath, began receiving heavenly visions in 1745, the first of which introduced him to "the worlds of spirits, heaven, and hell."[6] Apparently he possessed hitherto unsuspected mediumistic talents, a fact attested by his ability to recover information known only to the departed but later verified. The Swedenborg Foundation records one of the better-known incidents.

> In 1761, Swedenborg was presented at the court of Sweden's Queen Louisa Ulrika (1720—1782), and she asked him to relay a particular question to her deceased brother, Prince Augustus Wilhelm of Prussia (1722—1758). Swedenborg returned to court three weeks later and gave her the answer privately, upon which she was heard to exclaim that only her brother would have known what Swedenborg had just told her.[7]

His detailed accounts of the hereafter became the basis of several books. As with any mediumistic communications, much of the content was apparently influenced by the prevailing cultural atmosphere of his day. But in important respects, Swedenborg broke with convention.

He disagreed that angels had been created prior to the human race, stating instead that they were exalted human beings. Rejecting the idea that only Christians go to heaven, he said that many non-Christians lived more upright lives than some so-called Christians did; the important thing was not vagaries of doctrine but personal spiritual development. "There are wise and simple people among non-Christians just as there are among Christians,"[8] he wrote.

Similarly, he informed his readers that all children, not only those who have been baptized, are accepted into heaven. He showed respect for other cultures and ethnicities, at one point recounting an exchange with some Chinese spirits who had been shamefully abused by Christians during their time on earth. Moreover, he spoke of intelligent life on other planets. "It is common knowledge in the other life [i.e., the afterlife] that there are many planets with people on them and therefore angels and spirits from them … the human race is not just from one earth but from countless planets."[9]

In contrast to orthodox Christian teaching, he denied that a period of heavenly slumber preceded the Last Judgment. Nor would there be any physical resurrection. In fact, he was bold enough to say that the Last Judgment had already taken place in the spiritual realm.

Most relevant to our concerns are his many accounts of heaven itself. Here he makes no effort to disguise his break with established theology. Instead, he underlines his differences with the conventional thinking of his era.

> Many of the scholars of the Christian world are dumbfounded when they find themselves after death in bodies, wearing clothes, and in houses the way they were in this world. When they call to mind what they had thought about life after death, the soul, spirits, and heaven and hell, they are embarrassed and say that they had been thinking nonsense …
>
> Years and years of daily experience have witnessed to me that after separation from the body the human spirit is a person and is in a similar form. I have seen this thousands of times, I have heard such spirits, and I've talked with them … This is why almost all the people who arrive from this world are as astonished as they can be to find that they are alive and that they are just as human as ever, that they are seeing and hearing and talking, that their bodies are still endowed with the sense of touch, and that nothing at all has changed.[10]

Swedenborg's heaven is a collection of communities of like-minded spirits. And by communities, he means cities and towns complete with houses and gardens.

> At times, I have talked with angels about homes in heaven, telling them that nowadays hardly anyone would believe that they have homes and houses ... Whenever I have talked with angels face to face, I have been with them in their houses. Their houses were just like the houses on earth that we call homes, but more beautiful. They have chambers, suites, and bedrooms in abundance, and courtyards with gardens, flowerbeds, and lawns around them. Where there is some concentration of people, the houses are adjoining, one near another, arranged in the form of a city with streets and lanes in public squares, just like the ones we see in cities on our earth ... I have seen palaces in heaven that were so splendid as to be beyond description. Their upper stories shone as though they were made of pure gold, and the lower ones as though they were made of precious gems ... It was the same inside. The rooms were graced with such lovely adornments that neither words nor the arts and sciences are adequate to describe them. On the side that faced south there were parklands where everything sparkled in the same way, here and there the leaves like silver and the fruits like gold, with the flowers in their beds making virtual rainbows with their colors.[11]

People in heaven wear clothes. "We can tell that angels' clothes do not merely look like clothes but really are because they not only see them, they feel them as well. Further, they have many garments that they take off and put on, and they put away the ones they are not using and put back on the ones they are."[12]

They read books, they maintain their earthly marriages (at least for a time), and in most respects they lead lives similar to those they led on earth. There are differences, though. For one thing, their state of mind plays a direct role in what they see around them ...

> In the heavens, everything comes into being from the Lord in response to the deeper natures of the angels ... Since all the things that are responsive to angels' deeper natures also portray them, they are called representations ... To angels who are focused on intelligence there appear gardens and parks full of all kinds of trees and flowers. The trees there are laid out in the loveliest designs, joined into vaulted arches offering spaces for entrance, and with promenades around them. All this is so beautiful as to defy description. People who are focused on intelligence stroll there picking the flowers and weaving garlands to grace babies with. There are kinds of trees and

flowers there never seen, not even possible, in our world.[13]
... how they travel ...

> Whenever people move from one place to another, whether it is within their town, in their courtyards, in their gardens, or to people outside their own community, they get there more quickly if they are eager to and more slowly if they are not. The path is lengthened or shortened depending on their desire, even though it is the same path. I have often seen this, much to my surprise. We can see from all this again that distance in space itself depends wholly on the inner state of the angels; and since this is the case, no notion or concept of space can enter their minds even though they have space just the way we do in our world.[14]

... and what they wear.

> I have asked them where they got their clothes, and they have told me that their clothes come from the Lord and are given to them, and that sometimes they are clothed without noticing it. They have also said that their clothes change depending on the changes of their state, that their clothes are radiant and gleaming white in their first and second state, while in the third and fourth states they are somewhat dimmer.[15]

Angels, he tells us, "have all the senses we do—far more delicate ones, in fact."[16] But they "have no notion or concept of time and space ... There are no years or days, but only changes of state."[17]

Upon arrival, spirits find themselves in a "halfway place, ... neither heaven nor hell but a place or state between the two."[18] At first, many do not know they are dead and have trouble believing it even when they are told. Eventually they undergo an examination, not dissimilar to the life review. "In a word, all their evils, crimes, thefts, wiles, and deceptions are made clear to every evil spirit. They are drawn from their own memories and exposed ... Not just the general contents [of our memory] but even the smallest details that have entered our memory do last and are never erased ... Let no one believe, then, that there is anything we have thought or done in secret that will remain hidden after death. Believe rather than absolutely everything will come out into broad daylight."[19]

Those who are committed to evil migrate to one of several hells. They do this of their own volition. "People who have intended and loved what is evil in the world intend and love what is evil in the other life, and then they no longer allow themselves to be led away from it. This is why people who are absorbed in evil are connected to hell and actually are there in spirit; and after death they crave above all to be where their evil is. So after death, it is we, not the Lord, who cast ourselves into hell."[20]

In contrast to the teachings of modern spiritualism, there is no indication that those in hellish conditions will eventually be lifted up into the light of heaven. This light, Swedenborg tells us, is "vastly greater than noonday light on earth ... Heaven's light is not natural like the light of our world, but spiritual. It actually comes from the Lord as the sun, and that sun ... is divine love."[21]

Although Swedenborg's narratives don't always line up with more recent accounts, especially when he goes into the minutiae of the organization of afterlife communities and the theological implications to be drawn from his revelations, there is much in them that parallels the visions of NDErs, more modern and better tested mediums, and people on their deathbeds.

But no matter how much testimony we may read, how can we possibly believe in such an afterlife? For many folks, it sounds like the epitome of "bosh," and those who retail such stories are liable to public mockery.

Spiritualist teachings

Physicist Oliver Lodge learned this lesson the hard way when he published his 1916 book *Raymond, or Life and Death*, which presented many mediumistic communications purportedly originating with his son Raymond, who died in the battle of Ypres in 1915. His father, already convinced of an afterlife—in 1909 he'd published *The Survival of Man*, which argued for the reliability of mediumship—found additional proof in the new messages he received, many of which were highly evidential.

In *Raymond*, the eponymous communicator offered up a homey afterlife very similar to Swedenborg's. Many people found this hard enough to swallow, but one brief passage inspired special ridicule. (Here the medium, Gladys Osborne Leonard, speaks of Raymond in the third person as she conveys his messages.)

> People here try to provide everything that is wanted. A chap came over the other day, would have a cigar. "That's finished them," he thought. He means he thought they would never be able to provide that. But there are laboratories over here, and they manufacture all sorts of things in them. Not like you do,

out of solid matter, but out of essences, and ethers, and gases. It's not the same as on the earth plane, but they were able to manufacture what looked like a cigar. He didn't try one himself, because he didn't care to; you know he wouldn't want to. But the other chap jumped at it. But when he began to smoke it, he didn't think so much of it; he had four altogether, and now he doesn't look at one. They don't seem to get the same satisfaction out of it, so gradually it seems to drop from them. But when they first come they do want things. Some want meat, and some strong drink; they call for whisky sodas. Don't think I'm stretching it, when I tell you that they can manufacture even that. But when they have had one or two, they don't seem to want it so much …

He wants people to realize that it's just as natural as on the earth plane.[22]

Well, that tears it. Ghosts in heaven, drinking whisky sodas and smoking cigars! Oliver Lodge was an important scientist, knighted for his contributions to physics. How could he take such nonsense seriously?

Our departed loved ones living in houses, strolling through gardens, maintaining a wardrobe, and enjoying the occasional cocktail or stogie—it all seems too outlandish. Is there any way to make sense of it?

Intersubjective reality

A clue to the answer may be found in those channeled communications that purport to investigate the true nature of Summerland. In *The Blue Island*, deceased journalist and spiritualist W.T. Stead goes into detail about the postmortem environment that he and his companions inhabit—the Blue Island of the title. But in a follow-up book, *Life Eternal*, he reveals that his initial experience was more in the nature of a dream.

Have I disappointed you all by saying that in my sense of the term, The Blue Island was a delusion? Dreams are an essential for all of us during life on Earth, and are still more essential when we cast off the body. But for our dreams we could not continue our journey, for in the world of dreams the soul finds rest from the sharper realities within itself.[23]

A similar idea is presented in Geraldine Cummins's *The Road to Immortality* and *Beyond Human Personality*. In these texts, F.W.H. Myers calls the introductory stage of the afterlife the Plane of Illusion, comparable to the mythological land of the Lotus Eaters, who kept themselves in a perpetual state of intoxicated hallucination. Myers insists that however attractive the Plane of Illusion may be to its inhabitants, it is not ultimately real, and when an individual spirit recognizes this fact, he will be elevated to a higher plane.

The idea is not new. We've already encountered it in the *Tibetan Book of the Dead*, which warns that visions seen in lower spiritual realms may be merely projections of the deceased person's hopes or fears.

In his influential article "Survival and the Idea of 'Another World,'" philosopher H.H. Price puts forward a model of the afterlife consistent with these communications and traditions. This model, as summarized by Gregory Shushan in *The Next World*,

> posited a world of mental images, a mind-dependent reality that to the disembodied spirit would seem as real as life on earth. This would include the impression of having a quasi-physical presence complete with 'bodily' senses ... [I]t would be an "intersubjective" shared afterlife: an experience actually created by the deceased individual in conjunction with the minds of other human spirits. Like-minded individuals—with, for example, similar memories, ideas, values, or culture—would collectively create their surroundings, with each soul contributing to the group-afterlife while also bringing personal life and personal, idiosyncratic features into being.[24]

In this view, the early stage of the afterlife is a kind of communal dream state, exactly as both Stead and Myers suggest.

Shushan points to another philosopher, C.J. Ducasse, who argues in *Nature, Mind, and Death* that "the 'afterlife-as-dream' hypothesis would also account for the absurdities in the accounts, and for 'the lack of firmness and precision' in the descriptions conveyed by mediums." Similarly, reincarnation researcher Jim Tucker "wrote that the NDE is essentially 'a transition dream, involving an awareness of dying and moving on to another kind of experience.' The dream starts 'at the point of death, and the nature of the dream can vary from person to person,' and leads to a shared-dream otherworld."[25]

If this is true, the apparent absurdity of Raymond's cigars disappears. The afterlife comes down to subjective experience, the kind of experience we undergo when asleep and dreaming. And it is certainly possible to dream about smoking or drinking, or about living in a house, reading a book, composing music, or walking in a garden.

Crucial to this hypothesis is the idea of a pooled, shared, or collective consciousness. It's this group consciousness that creates the afterlife environment, with each member contributing a small part to the whole. Equally crucial is the idea that people at roughly similar stages of spiritual development tend to cluster together. Like attracts like. This accounts for the harmonious features of the environment. People of average moral development do not share the scene with serial killers and sadists. The "lower" types of personalities cluster together to create "lower" spheres characterized by darkness and fog, grime and ugliness, violence and fear. These are the "hells" reported by Swedenborg.

Similarly, people of similar backgrounds will cluster together, at least initially. In the early stages of postmortem existence, when the transition must be as smooth as possible, Britons will find themselves in the English countryside, not an Arabian oasis. One communicator explains:

> You can picture places with us which, in a way, correspond with lands on yours. Japan, for example. Our countries are like duplicates of yours: and England and France, and so on. You see, the English people like their English ways and progress more quickly, when first arriving, in surroundings to which they are accustomed. Think how strange a Japanese would feel if in England: so he is surrounded by familiar things in sites such as he was used to. Later he will mingle with other races and so progress. When one reaches a certain stage the racial differences are less noticed, because the highest in each becomes paramount. We have no hatred and no jealousy between different races, but tolerance and sympathetic understanding.[26]

In short, a given person's mental constitution, life history, and ingrained predilections determine the environment in which he'll most truly belong. But nobody stays in a given sphere forever. People can learn and advance to higher levels. This is true of ordinary people and also of those in the lower spheres, who (*contra* Swedenborg) are not doomed to hellish conditions for all time. They remain trapped in those conditions only as long as they feel they belong there; they will advance to better conditions when they recognize the need to let go of their worst impulses and begin to atone for past misdeeds. There is always an opportunity for redemption; it requires only the willingness to accept responsibility and reach out for guidance from above.

But let's not linger on the lower planes, which most of us, happily, will bypass. Instead let's look at the world created by the shared consciousness of normal people, those not crippled by moral failings. Spiritualists of the 19th century dubbed this the Summerland, because it is an Edenic place of perpetual light and peace.

Others know it by a name derived from the ancient Persian word for an enclosed garden: Paradise.

CHAPTER TWENTY:
Life on the Other Side

IN *BOTH SIDES OF THE VEIL* (1909), Anne Manning Robbins recounts sittings with Boston medium Leonora Piper, in which communications purportedly came through from Augustus P. Martin, known to his friends as the General. Here's some of what he had to say.

> When I first passed out my mind was cloudy, rather confused. I felt as though I was going into space, did not know where, drifting as it were, for a few hours—that was all—and then I felt as though there was a strong hand grasped me and said to me: "It is all right, it is all over." And I said: "What is over?" I could not seem to understand what it all meant, and after a little while, perhaps an hour, possibly an hour or two, I saw oh such a light! You cannot imagine it, cannot conceive what it is like. It is the most brilliant and yet the softest moonlight that you ever saw, and I thought, what a beautiful light it was! And all of a sudden I saw people moving about. I saw their heads, their figures. Then they seemed all clad in white, and I could not seem to make them out. They were moving in the air.
>
> And I said: "What is this place? Where am I? What am I? What has happened?" It was all such a puzzle to me.[1]

We can recognize many elements in common with near-death experiences: initial confusion, then the perception of a brilliant light, followed by encounters with spiritual figures. But all of this is somewhat misty and vague (perhaps owing to the temporary persistence of the intermediate body) compared to his account of his current existence.

> I have a mansion all my own and live in it just the same as you live in your place there, just the same. I have walls, I have pictures, I have music, I have books, I have poetry, I have everything ...

> It is not a *fac simile* of [earthly] life, but that life is a miserable shadow of what this really is, and when I get strong, as I become stronger, and, —that is, more accustomed to using this line [of communication], I can tell you more clearly about it.[2]

Here is the essential Platonic idea that the World of Forms (or Ideas) is the real world, with physical reality as its shadow. The General makes the same point later when he says, "Our castles, our homes, are real. They are as real to us as yours are to you. Yours is simply the imitation, ours is the real."

Another communicator, speaking through Gladys Osborne Leonard, says something similar.

> Father is always interested, when old acquaintances arrived, to see how surprised they are to find it has been little more than going from one house into another, just a removal. A little while back he reminded me of those words, "He hath awakened from the dream of life," and he thought how well those words fitted himself. Sometimes when we are walking together I say, "Aren't you happy now?" And he replies quite simply, "I have awakened!"[3]

Note, however, that this interpretation directly contradicts F.W.H. Myers's opinion of Summerland as the Plane of Illusion. In the view attributed to Myers, as in the philosophical speculations of H.H. Price and C.J. Ducasse, Summerland is not true reality but a collective dream. I suspect that Myers et al. are correct, and that the General and the other communicator quoted above were still in thrall to this overwhelmingly powerful collective hallucination when they conveyed these messages.

Whether his world is ultimately real or illusory, the General's description is still relevant to the subjective experience of Summerland. He goes on:

> After we have passed beyond [the veil], why the music, the flowers, the trees, the birds, the lakes, the rivers, the hills, the gardens, the walks, are perfectly magnificent, perfectly magnificent, and nothing in the earthly world hardly can even correspond to them. And we are taken up by perhaps a priest, or [a] man that acts in the capacity of what you would understand as a clergyman, and they say: "This is a state of

transition. You are now in the real life, in the new life." ...

And then I was surrounded by friends, by acquaintances, by old war veterans, by my intimate friends whom I know, members of my family and all, surrounded by them, welcoming me ...

And then I was taken—would you believe it if I should tell you? I was taken to an actual mansion. It would be what you would call a palace. There is a garden, [with] walks about it. It is divided into rooms, actual compartments. I was taken to that and [they] said: "Here is your home; occupy it, live in it; have what friends you choose with you, what relatives you choose with you, and as those whom you have left behind follow you, you may welcome them to this home as you may see fit." ...

I walked through a corridor and turned into a room at the right and actually walked without fatigue, without effort; I simply glided in. I saw beautiful pictures upon the walls, I saw beautiful flowers that we called in the body palms, growing about me. I heard this beautiful music ...

I said: "Now I would like to see if it is possible, I would like to see flowers about me." I went to the window, and would you believe, the flowers appeared to me in masses, en masse, I might say, and I never saw such flowers. There were lilies, roses, violets, geraniums, carnations, azaleas, hyacinths, tulips, poppies, of every conceivable description, not all intermingled, but each one in its own place. What could you find, what could one wish for better than that?[4]

Asked how he spends his time, the General replies that he assists new arrivals in acclimating to their environment: "We each lend a hand, show them their homes, settle them in it, go back and help another, and we are constantly doing that." He writes, he lectures, he takes walks, he engages in "devotional exercises." He adds, "And then all through what you would call evening ... there is chiefly music going on, entertainment and music. And after that passes, [during] what corresponds with your early morning or late at night, there are lectures and concerts of all kinds and descriptions going on, so that our lives are completely filled."[5]

Most of this material will be familiar to anyone who has studied the literature of Spiritualism. But there are certain idiosyncrasies in the General's account. For one thing, he claims there are actual pearly gates in heaven and sometimes the face of Christ smiles down from the sky. What are we to make of these elements?

My guess is that, if these details are genuine and not a product of

Mrs. Piper's subconscious mind, they constitute additional evidence that the General is still enthralled by the beautiful illusion of the Lotus Eaters' paradise. Raised in a Christian culture, he probably expected to find a Christ-centered version of paradise in line with biblical accounts. So did many of his friends. The world they share is consistent with their expectations and backgrounds. The experience of someone with different beliefs or from a different background will have different features.

There's also a strong likelihood that the original, unredacted communications were less in line with Christian orthodoxy. Robbins writes,

> At this point an account is given of his asking to know something about Christ, to know whether he had been deceived in the earthly world in what he had been taught about Christ, and a description is given of a certain vision that was vouchsafed him. I have thought best to omit this whole passage.[6]

Why not include this material? Presumably, unlike the pearly gates, it would go against the grain of conventional religious piety. The implication is that what was felt safe to print was only the content that would not alarm Christian readers.

In the garden

As I said, much of the description offered by the General matches other such reports. It is fascinating to see how often a beautiful garden, a meadow, flowers, etc. crop up in these accounts. The following examples, drawn from the writings of Robert Crookall, Peter and Elizabeth Fenwick, Bruce Greyson, Kenneth Ring, and Charles Drayton Thomas, could be multiplied indefinitely.

A communicator named Edgar in a Gladys Osborne Leonard séance:

> My idea of the Beyond ... had pictured a rather mysterious place which did not attract me. On coming here I found landscapes, trees and flowers. One could hardly believe at first that it was real. It is a happy life and more full of interest and opportunity than I am able to explain to you.[7]

A 1987 NDE reported by Dawn Gillott, recovering from surgery:

> The next thing was I was above myself near the ceiling looking down. One of the nurses was saying in what seemed like a frantic voice, "Breathe, Dawn, breathe." A doctor was pressing my chest, drips were being disconnected, everyone was rushing around... [I] then left on what I can only describe as the journey of a lifetime.
>
> I went down what seemed like a cylindrical tunnel with a bright warm inviting light at the end. I seemed to be traveling at quite a speed, but I was happy, no pain, just peace. At the end was a beautiful open field, a wonderful summery smell of flowers. There was a bench seat on the right where my Grampi sat (he has been dead seven years). I sat next to him ...
>
> [He asked how she and her family were doing, then said she had to go back.] My whole body seemed to jump. I looked around and saw I was back in the ITU.[8]

A 1961 account by Mary Errington, following removal of a brain aneurysm:

> I had returned from surgery and was still unconscious when my spirit left my body and I was up on the ceiling watching myself on the bed and the nurse bending over me as though she was stroking my face, but of course I couldn't feel anything. I then left the ceiling and went through the dark tunnel out into a beautiful bright meadow. It was so peaceful—a peace that I can only describe as heavenly—and I was floating on this meadow towards a tree that had its branches outstretched like arms waiting to welcome me. I was thinking that once I got to the tree I was safe, but I didn't get there because I came back down the tunnel, very fast, and onto the ceiling where the nurse still seem to be doing something to my face.[9]

Another NDEr, David Verdegaal, described his experience in even more vivid terms.

> This was an old-fashioned, typically English garden with a lush green velvet lawn, bounded by deep curving borders brimming with flowers, each flower nestling within his family group, each group proclaiming its presence with a riot of color and fragrance as if blessed by a morning dew. The entrance to the garden was marked by a trellis of honeysuckle so laden that you had to crouch down to pass beneath while at the other end a rustic garden gate led to the outside.[10]

Eleanor Cleator, suffering from pneumonia and pleurisy, also found herself in a pastoral world:

> I rose out of my body and went towards the front corner of the bedroom. I do not recall any tunnel or light, I was just in a wonderful peace and wellness in a beautiful landscape setting of grass, lawns and trees and brilliant light, diffused, not coming from any central source, with a feeling of being surrounded by wonderful love, joy and peace, no illness or pain.
>
> I was in a little bower corner, on my own. Between me and this place there was a low green trellis fence, which stopped, leaving a gap at the end. I could so easily have gone through. But I knew without anyone telling me that I could not stay there. I could see people walking around purposefully—I particularly remember seeing two nuns walking along together. I did not see anyone I knew; I would have wished to go to someone in particular had I seen him.
>
> The next thing I remember was floating along, passing through swathes of wonderful, beautiful, translucent colors, more beautiful than any I had ever seen on earth. I have no idea of time throughout this experience.
>
> I remember being horizontal, above my body in bed, back in my bedroom, when I slowly "clicked" back into my body.[11]

Vicki Umipeg had two NDEs, once during an attack of appendicitis and once after a car accident.

> She then discovered she had been sucked headfirst into a tube and felt that she was being pulled up into it. The enclosure itself was dark, Vicki said, yet she was aware that she was moving toward light. As she reached the opening of the tube, the music that she had heard earlier seemed to be transformed into hymns ... And she then "rolled out" to find herself lying on grass.
>
> She was surrounded by trees and flowers and a vast number of people. She was in a place of tremendous light, and the light, Vicki said, was something you could feel as well as see. Even the people she saw were bright. "Everybody there was made of light. And I was made of light."[12]

The most remarkable aspect of this last experience is that Vicki was born blind. As a premature baby she was given too much oxygen in the incubator, with the result that her optic nerves were destroyed. As she says, "Those two [near-death] experiences were the only time I could ever relate to seeing, and to what light was, because I experienced it. I was able to see … I've never been able to understand even the concept of light."[13] Nevertheless, she had no trouble seeing in her NDE. Kenneth Ring summarizes:

> Now finding herself in an illuminated field, covered with flowers, she sees two children, long deceased, whom she had befriended when they were all in a school for the blind together. Then, they were both profoundly retarded, but in this state, they appear vital, healthy, and without their earthly handicaps. She feels a welcoming love from them and tries to move toward them. She also sees other persons whom she had known in life, but who have since died.

Ring asked how her NDE compared to her dreams. "No similarity," she said. "No similarity at all." She had no visual perception in her dreams, "no color, no sight of any sort, no shadows, no light, no nothing … There's no visual impression at all in any dream I have."[14]

Brad Barrows, whom we met earlier, is another NDEr who was blind from birth.

> As he approached the end of the tunnel, he was aware of an "immense field" stretching before him for what seemed like miles. As he took in this scene, he says, "I knew that somehow I could sense and literally see everything that was around me." He noticed, for example, huge palm trees, with enormous leaves, and very tall grass as well.

> Brad was now walking on a path in this field and was overcome by the beauty of his surroundings and the feeling of homecoming it engendered in him …
>
> He was initially somewhat puzzled by his apparent ability to see in this realm, … but soon found it completely natural. Again, in connection with his awareness of the all-pervasive light, he makes these instructive comments: "It seemed to be all-encompassing. It seemed like everything, even the grass I had been stepping on seemed to soak in that light. It seemed like the light could actually penetrate through everything that was there, even the leaves on the trees. There was no shade, there was no need for shade. The light was actually all-encompassing.
>
> "Yet I wondered how I could know that because I had never seen before that point. At first I was taken aback by it. I did not understand what sensation I was experiencing."

> He was gently nudged back to his physical life, returning through the tunnel and into his physical body. "Later, he learned from a nurse that his heart had indeed stopped for four minutes, along with his breathing, and that only CPR had brought him back from death."[15]

Peter and Elizabeth Fenwick report that roughly one-quarter of the people who described NDEs to them spoke of a similar idealized landscape.

- Mrs. J. Johnston: "I floated upwards to a beautiful vivid green field."
- David Whitmarsh: "Suddenly I found myself standing in a field of beautiful yellow corn. The sky on the horizon was the deepest of sky blues that I have ever seen and I felt even more at peace in this lovely tranquil place. The brightness was strong but not overbearing and I felt

comfortable and appeared to be wearing a blue gown."
- Felicity Robinson describing her mother's NDE: "She spoke of going down a dark tunnel and there was at the end of it the most beautiful garden, filled with flowers which were beautiful—but she didn't actually enter the garden and the brightness, as the nurse or doctor was saying, 'Mrs. Robinson, Mrs. Robinson.' She said she hadn't wanted to come back but she felt very sad. She never forgot the experience."
- Mrs. G. U. Dunn saw "very high ornamental golden gates ... Inside was the most beautiful garden, no lawn, path or anything else, but flowers of every kind. Those that attracted me most were Madonna lilies, delphiniums and roses, but there were many, many more ... I pushed the gates and they gave way to my push, but try as I might I could not get in; there was something behind me on both sides which seemed to be stopping me from going in."
- Mrs. P. Morris, nearly a victim of drowning: "All my past life and incidents passed through my mind in a flash, things I had forgotten, right back to about two years of age, when I was given a rag doll. Then I entered this dark long tunnel, which had this bright fantastic light at the end. It took me a good while to float to the top but I made it and entered this wonderful garden, full of flowers, grass, shrubs, but it had no sky or birds and was completely empty. But the peace of it all and the brilliant light, much greater than sunlight and darker yellow, more of a gold. I wanted to stay, it was so peaceful."[16]

Recall also the case of Jack Bybee, whose nurse, Anita, was seen in his NDE:

> Then Anita was gone—gone through and over a very green valley and through a fence, where, she told me, "there is a garden on the other side. But you cannot see it. For you must return, while I continue through the gate."[17]

And here's a case from 1913, reported by Robert Crookall:

> "Don't you be afraid to die," a female patient said after having been pronounced dead (no pulse or respiration). "Oh, I've been so far away. I met mother (who had died twenty years before) and Tom Hobson (who had died thirty years before) and a great

many people who were so friendly ... It seems as though I saw trees and shrubbery ... I can never forget it. The light was so different from the light we have here. It was an indescribable glow, no shadows or dark places ... I would have liked to remain there if it had not been for [the need to return to] Pap and Maggie ... Happiness permeated everything."[18]

The Fenwicks find it surprising that such images so frequently reappear. They ask:

Is this vision of Paradise, this heightened and idealized pastoral world, simply the vision that feelings of peace evoke? If it is a personal vision then it's odd that there are not a few more disparate accounts. There must be plenty of people for whom spiritual peace is more likely to be found on a tropical island, for example, or a windblown Scottish moor, the top of a snow-clad mountain or even in the cloisters of a monastery. Although probably few people now really think of Heaven in terms of a bowered garden reminiscent of the biblical Garden of Eden, it may be that we are more culturally influenced by this myth than we realize.[19]

Or it may be that generations of Westerners who predeceased us, and who did believe in a garden paradise, shaped and molded this dream environment, which is now largely ready-made for us.

Experiences other than NDEs

It's not always necessary to die—or nearly die—in order to get a glimpse of the place we might call Otherwhere. Sometimes the shared death experiences that we looked at in connection with the tunnel can extend much further.

Earlier we read about Barbara Sherriff, whose shared death experience with her mother commenced with travel down a tunnel and into a light. Here's the rest of her story:

It seemed as though we were almost floating but the main thing was the light at the end of the tunnel was getting bigger and brighter. We traveled on and then all of a sudden it seemed as if I went into a plate glass window but looking across at my sister she just went through into the garden. She looked back at me and called me and said our gran was there. I could see a few of my relatives around the edge of the garden, which was raised ground with a white fence around. The people were on the other side. The flowers were beautiful and the grass reflected the gold from the sunshine. My sister was standing with her arms up above her head, turning around in circles and calling to me to come. I said I can't, they won't let me through. With that it was almost like a gust of wind took me backwards and the next thing I knew with a big thud my body started to move. I then looked at my sister who was quite quiet. This was around 11 a.m. and she passed away about 8 p.m. that night.[20]

Mrs. M.P. Cockerton had a similar experience, culminating in a vision of the hereafter.

Twenty years ago I lost my mother. I was with her very near the end, and had a wonderful—well, I didn't know what it was other than a "vision," that's what I've called it ever since ... What I saw was a wonderful place, I don't know if it was a garden or what, I only know it was beautiful and that there was a hill down which came my auntie who had died several years previously ... She held out her hands to my mother and they went away together. I really can't describe what peace of mind it gave me.[21]

There may be yet another way to visit the next world. It was discovered, quite by accident, by clinical psychologist Allan Botkin. Botkin specializes in Eye Movement Desensitization and Reprogramming, a technique that involves simulating rapid eye movement, characteristic of deep sleep, so as to place the patient in a trancelike state. In this condition, the patient seems able to process the memory of traumatic events with extreme speed and efficiency. Botkin says that patients who've suffered for years from post-traumatic stress have been significantly helped, even cured, by a single application of EMDR.

But when the EMDR procedure was modified in a rather minor way, an unexpected result occurred. Patients reported experiencing a strong sense of connection with a deceased friend or loved one, an experience that proved remarkably effective at healing grief. Botkin dubbed the procedure Induced After Death Communication, or IADC.

Perhaps the most striking feature of IADCs is their similarity to NDEs. Consider a physician named Pam who came to Botkin with unresolved issues pertaining to the death of her mother.

After she finished telling me about her mother, I used core-focused EMDR to go to her sadness and help her start to bring it down. Then I performed the IADC procedure.

After a minute, she opened her eyes and explained what had happened. She said she felt like she was going through a tunnel toward a bright light, but found herself becoming frustrated because she couldn't get to the end of the tunnel. I assured her that the IADC would unfold naturally; she just needed to relax and let it happen.

After some EMDR to relax her and help her move into a receptive stage, she was ready for the IADC experience. This time her mother was there. Pam kept her eyes closed for five minutes, a relatively long IADC. Tears rolled down her face as she sat quietly with her eyes closed. Finally, she opened her eyes and said, excitedly, "I saw my mother very clearly. She looked younger and thinner even though she had put on weight the last ten years of her life. She looked healthy, happy, peaceful, and she had a spark in her eyes that seemed to emanate a glow around her."

Pam laughed and said, "My mother was sitting on a large rock by the beach in one of those old-style bathing suits, but the surroundings were more beautiful than any beach I've ever seen. She communicated to me in a very clear way that she was very proud of what I had accomplished in my life. She said there was no reason for me to feel guilty about anything. I felt a warm connectedness like we used to have. When Mom was alive, there was always a touch of sadness in her smile, but that was gone and she looked genuinely happy."

When she was finished describing the IADC, she said, "I can't believe how peaceful I feel, like there's been a tremendous burden lifted off of me. And I have the sense that she is not gone and will always be with me."

As she was preparing to leave, she said she felt like all her issues related to the death of her mother had completely resolved. She emphasized more than once how unexpected her experience was.

Two months later she reported that she continued to feel much better, and that she could still experience the warm connectedness with her mother.[22]

Pam's IADC is atypical in one respect; most of them do not involve the sense of moving through a tunnel toward a light. Then again, the majority of NDEs don't feature a tunnel, either.

Though Botkin is careful not to assert that these experiences are metaphysically real, his fascinating case histories clearly indicate there's more to the IADC than a trick of the mind. In some instances, the patient received information during his IADC that was unknown to him but could be verified later. In other cases, an observer—or even the therapist himself—simultaneously experienced the IADC that the patient was undergoing, a phenomenon Botkin labels "shared IADCs." The similarities with shared death experiences are obvious.

Still another approach dates back to the ancient "theater of the mind" known as a psychomanteum, in which a spiritual seeker, properly initiated, would gaze deeply into the depths of a mirror or other polished surface to evoke a vision of a departed loved one or of the next world. After popularizing the NDE, Raymond Moody became interested in this lost art. He decided to construct his own psychomanteum and invite interested parties to try it.

In each case, he spent time with his visitor, talking about the loved one that the person most wished to contact, before ushering his guest into a darkened room and leaving him alone to gaze into a mirror. In the majority of cases, strikingly real and emotionally meaningful visions were reported. Some experiences were purely auditory, but most were visual, and a few even included tactile elements—a sense of being touched or hugged. Occasionally the apparitions seemingly emerged from the mirror or, even more remarkably, the visitor himself seemingly passed into the mirror, not unlike Alice in *Through the Looking Glass*. An experience of the latter type was reported by a 26-year-old woman:

> I saw visions first in the mirror, well, at first color patterns and little bright flickers or specks flashing. I saw this big mist just come up and fill up the whole mirror, just like a big fog blowing right up over the window, and after the mist was a bright light. I saw a light in the far distance and scenery, little brief scenes, but then my attention was drawn to a pathway …
>
> I can't say I went into the mirror because I didn't notice going through it, but I know for sure I was in this other dimension. The light and other scenes were all around, but I didn't pay them any attention because I knew I had to get down that passageway.
>
> I moved on through, and I saw these three people standing off a little to my left side, and I moved up closer to them, and there I saw that it was my grandmother and my favorite aunt, Betty, who died, and this other person I didn't recognize, but a woman definitely.

> Aunt Betty kind of indicated to me that this person was my great-grandmother Harriet and then I knew because I had seen her photographs. She didn't really look just like the pictures, though. She was more active-looking than in the pictures I saw or what I imagined ...
>
> I was so overjoyed during this whole meeting. I was so happy. There was not a doubt in the world they were there and that I saw them, and it was as real as meeting anyone ...
>
> This didn't last a very long time. Then I just came back into the chair, and the visions in the mirror faded away quickly.[23]

Naturally, the experience could be dismissed as an elaborate hallucination, perhaps the result of heightened suggestibility brought about by Moody's preparations. But not all people are susceptible to suggestion, and simple self-delusion seems inconsistent with the high rate of success reported by Moody (well above 50%), even with skeptical visitors. The historical persistence of the technique may also argue against an overly simple explanation. Moody traces its origins from the Oracle of the Dead at Ephyra in ancient Greece, through the Middle Ages, and up to the Elizabethan Era and the mirror scrying of John Dee. Dee's reported experiences, in particular, offer striking parallels to episodes reported by Moody's guests.

This is not to say that the visions are "objective" in the sense that a camera could photograph them. I suspect that a camera would record nothing of interest. The change that takes place is most likely an altered state of consciousness (which appears to be Moody's own view), and the visions are purely subjective.

"Subjective," however, does not necessarily mean unreal. After all, every experience is subjective by its very nature. The visions are, perhaps, a private window into another reality that our normal consciousness can't access. In themselves, they prove little, but in conjunction with NDEs, deathbed visions, crisis apparitions, and other phenomena, they are at least worth considering as another piece of the puzzle.

Return

Not everybody who experiences the joys of Summerland—or Paradise, or the Field of Reeds—is permitted to stay, at least on the first visit. People who've undergone near-death experiences, by definition, had to come back. That doesn't mean they were happy about it. In most cases, they weren't.

Still, a few did argue for a chance to continue their physical incarnation. One such person is Gillian McKenzie, who remembers:

> A voice at the end [of the tunnel] said, "Gill, you know who I am," and I thought, "Heavens, this is God and He knows my name." Then the voice chuckled and said, "Gill, there is someone here you do know." It was my grandfather, who died two years before. "Grandfather," I said, "I'm not staying here. Hamish can't cope, I've left a pile of shirts to be ironed and he doesn't know how to do them." ...
>
> And grandpa laughed and said, "Gill, it doesn't matter a damn. You'll have to put up a better case than that." So I said, "Grandpa, I'm only thirty-four, I've got so much more to do with my life. I haven't had my money's worth. I want to go back."[24]

There's an interesting postscript to this account. Gillian's mother later revealed that after learning of Gillian's precarious condition, she phoned an aunt, who reassured her with the words, "You don't have to worry about that, Gladys. Harry is looking after her." Harry was Gillian's grandfather.

As noted, Gillian's desire to return is atypical. But sometimes an NDEr will decide he must return, even though he doesn't really want to. Such was the case of Allan Pring, the RAF pilot we met earlier.

> And then, in a moment of utter despair, I realized I could not go on. I stopped and my companion ahead of me turned to look at me. No words were spoken but my predicament was completely understood. I loved my wife more dearly than life itself and I could not leave her like this ... I had to be able to tell her that there is no death and that it is possible to gain complete understanding. The journey back was desperate. Leaving was the worst experience of my existence and it will affect me for as long as I live.[25]

For the most part, however, the return is enforced by an implacable outside agency, much against the person's will. A patient known by the pseudonym "Stella" recounted an experience of this kind while weeping steadily.

> I began to realize that I was going to have to leave and I didn't want to leave ... I began to hear my name called. And the first time it happened, the drawing, the pulling force, and then I

heard a second time stronger and then I was outside the wall of the [astral] city and trying to hold on there. I didn't want to leave! Trying to find some way to stay there![26]

For a year afterward she felt angry "that I saw such a beautiful, beautiful place ... To gain that kind of knowledge and then ... to have to come back to these limitations."

A patient named Linda also remembers feeling angry.

> I was angry when I came back, and I remember thinking, If I could just talk to them [the doctors], I would tell them to leave me alone. Let me be back in that state I was in ...
> Nobody would want to be out of that state because it is so wonderful. I had left whatever had gone on in the past life; I wanted to stay there forever.[27]

Darrell, interviewed by Kenneth Ring, says,

> The most depressed, the most severe anxiety I've ever had was at the moment I realized I must return to this earth. That is the greatest depths of depression I personally have ever had since that time or before ... I did not want to come back. And now that I'm back, I'm absolutely assured of the fact that I did not want to come back ... This [earth] is a wonderful place to live if you don't know anywhere else.[28]

Mrs. J.H. Conant had an NDE in 1851.

> When ill she was prescribed a large overdose of morphine and went unconscious. The doctor thought she was going to die ... She went to "some beautiful place; she thought she was in heaven." There she met her mother, begged to be allowed to stay there, and was told she must return to Earth because "she had yet a mission to perform."[29]

Her mission, evidently, was to become a medium, which she did.

Jean Johnstone's father spoke of a dream he had shortly before he died in 1951:

> He said, "I have had a very vivid dream, more than a dream, it seemed. I was walking in the foothills of the Himalayas"—he had

served thirty-five years in Government service in India—"in the dawning, when suddenly all the dogs of our life, including the dog of my boyhood, came running to meet me, jumping and wagging their tails as they did to welcome me. I felt younger and stronger every minute, and the light grew behind the mountains, brighter and brighter. I was *so* happy. Then, there was a hand on my shoulder and a voice: "You must go back, it's not time," and I woke up. I *wish* I had not had to come back." He asked me not to tell anyone—"They'll think I'm finally in my dotage." He died not long afterwards.[36]

"The Door in the Wall"

There's even a short story, written in 1906, that may possibly concern an NDEr's deep, abiding regret. In *The Secret Life of Genius*, John Chambers recounts an early experience in the life of H.G. Wells. Shortly before his 21st birthday, while playing soccer, Wells suffered a potentially life-threatening kidney injury. He lingered for days but eventually recovered, though he suffered from tuberculosis for the rest of his life.

Chambers speculates that Wells had an NDE during his illness. Admittedly, Wells himself never mentioned anything of the sort. But twenty years later, he wrote the story in question, "The Door in the Wall."

The narrator informs us of a tale told by his friend Wallace, who confessed himself "haunted by something—that rather takes the light out of things, that fills me with longings." As a five-year-old boy, Wallace came across a green door in a white wall; stepping through, he found himself in a marvelous garden.

> It was very difficult for Wallace to give me his full sense of that garden into which he came.
> There was something in the very air of it that exhilarated, that gave one a sense of lightness and good happening and well-being; there was something in the sight of it that made all its color clean and perfect and softly luminous. In the instant of coming into it one was exquisitely glad ... And everything was beautiful there ...
> "And the size? [said Wallace] Oh! it stretched far and wide, this way and that. I believe there were hills far away ... And somehow it was just like coming home.
> "You know, in the very moment the door swung to behind me, I forgot the road with its fallen chestnut leaves, its cabs and tradesman's carts, I forgot the sort of gravitational pull back to

the discipline and obedience of home, I forgot all hesitations and fear, forgot discretion, forgot all the intimate realities of this life. I became in a moment a very glad and wonder-happy little boy—in another world. It was a world with a different quality, a warmer, more penetrating and mellower light, with a faint clear gladness in its air …

"Of course, I can convey nothing of that indescribable quality of translucent unreality, that difference from the common things of experience that hung about it all."[31]

He found himself in the company of "a tall, fair girl," smiling, "asking me questions in a soft, agreeable voice, and telling me things, pleasant things I know, though what they were I was never able to recall." There were other people as well, all of them "beautiful and kind. In some way—I don't know how—it was conveyed to me that they were all kind to me, glad to have me there, and filling me with gladness by their gestures, by the touch of their hands, by the welcome and love in their eyes."

Some children arrived, and together they played wonderful games, which subsequently, much to his distress, he was unable to remember in detail. "Then presently came a somber dark woman, with a grave, pale face and dreamy eyes, a somber woman wearing a soft long robe of pale purple, who carried a book." The book's pages contained his own life, set out in vivid moving images—"all the things that had happened to me since ever I was born … People moved and things came and went in them; my dear [deceased] mother, whom I had near forgotten; then my father, stern and upright, the servants, the nursery, all the familiar things of home."

He was forbidden to see what would come next in his life. Abruptly he found himself outside the green door, back on the shabby, commonplace street—"a wretched little figure, weeping aloud, for all that I could do to restrain myself, and I was weeping because I could not return to my dear play-fellows who had called after me, 'Come back to us! Come back to us soon!' … As I realized the fullness of what it happened to me, I gave way to quite ungovernable grief."

When he related the story to his family, he was punished "for telling lies … Everyone was forbidden to listen to me, to hear a word about it." Even so, he continued to yearn for his lost garden, often praying to go back, and throughout his life seeking "the door that goes into peace, into delight, into a beauty beyond dreaming, a kindness no man on earth can know."

Here we have many elements found in NDEs, including the ecstatic sense of homecoming, the immediate loss of interest in earthly life, the friendly people who convey their intentions without spoken words, the acquisition of important knowledge that is later forgotten, the life review, and of course the beautiful garden with its surreal, translucent, luminous quality. In addition, we have the harsh reality of return, the inability to convey one's experience or prove it, and the yearning to be uplifted again into that spiritual space.

Conclusion

Whether known as Summerland, Paradise, or A'aru, the afterlife environment has been pictured as an idealized replica of the physical world for thousands of years. While some details of these accounts are probably the result of confused communication or unconscious embellishment by the medium, the broad outline is consistent: Souls are drawn to a plane of existence corresponding to their level of moral development, and each plane is shaped by the collective unconscious of its inhabitants.

Arthur Conan Doyle sums it up nicely in the concluding lines of his two-volume work *The History of Spiritualism*:

> So workaday and homely a heaven may seem material to many minds, but we must remember that evolution has been very slow upon the physical plane, and it is slow also upon the spiritual one. In our present lowly condition we cannot expect at one bound to pass all intermediate conditions and attain to what is celestial. This will be the work of centuries—possibly of æons. We are not fit yet for a purely spiritual life. But as we ourselves become finer, so will our environment become finer, and we shall evolve from heaven to heaven until the destiny of the human soul is lost in a blaze of glory whither the eye of imagination may not follow.[32]

But this raises the question: What happens as we do become more fit for the "purely spiritual life"? It appears that we rise higher, leaving the beautiful dream of Summerland behind.

CHAPTER TWENTY-ONE:
Higher Planes

THE IDEA OF PROGRESSING in step-by-step fashion to ever higher levels of spiritual development does not seem to be part of the earliest traditions. For ancient peoples, the misty depths of Sheol or the resplendent pastures of the Field of Reeds were where you ended up; no further evolution was envisioned. Christianity and Islam similarly offered Paradise as a final destination for the saved, with Hell as the perpetual dungeon of the damned. Even Swedenborg had no place in his cosmology for progressively higher stages of spiritual growth.

By the 19th century, things had changed. The explosion of channeled literature and séances—what Arthur Conan Doyle called "the new revelation"—had spawned a radically different vision. In 1878 William Emmette was able to write, "The universal teaching of Spiritualism is, we all know, that the spirit-world is a progressive state of existence. By growth and effort the spirit passes from circle to circle, and from sphere to sphere."[1] Summerland was not a final destination, but only a way station along a road.

The most detailed exposition of this idea, at least among relatively early sources, is found in Geraldine Cummins's two books from the 1930s, *The Road to Immortality* and *Beyond Human Personality*, in which F.W.H. Myers outlines seven stages of spiritual development:

1. The Plane of Matter
2. The Intermediate Plane, or Hades
3. The Plane of Illusion (= Summerland)
4. The Plane of Color, or Eidos
5. The Plane of Flame, or Helios
6. The Plane of White (or Purified) Light
7. Out Yonder

Myers observes, "Between each plane there is [a] lapse into apparent oblivion, a stilling of all processes, a great calm."[2]

The channeled Myers insists that we are not meant to be content with Summerland, the shared dream world. We must be more ambitious:

> After death the aim of the highly developed man ... is to reach successively the Fourth and Fifth planes ...
>
> The Fourth state or world of Eidos [is where one lives] consciously in the realm of pure form ... This world, or realm, is a masterpiece of pure beauty which I have described as the prototype of earth.[3]

Unlike the third plane (Summerland), which is a version of earthly life re-created by shared memories, the fourth plane is said to be the ultimate source of earthly experience. Rather than a copy, it is the original, precisely corresponding to Plato's World of Forms.

The fifth plane involves an incarnation as a fire-being that inhabits the heart of a star—an idea that has struck most readers as pure fantasy. But who knows? Consider a recent speculative hypothesis by physicist Roger Penrose, who, with Stuart Hameroff, is the author of the theory of orchestrated objective reduction, or Orch-OR. Orch-OR posits that consciousness arises from quantum effects in the tiny microtubules of the brain. Could a similar process be at work in neutron stars?

> Penrose observed that interiors of neutron stars may have huge quantum superpositions which would reach OR with very large [energy], brief [time] and high intensity. By Orch-OR criteria such events would indeed be conscious. But because the conditions are presumably random, such conscious moments would lack cognitive information processing: OR without Orch.[4]

The idea, I gather, is that neutron stars can achieve a form of nonhuman consciousness on very brief time scales. For what it's worth, Myers's fire beings also live and pulsate with phenomenal speed, and their environment ("composed of a far heavier type of atom," Myers says) may possibly correspond to the dense interior of the neutron star.

On the sixth plane, the individual soul merges with a larger soul group. This sets the stage for the ultimate transformation on the seventh plane: "merging with the Idea, with the Great Source of spirit." Even at this point, there is no annihilation. "You still exist as an individual. You are as a wave in the sea; and you have at last entered into Reality and cast from you all the illusions of appearances."[5]

Another channeled book that appeared around the same time is *Life Eternal*, attributed to W.T. Stead and transmitted via the automatic writer Hester Dowden. *Life Eternal* agrees broadly with the Myers scripts on the existence of seven spheres of development, culminating with absorption into the Godhead. Stead tells us,

> The spheres are not shapes, they are not countries, they are not worlds, they are different states or conditions through which the soul passes on its way back to the great central force which is God ... The spheres are of different quality, and the duration of the soul's sojourn in each is of a different length. The state which I call a sphere is a mental condition. In each of the spheres we retain "form." Our bodies become more ethereal as we ascend ... These "forms" are given us so that we may preserve a shape until, the spirit being set free after we pass the seventh sphere, we are merely part of the great central plan and no longer preserve our personality.[6]

Besides channeled literature, there's another possible source of information on the higher planes—hypnotic regression to a state between earthly lives, a condition sometimes called the inter-life or intermission stage.[7]

Intermission

The earliest book dealing with hypnotically induced intermission memories that I'm aware of is *Life Between Life*, by Joel Whitton and Joe Fisher, published in 1986. The subject gained wider attention with Michael Newton's 1994 bestseller *Journey of Souls*. While the transcripts make fascinating reading, they describe an afterlife experience dramatically different from Summerland.

Instead of an idealized earthly world, the inter-life environment is typically described as an abstract geometrical or fluidic landscape inhabited by souls in the form of glowing blobs of color and light. While residents of Summerland normally remember only their most recent incarnation, and may doubt the reality of reincarnation altogether, souls in the inter-life realm remember *all* their incarnations, apparently because they're viewing things from the perspective of the higher self. They interact with other members of their group soul, addressing them by names that have no earthly counterparts.

The following passages are taken from *Journey of Souls*. All have been abridged, with the many ellipses in the original (signifying hesitation) deleted, and with some changes of punctuation for clarity.

> I see a variety of lights in patches, separated from each other by galleries. [The lights] are people, the souls of people within the bulging galleries reflecting light outward to me. That's what I'm seeing—patches of lights bobbing around. [The individual souls are] like dots. I see masses of dots hanging in clumps, as hanging grapes, all lit up. [The whole scene resembles] a long glow-worm, its sides bulging in and out. The movement is rhythmic, swaying as a ribbon in the breeze while I am going further away. Oh good! I'm coming in towards the site where my friends are attached. [I feel] fantastic! There is a familiar pulling of minds reaching out to me. I'm catching the tail of their kite, joining them in thought. I'm *home!* ... Will you let me stop talking now so I can meet with my friends?[8]

A different patient:

> I have come into a grand arena. I see many others crisscrossing around me. It's so vast. I'm carried forward rapidly, straight past the others. After a while I see nests of people, like hives—I see them as bunches of moving lights, fireflies. [I feel] warmth, friendship, empathy; it's dreamy. [Progress slows, and the subject begins to tremble.] There are bunches of people together off in the distance, but ... *there!* People I know, some of my family off in the distance, but (with anguish) I don't seem to be able to reach them! I don't know [why]! God, don't they know I'm here? *I can't reach my father!* ...
>
> [Calmer] He has to stay where he is. He does not belong in my hive. I have to work things out for myself with others like me ...
>
> Oh, *look!* My own people, it's wonderful to see them again. They are coming toward me! [They were involved with] more than one life, I can tell you. (with pride) These are *my* people! I haven't been with them for so long. Oh, it's fun seeing them all again. [Refusing to answer a question posed by the therapist about some other group.] I don't *want* to know. That is their business. Can't you see? I'm not attached to them. I'm too busy with the people I'm supposed to be with here. People I know and love.[9]

Accounts of a life between lives aren't limited to hypnotic regression. Some children who spontaneously recall a past life also remember the intermission phase.

Poonam Sharma and Jim B. Tucker found that 276 (23%) of 1,200 reincarnation cases in [Ian] Stevenson's collection at the University of Virginia included intermission memories. James Matlock and Iris Giesler-Petersen found intermission memories in 85 (21%) of 400 published reincarnation cases from twelve countries, seven in Asia and five in the West ...

Subjects with intermission memories made significantly more correct statements about the previous life, they remembered more names from the previous life, they were more likely to recall the death of the previous person and they recalled more past lives than did subjects without intermission memories.[10]

The intermission state reported in mediumship

The credibility of inter-life narratives would be strengthened if they were backed up by mediumistic accounts predating the reincarnation studies. In fact, there are such accounts.

In 1921, French artist Pierre Emile Cornillier published *The Survival of the Soul and Its Evolution after Death*. The book focuses on Cornillier's seances with a young model named Reine, who proved to be a naturally talented medium.

Reine said that the spirits she saw were differentiated by color. The lower spirits were reddish, the higher ones bluish, and the highest of all were white.[11] In her vision of the spirit world, there is no mention of gardens and cottages. Instead, what the book calls the "Au-Delà" (the Beyond) is an ethereal realm of shapeless spirits who can recall all their incarnations and in some cases assist in planning their next sojourn in the physical world. This is strikingly similar to regression inter-life accounts, though it predates them by six decades.[12]

Some of the Myers communications are also consistent with the inter-life accounts. Myers asserts that after leaving the Plane of Illusion, the individual becomes aware of his participation in a large and complex "group soul... [a] larger self [that] possesses the knowledge of all his anterior history as well as the history of those within his Group who are intimately bound to him and make a part of his personal pattern."

This higher sphere (corresponding to the fourth plane in Myers's scheme) is strikingly similar to the testimony of Michael Newton's subjects. According to Myers, the newly ascendant spirit

> realizes first of all that he has entered a world of myriad colors, lights and sounds. He is sensible of a body entirely dissimilar

from the human body. As regards appearance, it can only be described as being apparently a compound of light and colors unimaginable ...

In this many-colored region the form vibrates with extreme intensity, for now mind expresses itself more directly in form: so that we can hear the thoughts of other souls ... We dwell in a world of appearances in some respects similar to the earth. Only all this vast region of appearances is gigantic in conception, terrifying and exquisite according to the manner in which it presents itself to the Soul-man. It is far more fluidic, less apparently solid than earth surroundings ...

As we evolve here, we enter into those memories and experiences of other lives that are to be found in the existence of the souls that preceded us, and are of our group ....

The soul becomes sensible of the group-soul, and through the awareness there arises a great change.[13]

A point often made by Newton's patients is that, while in the intermission state, they plan out their earthly lives before birth, even choosing their parents. This, too, has parallels in the literature of mediumship. In *Letters from the Afterlife* (1914), Elsa Barker channels a deceased judge, David Hatch, who tells us:

You should get away from the mental habit of regarding your present life as the only one, get rid of the idea that the life you expect to lead on this side, after your death, is to be an endless existence in one state. You could no more endure such an endless existence in the subtle matter [of Hatch's world] then you could endure to live forever in the gross matter in which you are now encased. You would weary of it. You could not support it ...

I could probably force the coming back [to earth], but that would be unwise, for I should then come back with less power than I want ... It is better for me to rest in the condition of light matter until I have accumulated energy enough to come back with power. I shall not do, however, as many souls do; they stay out here until they are as tired of this world as they formerly were tired of the earth, and then are driven back half unconsciously by the irresistible force of the tide of rhythm. I want to guide that rhythm ...

When the soul enters matter, preparing for rebirth, it enters potentiality, if we may use such a term, and all its strength is needed in the herculean effort to form the new body and adjust to it.[14]

Hatch goes on to suggest a form of karma, saying that "the tendencies of any given life, the unexplained impulses and desires, are in nearly all cases brought over" to the new incarnation, though specific memories are usually forgotten.

The vicissitudes of life and the vagaries of free will often mean that the inter-life plan—mostly forgotten by the conscious mind while incarnated—is not carried out successfully. This concern, sometimes voiced by regression patients, is also found in Helen Greaves's *Testimony of Light*, a channeled book purportedly originating with a deceased nun, Frances Banks.

Here are the life plan and its somewhat disappointing outcome, as described by Frances:

> Somewhere in the deeps of my mind two "blueprints" are brought forward into my consciousness. These are so clear that I can (literally) take them out, materialize them and study them. One is the Perfect Idea with which my spirit went bravely into incarnation. The other is the resultant of only a partially-understood Plan ... in fact my life as it was actually lived ... First of all the mind looks at the whole comparison, and sets the blueprints side-by-side. This is the first shock; a true humbling of yourself to find that you did so little when you would have done so much; that you went wrong so often when you were sure that you were right. During this experience the whole cycle of your life-term unfolds before you in a kaleidoscopic series of pictures. During the crisis one seems to be entirely alone. Yours is the judgment. You stand at your own bar of judgment. You make your own decisions. You take the blame ... You are the accused, the judge and jury.[15]

Parallels to the in-depth life review are clear.

In one passage Frances describes her spontaneous transition from the Summerland plane to a higher sphere:

> Whilst I was meditating in my golden garden, I found myself 'transported' to ... a cluster of entities about a Teacher. Immediately I experienced a rise of consciousness, an upsurge of joy, a mingling of unity and harmony which colored my whole being. I cannot explain this in any other terms, though I doubt whether they will have the same connotation for you. I knew this was right for me. I had come into my own. There was no definite acceptance, the entire operation was unobtrusive and simple, yet I had the conviction that all was well, that I was

amidst my fellow-travelers on the Way.[16]

As we saw in inter-life regression transcripts, this "upsurge of joy" and immediate sense of belonging are typical of the reactions of hypnotized patients, often expressed in highly emotional terms. But *Testimony of Light* was first published in 1969, predating both *Life Between Life* and *Journey of Souls*.

If there is any truth in these various accounts, it would appear that different levels of the afterlife experience are being accessed—that, somehow, regression therapy and spontaneous past-life memories can put the individual in touch with the higher self, which encompasses all its incarnations, while, for the most part, mediumship and NDEs allow contact with only the most recent incarnated personality.[17]

CHAPTER TWENTY-TWO:
Reincarnation

DISCUSSION OF A LIFE between lives naturally leads to the question of reincarnation, which has long been controversial even among people who accept evidence for postmortem survival. Doubters point out that many spirits communicating through mediums either deny reincarnation outright or appear to know nothing about it. Other spirits, however, are quite committed to the idea of incarnation.

Cornillier's medium Reine was asked about this vexing problem. The answer she conveyed was that spirits at different levels of development have different levels of knowledge.

> By their fixed and persistent ideas Spirits, unconsciously, produce images around them—illusions of which they themselves are the first dupes and which also mislead the disincarnated souls in their environment ... And this is a ... source of errors in communications that are quite sincere but which, as information, are no more dependable than is any other hallucination ... In astral life Spirits of slight evolution seem as a rule to perceive only these image illusions.[1]

As we've seen, this explanation is broadly consistent with the teachings of the *Tibetan Book of the Dead*, which warns against being taken in by thought-forms, and with channeled statements that characterize Summerland as a "plane of illusion."

Regardless of the discrepancies in channeled messages, the evidence for reincarnation is surprisingly good—good enough to convince even those, like me, who don't relish the prospect of going through high school all over again. This evidence takes several forms: hypnotic regression, spontaneous recollection, and some communications via mediums.

Hypnotic regression

There's a long-standing debate over how much credence can be put in regression therapy. It's well known that the subconscious mind is prone to confabulation—making things up—in order to follow the lead of an authority figure, who in this case is the hypnotist. Confabulation accounts for those "recovered memories" of childhood abuse that have proved spurious. It also accounts for memories of past lives that have been definitively traced to novels, movies, and even a radio drama—material that the patient consciously forgot but was able to subconsciously recall (a phenomenon known as cryptomnesia). Scott Rogo's book *The Search for Yesterday* analyzes many cases of this type.

That's not to say there aren't compelling examples of hypnotic regression. The famous case of Bridey Murphy, which ignited the American public's interest in regression therapy in the 1950s, still holds up reasonably well. Much-publicized efforts to debunk it have themselves been largely discredited.[2]

A more recent case is presented by Carol Bowman in *Children's Past Lives*. It involves her son Chase, who underwent hypnotic regression on two occasions. Chase's story led his mother to pursue an active interest in past-life regression, resulting in several books.

When he was five, Chase began exhibiting a hysterical fear of loud booming noises, like fireworks. A hypnotherapist offered to regress him. Under hypnosis, Chase reported:

> I'm carrying a long gun with a kind of sword at the end ... I have dirty, ripped clothes, brown boots, a belt. I'm hiding behind a rock, crouching on my knees and shooting at the enemy. I'm at the edge of a valley. The battle is going on all around me ... I don't want to look, but I have to when I shoot. Smoke and flashes everywhere. And loud noises: yelling, screaming, loud booms. I'm not sure who I'm shooting at—there's so much smoke, so much going on. I'm scared. I shoot at anything that moves. I really don't want to be here and shoot other people ... I'm hit in the right wrist by a bullet someone shot from above the valley. I slide down behind the rock, holding my wrist where I was shot. It's bleeding—I feel dizzy.
>
> Someone I know drags me out of the battle and takes me to a place where they took soldiers that are hurt—not like a regular hospital, just big poles, like an open tent, covered with material. There are beds there, but they're like wooden benches. They're very hard and uncomfortable ...
>
> I'm walking back to battle. There are chickens on the road. I see a wagon pulling a cannon on it. The cannon is tied onto the wagon with ropes. The wagon has big wheels.[3]

Chase's fear of loud noises cleared up immediately after this session.

His narrative doesn't seem like the shoot-'em-up heroics of a child. Instead, it's an account of a frightened man who doesn't "want to be here" and who's not sure who he's shooting at. His descriptions—the makeshift field hospital, a cannon "tied onto the wagon with ropes," "chickens on the road"—possess a certain verisimilitude.

Could he have seen these details in a movie? Bowman says the five-year-old's TV watching was carefully monitored and did not include programs about war. Of course we can't be sure he never caught a glimpse of a war movie, but his account seems to go beyond the memory of a film.

In subsequent years, some of Chase's offhand comments led his mother to speculate that her son's past life took place during the Civil War. However, she did not pursue the matter until Chase expressed the desire for another regression. This was during the 1991 Persian Gulf War, when news coverage reawakened old fears in the now eight-year-old boy. By this time Bowman had learned hypnosis, and she regressed her son.

Observe how closely his second, more sophisticated rendition of the tale dovetails with the first:

> Can't hear sounds, but can see it. I see horses coming in the valley. Men with guns with spears on the ends. I see myself crouching behind a rock, looking up at them. I'm feeling sad, scared, proud. There are soldiers on horses on my side. I'm now kneeling behind a rock. Waiting.
>
> There's a battle going on. Smoke everywhere. I'm not shooting, I'm waiting. I start to shoot at the enemy—I don't have any choice, I want to protect myself. The people on the horses are white, I'm black. White soldiers are on my side. There's too much going on. Confusion everywhere. I'm scared half to death. Oh—he gets my wrist with a shot. It hardly hurts. Everything goes black ...
>
> Now I'm going back to fight with a bandage on my wrist. I see horses pulling a cannon, making a lot of dust. The cannon is on a wagon with big wheels—it's tied down with heavy ropes. There's chickens walking along the road. It's a time between fighting. I'm thinking of how unhappy I am about going to war. I didn't know what I was getting into ...
>
> I'm back in battle. I'm shooting a cannon from the top of the valley. I pull a string, the cannon fires. I'm not loading it, though. I can't shoot a gun because of my arm. I'm scared shooting the cannon. Now I know how the others feel to be shot at. They're scared too ...

> I'm sad to go back to battle. I miss my family. I'm behind the cannon. I'm hit! ...
>
> I'm floating above the battlefield. I feel good that I'm done. I see the battle and smoke below. As I look down on the battlefield, everything is still and smoky—nothing is moving down there. I feel happy that I'm done. I get to go to a happier life. I float over my house. I see my wife and kids. I say goodbye to my family. They don't see me because I'm in spirit, but they know that I'm dead ...
>
> Everyone has to be in a war. It balances everything out. Not necessarily die in a war, but experience it. It teaches you about feelings. It gives you a sense of how other people feel. It's a bad place. I skipped World War II. I was up. I was waiting for my turn to go back to a more peaceful time. I had a short life in between.[4]

The account is remarkably realistic, even down to the detail of firing a cannon by pulling a string, a fact Bowman later verified. She adds that Chase's anxiety about the Gulf War was alleviated by this second session. Note also the implication of an intermission state: "I was up. I was waiting for my turn to go back."

Xenoglossy

A few regression cases involve xenoglossy—the ability to speak in languages ordinarily unknown to the speaker. Dr. Joel Whitton handled a case of this type.

> When Harold was reexperiencing his life as Thor (a Viking), Dr. Whitton instructed him to write down, phonetically, the vocal exchanges that were taking place. Harold responded by writing twenty-two words and phrases, none of which he understood. Working independently, linguistic authorities who spoke Icelandic and Norwegian subsequently identified and translated ten of these words as being Old Norse, the language of the Vikings and the precursor of modern Icelandic. Several other words seemed to have Russian, Serbian, or Slavic derivation and these were also identified. Most of the words relate to the sea—precisely the type of verbal communication that could be expected from a Viking warrior.
>
> Dr. Thor Jakobsson, a research scientist with Canada's Department of the Environment and an expert on the Icelandic language, studied the transcripts produced by Harold and

concluded that many of the words—including those for "storm," "heart," and "iceberg"—were "definitely of Icelandic origin." That some of the words had their origins in other languages only added to the authenticity of the script, said Dr. Jakobsson, because the restless, warlike Vikings roamed to the far corners of Europe.[5]

When retrieving memories of another of Harold's purported lives, this one in Mesopotamia, Whitton asked him to write down the words for common concepts, such as "brother," "house," and "clothing."

> Holding the pencil very lightly, Harold carefully created a mysterious, Arabic-style script in a spidery, childlike hand ...
> Unsuccessful in matching his patient's supposed calligraphy with ancient scripts in library books, [Whitton] eventually submitted the pencil markings to Dr. Ibrahim Pourhadi, an expert in ancient Persian and Iranian languages at the Near Eastern Section of Washington's Library of Congress. After close examination of the samples, Dr. Pourhadi maintained that [they] were an authentic representation of the long-extinct language called Sassanid Pahlavi, which was used in Mesopotamia between A.D 226 and 651 and bears no relation to modern Iranian.[6]

Another case of xenoglossy under hypnosis, reported by Dr. Robert Bobrow, concerns Dolores Jay of Mount Orab, Ohio. In 1970 her husband—a Methodist minister and amateur hypnotist—hypnotized Delores in the hope of curing her back pain. While in trance, she answered a question by saying, "Nein," German for *no*. This in itself was trivial, but when her husband re-hypnotized Dolores three days later he prompted her to speak German, which she did.

> The minister asked questions in English; his wife replied largely in German, and in the voice of a young child ...
> Dolores spoke German, under hypnosis, responsively, meaning she answered in German whether the query was posed in English or in German (some sessions were attended by German-speakers). Only she wasn't Dolores; she was Gretchen. And the time in which she lived, placed by events of which she spoke, would have been the late 19th century.[7]

Bobrow acknowledges the difficulties in confirming past-life regressions, not least of which is the scarcity of historical records necessary to verify the patients' claims. He goes on,

> Suffice it to say that Gretchen's accounts were more or less consistent, including her last name (Gottlieb), the town in which she lived (Eberswalde), and her death—a murder—at about the age of sixteen. Not to mention the fact that she could speak German, and even used some archaic and obscure words.[8]

Ian Stevenson, known for his investigations of children's past lives, became involved after learning of the case in a magazine.

> Stevenson speaks German, and first ascertained that [Dolores] was, in fact, responding to coherent German in her "Gretchen" mode. He then obtained assurances from the couple that neither had ever had any prior knowledge of the language; they even signed affidavits to this effect. Mrs. Jay would eventually take a lie-detector test in New York City, which showed that she believed she was telling the truth about never having learned German.
>
> [Stephenson looked] into whether Dolores Jay could have learned to speak German at some juncture in her past, and perhaps had forgotten about it. She was born in Clarksburg, West Virginia, and at the age of two moved to a neighboring town. Her only German ancestry consisted of two great-great-grandparents on her mother's side, who had died many years before her birth. Stephenson interviewed [Dolores's] mother, who told him that she had never heard any family members speak German …
>
> Stevenson went back to the Clarksburg area where both Jays had grown up and interviewed nineteen relatives and neighbors of Dolores Jay, including her parents and a younger sister. All denied having any family or acquaintances who spoke German. No German books had ever been in the house …
>
> Even the schools of Harrison County did not teach German at the time the Jays were enrolled there.[9]

Stevenson's cautious conclusion with regard to Dolores Jay is "that responsive xenoglossy derives from some paranormal process."

Spontaneous memories

Children who spontaneously articulate memories of a past life typically remember a comparatively recent lifetime that ended too soon—a life snuffed out by violence, sudden illness, or some other tragedy. It seems that, in some cases, an individual whose mission on earth is interrupted will dive back into life almost immediately, while retaining memories of the previous incarnation until about age ten.[10]

The classic work in this field is Ian Stevenson's *Twenty Cases Suggestive of Reincarnation*, from which both of the following cases are taken. First up is the celebrated case of Swarnlata Mishra.

> When Swarnlata was between three and three and a half years old, ... her father took her with him on a trip to Jabalpur, ... which lies about 170 miles south of [their hometown of] Panna. On the return journey, as they passed the city of Katni (57 miles north of Jabalpur), Swarnlata unexpectedly asked the driver of the truck they were in to turn down the road toward "my house." A little later, when the group was taking tea at Katni, Swarnlata proposed that they could obtain much better tea at "her" house nearby. These statements puzzled [her father] Sri Mishra and the more so when he learned that Swarnlata later told other children of the family further details of a previous life in Katni as a member of a family named Pathak ...
>
> During the next few years, Swarnlata revealed fragments of her apparent memories, mostly to her brothers and sisters, but to some extent to her parents. In 1958, Swarnlata ... met the wife of Professor R. Agnihotri, who came from the area of Katni and whom Swarnlata claimed to recognize from having known her during the previous life in that city. In this way, Sri Mishra first confirmed the accuracy of some of his daughter's numerous statements about her previous life in Katni.[11]

An investigator, H.N. Banerjee, met the Pathak family and confirmed nine statements Swarnlata had made about them. In fact, he said he was guided to the house of the correct family (there was more than one by that name) by Swarnlata's statements. The lifetime she described corresponded closely with that of a woman named Biya who died twenty years earlier, in 1939.

A little later, some of the Pathaks, as well as Biya's in-laws, visited Swarnlata at home. The Pathaks tested her claims in various ways. "Swarnlata was obliged to give a name or state relationship between

Biya and the person in question. It was not a question of 'Am I your son?' but of 'Tell me who I am.' And on several occasions serious attempts were made to mislead her or deny that she gave the correct answers. And her recognitions usually came quickly."[12] Swarnlata is said to have wept when she met the Pathaks and again when they parted.

Subsequently, Swarnlata went with some of her family members to Katni and to other towns where Biya had spent her married life.

> At Katni, among the Pathaks, she behaved like an older sister of the house, and this with men forty or more years her senior, as the Pathak brothers were. They, moreover, completely accepted her as Biya reborn ... It is perhaps worth noting that the Pathaks are ... rather "Westernized." Sri R.P. Pathak stated that he had had no convictions whatever about reincarnation prior to Swarnlata's visit, which had quite changed his mind.[13]

Stevenson personally investigated the case two years later, interviewing many of the people involved. He observes that the distances between towns are considerable, making travel between Panna and Katni uncommon.

While her memories of Biya's life are interesting, the most compelling aspect of the case is Swarnlata's ability to sing in an unknown language and to accompany this recitation with a dance. This musical performance, which reportedly never varied, was apparently left over from a different lifetime, one that took place after Biya's death and before Swarnlata's birth. Unfortunately, this past-life personality was never identified.

Stevenson writes, "Professor Pal, who was a native of Bengal, identified the songs as Bengali and upon returning to his home in West Bengal he learned that two of them derived from poems by Rabindranath Tagore." The Mishra family did not own a phonograph or radio when Swarnlata began performing her song-and-dance routine, nor had she ever been to a movie. Her parents did not speak Bengali; the songs were, to them, unintelligible.[14]

Another famous case, also from India, involves Ravi Shankar. In July of 1951, Ravi was born in the city of Kanauj. When he was between two and three years old, he identified himself as the son of Jageshwar, a barber in a nearby district. He described the son's murder, identifying the killers and the location of the crime.

In fact, six-year-old Ashok Kumar (known as Munna), the only son of a barber named Jageshwar Prasad, had been murdered a few years before, allegedly by two neighbors, one of whom was a relative, as part of an inheritance scheme. The accused murderers were arrested, but the case against them was dropped.

> [Ravi's] family and neighbors testified to his repeated demand for Munna's toys which he said were in his other home, and to his wish to be taken to that home. He said he needed the toys. He complained that the house in which he lived was not "his house." At least once, when rebuked, he ran out of his house, saying he would go to his former house. He often spoke spontaneously about Munna's murder to members of his family ...
>
> He himself said (in 1962) he was afraid of the two men who had murdered him (Munna), even though he could not explain why he was afraid of them. His mother testified to his extreme fear when he first saw and recognized one of the murderers ... Ravi Shankar's mother testified also to his showing marked fear whenever she took him to the Chinatimini Temple, located in the area of the murder of Munna.[15]

Munna's father Jageshwar learned of the boy's claims and pursued the matter, much to the distress of Ravi's family, who wanted him to keep silent. Ravi's father even beat him as punishment for continuing to speak of a past life. "Such opposition," Stevenson notes, "certainly makes it extremely unlikely that the case could have been worked up for fraudulent purposes by Ravi Shankar's family."[16]

Nevertheless, Jageshwar did succeed in meeting four-year-old Ravi, who volunteered details of the murder that appeared to match up with the retracted confession of one of the suspects.

Could Ravi have learned these things by normal means? While the two families did not know each other, they resided only about half a mile apart, though getting from one house to the other required taking a complicated route down many side streets. The murder was notorious throughout the city, and Ravi's family certainly had heard of it. But of course it occurred before Ravi was born, and there's no evidence his family ever mentioned it to him. Moreover, many of the details supplied by Ravi were known only to the family of the murdered boy and were not public knowledge.

Perhaps the most interesting aspect of the case involves a birthmark that appeared to match the wound inflicted on Munna, whose murderers had slit his throat with a knife or razor. Ravi bore a congenital linear mark across the neck. Ravi himself claimed that the mark in some way represented the fatal cut.

Birthmark and birth defect cases, while uncommon, do crop up in reincarnation research. Perhaps the most striking case involved a boy born with stunted fingers on one hand, who remembered a past life in another village. Investigation revealed that the previous-life personality had suffered a nonfatal industrial accident resulting in the amputation of the fingers of that hand. Other cases have involved unusual puckered birthmarks corresponding to fatal gunshot wounds in the previous life. In some cases, autopsy photos have confirmed an approximate correlation between the locations of the fatal wounds and the birthmarks.[17]

Reincarnation in mediumship

It's sometimes said that reincarnation wasn't part of 19th-century mediumship, and that the topic arose only after reincarnation became trendy in the West, largely owing to the influence of Madame Blavatsky's occult system, Theosophy, and the teachings of the Masons, Rosicrucians, and some Transcendentalists. This is only partly true. Many early communications either deny reincarnation or, as with Swedenborg, make no mention of it; but some explicitly acknowledge it. In general, the idea seems to have met with a more favorable reception on the European continent than in the UK or the US.

One of the earliest systematic studies of mediumship is *The Spirits' Book*, published in 1857 by Hippolyte Rivail under the pen name Allan Kardec. Kardec's communicating spirits view reincarnation as a natural part of spiritual evolution.

Asked, "How can the soul that has not attained to perfection during the corporeal life complete the work of its purification?", the spirits answer: "By undergoing the trial of a new [physical] existence."

> The soul, in purifying itself, undoubtedly undergoes a transformation; but, in order to effect this transformation, it needs the trial of corporeal life ... He who advances quickly spares himself many trials. Nevertheless, these successive incarnations are always very numerous, for progress is almost infinite.[18]

Despite Kardec's work, the idea of reincarnation struggled to gain ground in Great Britain and North America. Writing in 1920, Hereward Carrington observes:

The early French school of spiritists, led by Allan Kardec, accepted reincarnation; the majority of British and American spiritists reject it. Andrew Jackson Davis, for example, was particularly bitter in his denunciation of this doctrine—contending that it was "a magnificent mansion built upon the sand."[19]

Carlos Alvarado offers a thorough rundown of early attitudes toward reincarnation among American and British spiritualists:

> In 1865 an author in the *Spiritual Magazine*, published in England, referred to reincarnation as an "absurd doctrine," an "excrescence on Spiritualism" with nothing to support it, and dispensing with the comfort of finding our loved ones in the beyond ...
>
> The famous trance speaker and writer Emma Hardinge Britten entered the debate [in 1875] ... "The most remarkable and certainly not the least indefensible part of the Re-incarnationist's [sic] theory is, however, not only that they have no facts on which to ground their assertions, like the majority of their fellow believers in Spiritualism, but that they infer there must be countless millions of spirits communicating through other channels who have no knowledge of Re-incarnation, and even emphatically deny its truth."[20]

Some spiritualists used stronger language. Englishman William Howitt wrote, "Lord deliver Spiritualism from the slime and venom of this devil's creed," and, on another occasion, "We may, therefore, ... pronounce the dogma of Reincarnation false as the hell from which it sprung."

Not to be outdone, an American, William Emmette Coleman, denounced reincarnation as a "fungus growth," saying the doctrine "leads to the grossest immoralities, and to general demoralization and laxity of conduct" and would inevitably destroy "all family relationship," a reason "sufficient in itself to everlastingly damn the vile enormity in its entirety."[21]

Arthur Conan Doyle devotes a chapter of his *History of Spiritualism* to reincarnation. He observes that

> spiritualists in England have come to no decision with regard to reincarnation. Some believe in it, many do not, and the general attitude may be taken to be that, as the doctrine cannot be proved, it had better be omitted from the active politics of Spiritualism.

Nevertheless, Doyle concludes:

> On the whole, it seems to the author that the balance of evidence shows that reincarnation is a fact, but not necessarily a universal one. As to the ignorance of our spirit friends upon the point, it concerns their own future, and if we are not clear as to our future, it is possible that they have the same limitations ... As to the natural question, "Why, then, do we not remember such [past-life] existences?" we may point out that such remembrance would enormously complicate our present life, and that such existences may well form a cycle which is all clear to us when we have come to the end of it, when perhaps we may see a whole rosary of lives threaded upon the one personality.[22]

In the same chapter, Doyle also quotes medium Daniel Dunglas Home as saying caustically:

> I meet many who are reincarnationists, and I have had the pleasure of meeting at least twelve who were Marie Antoinette, six or seven Mary Queen of Scots, a whole host of Louis and other kings, about twenty Alexander the Greats, but it remains for me yet to meet a plain John Smith, and I beg of you, if you meet one, to cage him as a curiosity.

Home's objection, often voiced by skeptics even today, is not consistent with modern findings. I've read of no children who spontaneously recall the life of a famous person, and almost no instances of hypnotized patients who make this claim. The idea that anyone remembers a past life as Cleopatra or Napoleon (or their equivalent) has as far as I know, no support in the literature. Most "past lives" are remarkable only for their mundanity.

Therapist Helen Wambach hypnotically regressed 1,088 subjects and analyzed the resulting data in terms of economic classes. In every time period, the lower class (defined as slaves, tribesmen, peasants, and common soldiers) ranged from 59% to 77%. "If my subjects were fantasizing," she writes, "their fantasies were bleak and barren. The great majority of my subjects went through their lives wearing rough homespun garments, living in crude huts, and eating bland cereal grain with their fingers from wooden bowls ... The majority of [hypnotically evoked] lower class lives at all time periods belonged to people who farmed the land."

As for how many people "seemed to have been Cleopatra or high priests in Egypt in past lives," as Wambach puts it, the answer is: remarkably few.

> None of my subjects reported a past life as a historical personage. It is possible that if they had recalled such a life, they might have been embarrassed to report it. I had several high priests and one person who reported seeing himself as a Pharaoh of Egypt, but their percentage in the sample was very low. The 7% [on average] who reported upper class lives did not feel them to be particularly pleasant.[23]

Although most of her subjects were "white middle class Californians," Wambach found a complicated distribution of races and ethnicities in past-life accounts, with Caucasians in the minority. And while women made up 78% of the first test group and 55% of the second group, past-life personalities reported by each group were evenly split between males and females.[24]

The overall percentages in Wambach's study roughly match historical breakdowns in terms of economic status and sex, and don't unduly favor one race or ethnic type over another. And, contrary to D.D. Home, the celebrities of history are scarcely represented at all.

On the whole—to borrow Arthur Conan Doyle's judicious phrase—it appears that American and British attitudes toward reincarnation in the 19th century were so hostile as to discourage the subject from even coming up in the séance room or, perhaps, being reported if it did come up. (Recall that Anne Manning Robbins "thought best to omit [a] whole passage" of channeled material from her 1909 book, apparently because it contradicted Christian orthodoxy.[25])

There is, however, another possible explanation for the contradictory accounts given by spirit communicators. Reincarnation may be more complex than we assume. It could be argued that reincarnation both *is* and *is not* a reality, depending on how you look at it.

Many selves

How would reincarnation work? We might imagine a simple linear model in which life A terminates and, usually after a period of rest and recuperation, life B begins. But many channeled sources draw a more complicated picture.

Seth, speaking through Jane Roberts, takes issue with the idea that linear time as we understand it is even real.

> Your idea of time is false. Time as you experience it is an illusion caused by your own physical senses ... The physical senses can only perceive reality a little bit at a time, and so it seems to you that one moment exists and is gone forever, and the next moment comes and like the one before also disappears.
>
> But everything in the universe exists at one time, simultaneously. The first words ever spoken still ring through the universe, and in your terms, the last words ever spoken have already been said, for there is no beginning. It is only your perception that is limited.
>
> There is no past, present, and future. These only appear to those who exist within three-dimensional reality. Since I am no longer in it, I can perceive what you do not. There is also a part of you that is not imprisoned within physical reality, and that part of you knows that there is only an Eternal Now. The part of you who knows this is the whole self.[26]

This idea is not new. Immanuel Kant hypothesized that space and time are not ultimately real; in his system, they are "phenomenal" (empirical) constructs, not part of "noumenal" (transcendent) reality.

To put it in Platonic terms, space and time are merely shadows we mistake for reality, while the World of Forms is spaceless and timeless.

Essentially, Seth is telling us that past, present, and future are concepts that don't apply to the higher self (an idea consistent with the timelessness characteristic of immersion in the light, as discussed in Chapter 14). Accordingly, all incarnations are lived simultaneously, even though, as a matter of convenience, they can be described as past or future lives from our current perspective. Moreover, each incarnation is experienced by a different ego, so it is not "I" who will reincarnate, but another split-off fragment of my higher self, or (to put it differently) another member of my group soul.

> The various reincarnational selves can be superficially regarded as portions of a crossword puzzle, for they are all portions of the whole, and yet they can exist separately ...
>
> What you have instead [of sequential time] is something like the developments narrated in *The Three Faces of Eve* [a book and movie about multiple personality disorder]. You have dominant egos, all a part of an inner identity, dominant in various existences. But the separate existences exist simultaneously. Only the egos involved make the time distinction. 145 BC, AD 145, a thousand years in your past, and a thousand years in your future—all exist now ...
>
> It is interesting that the personalities [in *The Three Faces of Eve*] did alternate, and all were in existence at once, so to speak, even though only one was dominant at any given time. In the same way, so-called past personalities are present in you now but not dominant ... Since all events occur at once in actuality, there is little to be gained by saying that a past event causes a present one. Past experience does not cause present experience. You are forming past, present, and future—simultaneously. Since events appear to you in sequence, this is difficult to explain.
>
> When it is said that certain characteristics from a past life influence or cause present patterns of behavior, such statements—and I have made some of them—are highly simplified to make certain points clear.
>
> The whole self is aware of all of the experiences of all of its egos, and since one identity forms them, there are bound to be similarities between them and shared characteristics. The material I have given you on reincarnation is quite valid, particularly for working purposes, but it is a simplified version

of what actually occurs.[27]

Each incarnated personality, then, represents only the tip of the iceberg of the total personality, which is the sum of all its parts. The higher self chooses when and where to be incarnated, each time assuming a different ego-persona to carry out the mission. Though it has a plan, it cannot control the course of the incarnated personality's life, which is largely determined by the particular ego's free-will choices. As a result, some incarnations are more successful than others; some ego-personas will learn the lessons they were intended to learn and contribute this knowledge to the total personality (higher self, group soul), while others will not. In the event that a necessary lesson is not learned, a new incarnation by a new ego-persona is necessary.

Karma exists, but, Seth says, it is not punishment; instead, it "presents the opportunity for development. It enables the individual to enlarge understanding through experience, to fill in gaps of ignorance, to do what should be done."[28]

Or as the channeled voice of F.W.H. Myers puts it:

> The fact that we do appear on earth to be paying for the sins of another life is, in a certain sense, true. It was our life, and yet not our life. In other words, a soul belonging to the group of which I am a part lived that previous life which built up for me the framework of my earthly life, lived it before I had passed through the gates of birth ...
>
> There may be contained within that spirit [= higher self, group soul] twenty souls, a hundred souls, a thousand souls. The number varies. It is different for each man. But what the Buddhists would call the karma I had brought with me from a previous life is, very frequently, not that of my life, but of the life of a soul that preceded me by many years on earth and left for me the pattern which made my life. I, too, wove a pattern for another of my group during my earthly career. We are all of us distinct, though we are influenced by others of our community on the various planes of being ...
>
> I shall not live again on earth, but a new soul, one who will join our group, will shortly enter into the pattern or karma I have woven for him on earth.[29]

Returning to the metaphor of the higher self as a diamond, which we looked at in Chapter 15, we might say that each shining facet is a separate ego-persona requiring a separate incarnation, all timelessly coexisting, all contributing to the perfection of the whole.

AFTERWORD

> I am a part of all that I have met;
> Yet all experience is an arch wherethro'
> Gleams that untravell'd world whose margin fades
> For ever and for ever when I move.
>
> —Tennyson, "Ulysses"

IN SPY THRILLERS and military adventure stories, there often comes a point where the hero, operating behind enemy lines, has completed his mission, or as much of it as possible. He now requires an extraction —a way out.

Likewise, to be born is to begin an undercover mission, a dangerous foray into hostile territory with an unpredictable outcome. We go in with a plan, but we can't be sure of following it. Life, as we say, gets in the way.

At a certain point, having accomplished all we can, extraction becomes necessary. Maybe we make the call; some people really do seem to choose when and how they pass on, even without committing suicide. Or maybe the call is made for us by our superiors at headquarters, our group soul and higher self.

One way or the other, we are lifted out of enemy territory and escorted home to rest, recuperate, and assess the success (partial or complete) of our mission.

Death, then, is not a defeat. It is simply the end of one experience and the beginning of another. Or to put it a little differently, it is a transition from one state of mind to another.

The arch of experience

I'm not sure we appreciate what a remarkable thing it is to be conscious. Most of the physical universe consists of empty space, and much of the rest consists of clouds of interstellar dust, the compacted agglomerations of gas that we call stars, and the barren, mostly lifeless chunks of rock called planets. Life—no matter how common it may prove to be, and even if, like Myers's flame-beings, it flickers at the heart of the neutron star—must make up a very small part of the universe; life capable of self-aware consciousness must be even more rare.

To exist as a sentient, conceptualizing, self-knowing being in a universe of dust, gas, and rock, of microbes, worms, and termites, is an exceptional privilege. Every one of us is the winner of a cosmic lottery that allows us to stand out from the monotonous insensate physicality and robotic programmed instincts that surround us.

Consciousness not only defines us; it *is* us. It is not only all our thoughts, but all our experiences, observations, and actions. Even our unconscious behaviors become real to us only through our faculty of awareness. Tennyson writes of the arch of experience "wherethro' gleams that untravell'd world whose margin fades for ever and for ever when I move." That arch is our subjective outlook, which frames everything we know and everything we have.

The survival of consciousness after death does not, therefore, involve merely the survival of a *part* of us. It is the survival of the *whole* of us. Our physical body exists, for us, only in our own mind. Discarding that body makes very little difference. It's merely taking off a costume, which is immediately replaced by another body, one we perceive as every bit as physical, tangible, and real as the one we've cast aside. And in each case the body in question exists, for us, only through our subjective awareness. In effect, we are trading one mental experience for another. That doesn't sound particularly traumatic, does it?

Yes, the process leading up to death may be difficult and painful. I don't discount the emotional and physical suffering experienced by many people in their final stages of biological life. The physical part of the dying process can be agonizing, the short-term emotional effects hard to bear. What I want to focus on, however, is the spiritual transformation we all undergo.

When my father lay dying, immobile and comatose, a hospice nurse commented to me that while he looked nearly dead, he was actually more alive than he had ever been. What the nurse meant was that new potentialities were opening up to his expanding consciousness.

I think this is true. And this is what ultimately matters.

Bodily pain will pass. Earthly suffering will fade.

But consciousness is forever.

postscript

Leo Tolstoy, *The Death of Ivan Ilych*[1]:

>Till about three in the morning he was in a state of stupefied misery. It seemed to him that he and his pain were being thrust into a narrow, deep black sack, but though they were pushed further and further in they could not be pushed to the bottom ...
>
>He felt that his agony was due to his being thrust into that black hole and still more to his not being able to get right into it ...
>
>Suddenly some force struck him in the chest and side, making it still harder to breathe, and he fell through the hole and there at the bottom was a light ...
>
>At that very moment ... it was revealed to him that though his life had not been what it should have been, this could still be rectified. He asked himself, "What is the right thing?" and grew still, listening. Then he felt that someone was kissing his hand. He opened his eyes, looked at his son, and felt sorry for him. His wife came up to him and he glanced at her. She was gazing at him open-mouthed, with undried tears on her nose and cheek and a despairing look on her face. He felt sorry for her too ...
>
>And suddenly it grew clear to him that what had been oppressing him and would not leave him was all dropping away at once from two sides, from ten sides, and from all sides. He was sorry for them, he must act so as not to hurt them: release them and free himself from these sufferings. "How good and how simple!" he thought. "And the pain?" he asked himself. "What has become of it? Where are you, pain?"
>
>He turned his attention to it.
>
>"Yes, here it is. Well, what of it? Let the pain be.
>
>"And death ... where is it?"
>
>He sought his former accustomed fear of death and did not find it. "Where is it? What death?" There was no fear because there was no death.
>
>In place of death there was light.

BIBLIOGRAPHY

Books

Abbott, Edwin A., *Flatland: A Romance of Many Dimensions*, Dover 1992 (1884); https://www.gutenberg.org/ebooks/201

Alexander, Eben & Tompkins, Ptolemy, *Map of Heaven*. Simon & Schuster 2014)

Atwater, PMH, *We Live Forever*. A.R.E. Press 2004

Baird, A.T. (ed), *One Hundred Cases for Survival after Death*. Ruttle, Shaw & Wetherill 1944; https://ia600307.us.archive.org/27/items/onehundredcasesfoobair/onehundredcasesfoobair.pdf

Barrett, Florence Elizabeth, *Personality Survives Death*. White Crow 2020 (1937)

Barrett, Sir William, *Death-Bed Visions*. Methuen & Co 1926; https://archive.org/details/b29813992/mode/2up

Betty, Stafford, *The Afterlife Unveiled*. O-Books 2011

Bobrow, Robert S., *The Witch in the Waiting Room*, Thunder's Mouth Press 2006

Botkin, Allan L. & Hogan, R. Craig, *Induced After Death Communication: A New Therapy for Healing Grief and Trauma*. Hampton Roads 2005

Bowman, Carol, *Children's Past Lives*. Bantam 1998

Bucke, Richard Maurice, *Cosmic Consciousness: A Study in the Evolution of the Human Mind*. Innes & Sons 1901

Brown, John, *Mediumistic Experiences of John Brown, the Medium of the Rockies*. Office of the Philosophical Journal 1897

Buhlman, William, *Adventures Beyond the Body*. HarperCollins 1996

Buhlman, William, *The Secret of the Soul*. HarperCollins 2001

Bush, Nancy Evans, *Dancing Past the Dark: Distressing Near-Death Experiences*. 2012

Callanan, Maggie & Kelley, Patricia, *Final Gifts*. Simon & Schuster 1993

Carter, Chris, *Science and the Afterlife Experience*. Inner Traditions 2012

Carter, Chris, *Science and the Near-Death Experience*. Inner Traditions 2010

Chambers, John, *The Secret Life of Genius*. Destiny 2009

Chism, Stephen, *The Afterlife of Leslie Stringfellow*. University of Arkansas Press 2005

Contenau, Georges, *Everyday Life in Babylon and Assyria* W.W. Norton & Co 1966

Cornillier, Pierre-Emile, *The Survival of the Soul and Its Evolution after Death*. White Crow Books 2017 (1921)

Crookall, Robert, *The Supreme Adventure*. James Clarke & Co 1961

Crookall, Robert, *More Astral Projections*. Aquarian Press 1964

Crookall, Robert, *Out of the Body Experiences*. Citadel Press 1992 (1970)

Cummins, Geraldine & Gibbes, E. B. (ed.), *The Road to Immortality*. Ivor Nicholson & Watson 1933;
http://iapsop.com/ssoc/1933__gibbes_cummins__the_road_to_immortality.pdf

Cummins, Geraldine, *Beyond Human Personality*. Ivor Nicholson & Watson 1935;
http://v-j-enterprises.com/myers/BeyondHumanPersonality.pdf

DeSalvo, John, *Andrew Jackson Davis: The First American Prophet and Clairvoyant*. Lulu.com 2005

Dostoevsky, Fyodor (trans. Constance Garnett), *Crime and Punishment*. 1866;
http://www.literaturepage.com/read/crimeandpunishment.html

Dostoevsky, Fyodor (trans. Richard Pevear & Larissa Volokhonsky), *Crime and Punishment*. Vintage Classics 2021

Doyle, Arthur Conan, *The History of Spiritualism*. Cassell & Co 1926;
https://www.arthur-conan-doyle.com/index.php/The_History_of_Spiritualism

D'Souza, Dinesh, *Life After Death: The Evidence*. Salem Books 2015

Emmons, Charles & Emmons, Penelope, *Guided by Spirit*. Writers Club Press 2003

Erman, Adolf, *Life in Ancient Egypt*. Dover 1971 (1894)

Everitt, Anthony, *Augustus*. Random House 2006

Farr, Sidney Saylor, *What Tom Sawyer Learned from Dying*. Hampton Roads 1993

Fenwick, Peter & Fenwick, Elizabeth, *The Truth in the Light*. Berkley 1997

Fenwick, Peter & Fenwick, Elizabeth, *Past Lives: An Investigation Into Reincarnation Memories*. Berkley 2001

Everard Feilding et al., *Sittings with Eusapia Palladino & Other Studies*. University Books 1963

Findley, Arthur, *On the Edge of the Etheric*. Rider & Co 1931

Finkel, Irving, *The First Ghosts*. Hodder & Stoughton 2021

Fiore, Edith, *The Unquiet Dead: A Psychologist Treats Spirit Possession*. Ballantine 1995 (1987)

Fisher, Joe, *The Siren Call of Hungry Ghosts*. Paraview Press 2001

Greaves, Helen, *Testimony of Light*. Rider 1969

Greyson, Bruce, *After: A Doctor Explores What Near-Death Experiences Reveal about Life and Beyond*. St. Martin's Essentials 2021

Gurney, Edmund; Myers, Frederic W.H.; Podmore, Frank, *Phantasms of the Living*. E. P. Dutton 1918 (2nd ed., abr.);
https://archive.org/details/phantasmsoflivinoogurn/mode/2up

Hancock, Graham, *Supernatural*. Disinformation Co. 2007

Hansel, C.E.M., *ESP: A Scientific Evaluation*. Charles Scribner's Sons 1966

Heath, Pamela Rae & Klimo, Jon, *Suicide: What Really Happens in the Afterlife?* North Atlantic Books 2006

Holt, Henry, *The Cosmic Relations and Immortality*, vol 2. Houghton Mifflin 1919

Hunter Jack (ed), *Deep Weird: The Varieties of High Strangeness Experience*. August Night 2023

Kardec, Allan, *The Spirits Book*. Cosimo 2006 (1856)

Kardec, Allan (trans. Darrell W. Kimball, Marsha M. Seiz, Ily Reis), *Heaven and Hell: Divine Justice according to Spiritism*. International Spiritist Council 2011 (1865)

Keene, M. Lamar & Spraggett, Allen, *The Psychic Mafia*. St. Martin's Press 1976; https://archive.org/details/psychicmafia00keen/page/n5/mode/2up

Kelly, Edward; Kelly, Emily Williams; et al., *Irreducible Mind*. Rowman & Littlefield 2007

Lanza, Robert, *Biocentrism: How Life and Consciousness are the Keys to Understanding the True Nature of the Universe*, BenBella Books 2010

Leland, Kurt, *The Unanswered Question*. Hampton Roads 2002

Lodge, Oliver, *Raymond, or Life and Death*. George H. Doran Co 1916; https://www.gutenberg.org/ebooks/51086

Mack, John, *Abduction: Human Encounters with Aliens*. Simon & Schuster 1994

McLuhan, Robert, *Randi's Prize*. Matador 2010

Miller, Francis Trevelyan, *Thomas A. Edison, Benefactor of Mankind*. John C. Winston 1931

Monroe, Robert, *Journeys out of the Body*. Broadway Books 1992

Moody, Raymond, *Life After Life*. Bantam 1976

Moody, Raymond (with Paul Perry), *The Light Beyond*. Bantam 1988

Moody, Raymond (with Paul Perry), *Reunions: Visionary Encounters with Departed Loved Ones*. Ivy 1993

Moorjani, Anita, *Dying to be Me*. Hay House 2012

Moreira-Almeida, Alexander; Costa, Marianna de Abreu; & Coelho, Humberto Schubert; *Science of Life after Death*. SpringerBriefs in Psychology 2022

Morse, Melvin (with Paul Perry), *Closer to the Light*. Ivy Books 1990

Myers, Frederic W.H., *Human Personality and Its Survival of Bodily Death*. Longmans, Green & Co. 1906

Neihardt, John G., *Black Elk Speaks*. William Morrow & Co 1932;

Newton, Michael, *Journey of Souls*. Llewellyn 2010 (rev. ed.)

Playfair, Guy Lyon, *If This Be Magic*. White Crow 2011

Randi, James, *Flim-Flam!* Prometheus 1982

Radin, Dean, *Supernormal: Science, Yoga, and the Evidence for Extraordinary Psychic Abilities*. Deepak Chopra Books 2013

Riggs, Christina, *Ancient Egyptian Magic: A Hands-On Guide*. Thames & Hudson 2020

Ring, Kenneth, *Life at Death*. William Morrow & Co 1980

Ring, Kenneth, *Heading toward Omega*. Quill/William Morris 1985

Ring, Kenneth, *The Omega Project*. William Morrow 1992

Ring, Kenneth, *Lessons from the Light*. Moment Point 2006

Ring, Kenneth & Cooper, Sharon, *Mindsight*. William James Center for Consciousness Studies 1999

Roberts, Jane, *The Seth Material*. Fireside 1972

Robbins, Anne Manning, *Both Sides of the Veil*. Sherman, French and Co. 1909; https://www.google.com/books/edition/Both_Sides_of_the_Veil/CdcRAAAAYAAJ

Rogo, D. Scott, *Leaving the Body*. Prentice Hall 1983

Rogo, D. Scott, *The Search for Yesterday*. Anomalist Books 2005

Rommer, Barbara R., *Blessing in Disguise*. Llewellyn 2000

Rubenstein, Ian, *Consulting Spirit*. Anomalist 2011

Sabom, Michael, *Recollections of Death*. Harper & Row 1982

Sabom, Michael, *Light and Death*. Zondervan 1998

Sacks, Oliver, *Musicophilia*. Knopf 2007

Saltmarsh, H.F., *Evidence of Personal Survival from Cross Correspondences*. G. Bell & Sons 1938

Schwartz, Stephan A., *The Secret Vaults of Time*, Hampton Roads 2005

Sherwood, Jane, *The Country Beyond*. C.W. Daniel 2004

Shushan, Gregory, *The Next World*. White Crow 2022

Snell, Joy, *The Ministry of Angels*. G. Bell and Sons 1920

Stead, W.T., *Life Eternal*. White Crow 2020 (1933)

Stevenson, Ian, *Twenty Cases Suggestive of Reincarnation*. University Press of Virginia 1974

Strassman, Rick, *DMT: The Spirit Molecule*. Park Street Press 2001.

Swedenborg, Emanuel (trans. George F. Dole), *Heaven and Hell*. Swedenborg Foundation 2000

Tart, Charles, *The End of Materialism*. New Harbinger 2009

Taylor, Greg, *Stop Worrying: There Probably Is an Afterlife*. Daily Grail 2013

Thomas, Rev. Charles Drayton, *From Life to Life*. White Crow 2018 (1945)

Tolstoy, Leo, (trans. Louise Maude & Aylmer Maude), *The Death of Ivan Ilych* 1886; https://open.lib.umn.edu/ivanilich/chapter/full-text-english/

Tolstoy, Leo, (trans. Louise Maude & Aylmer Maude), *Hadji Murad*. MobileReference 2010 (1912)

Varghese, Roy Abraham, *There Is Life After Death*. Weiser 2009

Wade, Jenny, *Changes of Mind: A Holonomic Theory of the Evolution of Consciousness*. State University of New York Press 1996

Wambach, Helen, *Reliving Past Lives*. Barnes & Noble 2000 (1978)

Wedgwood, C.V., *The Thirty Years War*. New York Review of Books 2005 (1938)

Weiss, Brian L, *Many Lives, Many Masters*. Fireside/Simon & Shuster 1988

Weiss, Jess E. (ed.), The Vestibule. Pocket 1997 (1972)

Wells, H. G., *The Door in the Wall and Other Stories*; Project Gutenberg 1996; https://www.gutenberg.org/files/456/456-h/456-h.htm

Whitton, Joel L. & Fisher, Joe, *Life Between Life*. Doubleday 1986

Wickland, Carl, *Thirty Years Among the Dead*. National Psychological Institute 1924; 1980 edition @ https://archive.org/details/thirty-years-among-the-dead-1980-353pp-carl-wickland/mode/2up

Zaleski, Carol, *The Life of the World to Come*. Oxford University Press 1996

Articles and web posts

Alvarado, Carlos S., "Attending to the Past: William G. Roll and the Old Psychical Research Literature," *Paranormal Review* No 68. October 2013

Alvarado, Carlos. S. "Out-of-Body Experience (OBE)," *Psi Encyclopedia*. Society for Psychical Research. 2015; https://psi-encyclopedia.spr.ac.uk/articles/out-body-experience-obe

Alvarado, Carlos S., "Skepticism about Reincarnation in Nineteenth-Century Spiritualist Articles," *Parapsychology* (blog) January 8, 2020; https://carlossalvarado.wordpress.com/2020/01/08/skepticism-about-reincarnation-in-nineteenth-century-spiritualist-articles/

Awaken, "Ernest Hemingway's Near Death Experience." November 15 2020; https://awaken.com/2019/11/ernest-hemingways-near-death-experience/

Belmonte, Adriana, "Nine of the Most Chilling Last Words in History," *Insider*. June 19, 2018; https://www.insider.com/chilling-last-words-history-2018-6

Benedict, Mellen-Thomas, "The Light Kept Changing into Different Figures..." *Light Ascension*; https://www.lightascension.com/arts/Throughthelight.htm

Bonenfant, Richard J., "A Near-Death Experience Followed by the Visitation of an 'Angel-Like' Being," *Journal of Near-Death Studies*, Vol 19 No 2, Winter 2000, pp 103ff; https://digital.library.unt.edu/ark:/67531/metadc798984/

Broughton, Richard S., & Cheryl H. Alexander. "An Attempted Replication of the PRL Ganzfeld Research." *The Journal of Parapsychology* Vol 61 No 3, Sept. 1997, pp. 207ff

Carroll, Robert Todd, "Ectoplasm," *The Skeptic's Dictionary*. October 18, 2015; https://skepdic.com/ectoplasm.html

Cassol, Helena, et al., "Near-Death Experience Memories Include More Episodic Components Than Flashbulb Memories," *Frontiers in Psychology*, Vol 11, May 13, 2020; https://www.frontiersin.org/articles/10.3389/fpsyg.2020.00888/full

CBS News, "What Made Him 3-Time Lottery Winner?" May 3, 2006; https://www.cbsnews.com/news/what-made-him-3-time-lottery-winner/

Cicoria, Tony & Cicoria, Jordan, "Getting Comfortable With Near-Death Experiences," *Missouri Medicine*, July-August 2014; Vol 111 No 4, pp 304—307; https://www.ncbi.nlm.nih.gov/pmc/articles/PMC6179462/

Cox, Benjamin R. III, "The Science of Mediumship and the Evidence of Survival" (2009). Master of Liberal Studies Theses. 31. http://scholarship.rollins.edu/mls/31

Douven, Igor, "Abduction," *Stanford Encyclopedia of Philosophy*. 2021; https://plato.stanford.edu/entries/abduction

Fitzgerald, Rory, "As I Lay Dying a Voice Said: 'Let's Go,'" *Catholic Herald*. April 9, 2012; https://catholicherald.co.uk/as-i-lay-dying-a-voice-said-lets-go/

Graveland, Bill, "Five-Time Lotto Winner Gets Another $17M," *Toronto Star* Nov. 3, 2009; https://www.thestar.com/news/canada/2009/11/03/fivetime_lotto_winner_gets_another_17m.html

Greyson, Bruce, "Seeing Dead People Not Known to Have Died: 'Peak in Darien' Experiences," *Anthropology & Humanism*. Vol 35, No 2. December 2010; https://www.researchgate.net/publication/229658803_Seeing_Dead_People_Not_Known_to_Have_Died_Peak_in_Darien_Experiences

Greyson, Bruce, Kelly, Edward F., & Ross, W. J., "Surge of Neurophysiological Activity in the Dying Brain," *The Proceedings of the National Academy of Sciences*. Vol 110 No 47. November 6, 2013; https://www.pnas.org/doi/full/10.1073/pnas.1316937110

Hamilton, Trevor, "Gladys Osborne Leonard," *Psi Encyclopedia*. Society for Psychical Research 2022; https://psi-encyclopedia.spr.ac.uk/articles/gladys-osborne-leonard

Haraldsson, Erlendur. "Survey of Claimed Encounters with the Dead." *Omega* No 19, pp 103—113. 1988—89

Haraldsson, Erlendur & Stevenson, Ian, "A Communicator of the 'Drop In' Type in Iceland: The Case of Runolfur Runolfsson," *Journal of the American Society for Psychical Research*, Vol 69, pp 35—39. January 1975

Heim, Albert, "The Experience of Dying from Falls" (original: "Notizen über den Tod durch Absturz"), *Yearbook of the Swiss Alpine Club*. 1892

Hoffman, Jan, "A New Vision for Dreams of the Dying." *The New York Times*. February 2, 2016

Hodgson, Richard, "A Further Record of Observations of Certain Phenomena of Trance." *Proceedings of the Society for Psychical Research*, No 13, pp 284—582. February 1898

Huddleston Jr, Tom, "These People Won the Lottery Multiple Times, Taking Home Millions—a Harvard Prof. Talks Odds," CNBC. June 1, 2019; https://www.cnbc.com/2019/05/31/harvard-prof-on-odds-of-winning-multiple-lotteries-like-these-people.html

Hyman, Ray, "Evaluation of Program on Anomalous Mental Phenomena." University of Oregon. 1995. https://www.ics.uci.edu/~jutts/hyman.html

Irwin, Lee, "Reincarnation in America: A Brief Historical Overview." *Religions*, Vol 8 No 10 p 222ff. 2017; https://doi.org/10.3390/rel8100222

James W (pseud.), "James W NDE," NDE1255 James W NDE 3168, Near-Death Experience Research Foundation;
https://www.nderf.org/Experiences/1james_w_nde.html

James, William, *The Varieties of Religious Experience*. Longmans, Green, & Co 1902

Jansen, K.L.R., "Ketamine and Quantum Psychiatry," *Asylum Magazine*, Vol 11 No 3 1999; https://bibliography.maps.org/resource/16239

Janssen, Scott, "Near the End of Life My Hospice Patient Had a Ghostly Visitor." *The Washington Post*. January 2, 2021

Johns Hopkins Medicine, Media Relations and Public Affairs, "Hopkins Scientists Show Hallucinogen in Mushrooms Creates Universal 'Mystical' Experience." July 11, 2006;
https://www.hopkinsmedicine.org/Press_releases/2006/07_11_06.html

Johnson, Alice, "On the Automatic Writing of Mrs. Holland," *Proceedings of the Society for Psychical Research*. Vol 21. Robert Macleose & Co Ltd 1909;
https://www.google.com/books/edition/Proceedings_of_the_Society_for_Psychical/RttvRGGcjLgC

Jones, Chris, "Oral Histories of 2013: Roger Ebert's Wife, Chaz, on His Final Moments," *Esquire*, Dec 2013

Khanna, Surbhi & Greyson, Bruce, "Near-Death Experiences and Posttraumatic Growth," *The Journal of Nervous and Mental Disease*. Vol 203 No 10, pp 749-755, October 2015.

LaMotte, Sandee, "Near-Death Experiences Tied to Brain Activity after Death, Study Says," CNN. September 14, 2023; https://www.cnn.com/2023/09/14/health/near-death-experience-study-wellness/index.html

Lopez, Ursula; Forster, Alain; et al., "Near-Death Experience in a Boy Undergoing Uneventful Elective surgery under General Anesthesia," *Pediatric Anesthesia* No 16 pp 85—88. January 2006; https://www.newdualism.org/nde-papers/Lopez/Lopez-Pediatric%20Anesthesia_2005-16-85-88.pdf

Mark, Joshua J., "Egyptian Afterlife—The Field of Reeds." *World History Encyclopedia*. March 28, 2016;
https://www.worldhistory.org/article/877/egyptian-afterlife--the-field-of-reeds/

Matlock, J. G., "Reincarnation Intermission Memories," *Psi Encyclopedia*. Society for Psychical Research. 2017; https://psi-encyclopedia.spr.ac.uk/articles/reincarnation-intermission-memories

McLuhan, Robert, "Miami Poltergeist." *Psi Encyclopedia*. Society for Psychical Research. 2017; https://psi-encyclopedia.spr.ac.uk/articles/miami-poltergeist

McNear, Tom, "Analytical Overlay in Remote Viewing." *Remote Viewing Instructional Services*. Feb 28, 2017; https://rviewer.com/analytical-overlay-in-remote-viewing/

Meredith, Fionola, "Going into the Light." *The Irish Times*. March 22, 2011

Nahm, Michael, "Terminal Lucidity in People with Mental Illness and Other Mental Disability." Journal of Near-Death Studies, Vol 28 No 2, winter, pp 86—106; https://digital.library.unt.edu/ark:/67531/metadc461761/

Nahm, Michael & Greyson, Bruce, "Terminal Lucidity in Patients with Chronic Schizophrenia and Dementia: A Survey of the Literature." *Journal of Nervous and Mental Disease*. Dec 2009. Vol 197, No 12, pp 942-4; https://journals.lww.com/jonmd/Abstract/2009/12000/Terminal_Lucidity_in_Patients_With_Chronic.12.aspx

Pearson, Patricia; Mossbridge, Julia; Beischel, Julie, "Crisis Impressions: A Historical and Conceptual Review," *Threshold: Journal of Interdisciplinary Consciousness Studies*. Vol 5 No 2, 2023; https://www.windbridge.org/papers/TJICS-Crisis-Impressions-2023.pdf

Peter N (pseud.), "Peter N NDE," 3253 Peter N NDE 6584/10105, Near-Death Experience Research Foundation; https://www.nderf.org/Experiences/1peter_n_nde_6584.html

Penman, Danny, "Could There Be Proof to the Theory that We're ALL Psychic?" *The Daily Mail*. 28 January 2008; https://www.dailymail.co.uk/news/article-510762/Could-proof-theory-ALL-psychic.html

John Piippo, "A.J. Ayer Was Nicer After He Died." JonPiippo.com, March 25, 2010; https://www.johnpiippo.com/2010/03/aj-ayer-was-nicer-after-he-died.html

Poets.org, "Famous Last Words"; https://poets.org/text/famous-last-words

Potter, Linda, "Proof of Heaven: An Interview with Dr. Eben Alexander," *BellaSpark Magazine*. Jul/Aug 2013; https://bluetoad.com/publication/?i=165256&article_id=1441491

Prescott, "Palladino," *Michael Prescott's Blog*. July 17, 2006; https://michaelprescott.typepad.com/michael_prescotts_blog/2006/07/palladino.html

Prescott, Michael, "Under the Table," *Michael Prescott's Blog*. November 06, 2009; https://michaelprescott.typepad.com/michael_prescotts_blog/2009/11/under-the-table.html

Prescott, Michael, "The Diamond," *Michael Prescott's Blog*. December 22, 2012; https://michaelprescott.typepad.com/michael_prescotts_blog/2012/12/the-diamond.html

Project Hyakumeizan (pseud.), "I Noted the Situation Was Serious." *One Hundred Mountains*. July 6 2016; https://onehundredmountains.blogspot.com/2016/07/i-noted-situation-was-serious.html

Radin, Dean, "Skeptic Agrees that Remote Viewing Is Proven." *Entangled Minds* blog, Sept 14, 2009; http://deanradin.blogspot.com/2009/09/skeptic-agrees-that-remote-viewing-is.html

Ring, Kenneth, & Cooper, Sharon, "Near-Death and Out-of-Body Experiences in the Blind: A Study of Apparent Eyeless Vision," *Journal of Near-Death Studies*. Vol 16 No 2 Winter 1997 pp 101—147

Ring, Kenneth & Lawrence, Madelaine, "Further Evidence for Veridical Perception During Near-Death Experiences," *Journal of Near-Death Studies,* Vol, 11 No 4. Summer 1993

Sabom, Michael, "Response to Gracia Fay Ellwood's 'Religious Experience, Religious Worldviews, and Near-Death Studies,'" *Journal of Near-Death Studies.* Vol 19, No 1. September 2000

Sanderson, Alan, "Spirit Releasement Therapy in a Case Featuring Depression and Panic," *European Journal of Clinical Hypnosis,* April 4, 1998

Sanderson, Alan, "Spirit Release in Clinical Psychiatry—What Can We Learn?" *International Journal of Regression Therapy* 2014

Schwartz, Stephan A., "Finding Saddam Hussein: A Study in Applied Remote Viewing," *EdgeScience* No 36, pp 5—10, December 2018; https://netwerknde.nl/wp-content/uploads/Finding_Saddam_Hussein_Remote_Viewing.pdf

Silva, Lee A., "The Mysterious Morgan Earp," *HistoryNet*. January 16, 2018; https://www.historynet.com/mysterious-morgan-earp/

Stevenson, Ian, "Birthmarks and Birth Defects Corresponding to Wounds on Deceased Persons," *Journal of Scientific Exploration*, vol 7, no 4, pp 403-410. 1993; https://med.virginia.edu/perceptual-studies/wp-content/uploads/sites/360/2016/12/STE39stevenson-1.pdf

Stevenson, Ian, "The Contribution of Apparitions to the Evidence for Survival." *Journal of the Society for Psychical Research* no 76, pp 341—358. 1982

Swedenborg Foundation, "Swedenborg's Life"; https://swedenborg.com/emanuel-swedenborg/about-life/

Taylor, Greg, "The Dude's Mind Abides," *The Daily Grail* blog, September 30, 2008; https://www.dailygrail.com/2008/09/the-dudes-mind-abides/

Tennyson, Alfred, "Ulysses"; https://www.poetryfoundation.org/poems/45392/ulysses

Thomas, Charles Drayton, *An Amazing Experiment*. Two Worlds Publishing Company Ltd 1904; http://www.survivalafterdeath.info/library/thomas/amazing/contents.htm

Thomason, Sarah Grey, "Xenoglossy," University of Pittsburgh 1995; http://www-personal.umich.edu/~thomason/papers/xenogl.pdf

Tucker, Jim B., "Children Who Claim to Remember Previous Lives: Past, Present, and Future Research," *Journal of Scientific Exploration*, vol 21, no 3, pp 543-552. 2007

Tymn, Michael, "Opera Composer Tells of Psychic & Mediumistic Experiences," *Michael Tymn's Blog*. Jan 4, 2021 ; http://whitecrowbooks.com/michaeltymn/entry/opera_composer_tells_of_psychic_mediumistic_experiences

Tymn, Michael, "Lurancy Vennum," *Psi Encyclopedia*. Society for Psychical Research. 2015; https://psi-encyclopedia.spr.ac.uk/articles/lurancy-vennum

Wetenhall, John, "Who Is The Lucky Four-Time Lottery Winner?" *ABC News*, July 7, 2010; https://abcnews.go.com/Business/texas-woman-wins-millions-lottery-fourth-time/story?id=11097894

Whitworth, Brian, "Quantum Realism," https://brianwhitworth.com/quantum-realism/

Woerlee, Gerald, "Review of 'Evidence of the Afterlife,'" undated; http://neardth.com/evidence-of-the-afterlife.php

Zingrone, N. L., "Pleasurable Western Adult Near-Death Experiences: Features, Circumstances, and Incidence." In Holden, J. M. et al (eds.), *The Handbook of Near-Death Experiences: Thirty Years of Investigation*, Praeger-ABC-CLIO 2009

NOTES

Introduction

1. Hugo & Jobs: Belmonte, "Most Chilling Last Words"; Ebert: Jones, "Oral Histories of 2013"; Browning: *Poets.org*, "Famous Last Words"; Edison: Miller, *Thomas A. Edison*, 295; Earp: Silva, "Mysterious Morgan Earp"
2. Archbishop Richard Whately, *Rhetoric* chap. 1, quoted in Barrett, *Death-Bed Visions*, 5–6
3. Alan Murdie, "Poltergeists and High Strangeness" in *Deep Weird*, ed. Hunter
4. Ibid.
5. Randi, *Flim-Flam!*, 227
6. Carroll, "Ectoplasm"
7. Hyman, "Evaluation of Program." Also relevant is a statement by philosopher C.J. Ducasse: "Although the evidence offered by addicts of the marvelous for the reality of the phenomena they accept must be critically examined, it is equally necessary on the other side to scrutinize just as closely and critically the skeptic's allegations of fraud, or of mal-observation, or of misinterpretation of what was observed, or of hypnotically induced hallucinations. For there is likely to be just as much wishful thinking, prejudice, emotion, snap judgment, naïveté, and intellectual dishonesty on the side of orthodoxy, of skepticism, and of conservatism, as on the side of hunger for and belief in the marvelous. The emotional motivation for irresponsible disbelief is, in fact, probably even stronger—especially in scientifically educated persons, whose pride of knowledge is at stake—than is in other persons the motivation for irresponsible belief. In these matters, nothing is so rare as genuine objectivity and impartiality of judgment—judgment determined neither by the will to believe nor the will to disbelieve, but only by the will to get at the truth irrespective of whether it turns out to be comfortably familiar or uncomfortably novel, consoling or distressing, orthodox or unorthodox." Quoted in Kelly et al., *Irreducible Mind*, xxvii
8. Sidgwick, Eleanor, *Proceedings of the Society of Psychical Research* 1885, p 69, quoted in Barrett, *Death-Bed Visions*, 7–8
9. Douven, "Abduction"
10. Moreira-Almeida, *Science of Life*; Darwin quote attributed to Candolle, A de D. -13 M 2021, letter no. 3603 in the Darwin Correspondence Project
11. The author in question is identified as Larry Dossey in Ring & Lawrence, "Further Evidence," 225

12. Ring & Cooper, *Mindsight*, 4; no doubt Moody, author of the all-time NDE bestseller *Life After Life*, has been deluged with thousands of NDE accounts; while he has personally followed up on many, he cannot be expected to keep track of

them all.

13. McLuhan, *Randi's Prize*, 15. A.T. Baird makes a similar point in his book *One Hundred Cases for Survival*, 7–8: "The reader must not for one moment imagine that the case for survival rests solely on the hundred examples quoted in this book; a thousand equally good cases could be produced as easily; in fact, at times I was embarrassed with the wealth of material at my disposal and I may mention that my difficulty was in rejecting! Perhaps later, someone more energetic and enthusiastic, with more time and patience than I have, may publish *Five Thousand Cases for Survival*, and even then there will be plenty in reserve."

14. Samantha Lee Treasure, "Out-of-Body Experiences in the Screen Age," in *Deep Weird*, ed. Hunter; quoting Fenwick, 2005 p. 2 for the 10% estimate and citing van Lommel et al, 2001 for the 12-18% estimate

15. Other prominent figures who explored the paranormal included writers Victor Hugo, who engaged in regular séances, and André Breton, who corresponded with Richet and Flournoy; philosopher Henri Bergson; and physicists Pierre and Marie Curie. Of course, other leading intellectuals of that era showed no interest in parapsychology and sometimes rejected it out of hand. Pioneering physicist Michael Faraday tried to explain table tilting (in séances) in purely mechanistic terms, while another great physicist, Hermann von Helmholtz, famously dismissed telepathy with the words: "I cannot believe it. Neither the testimony of all the Fellows of the Royal Society, nor even the evidence of my own senses, would lead me to believe in the transmission of thought from one person to another independently of the recognized channels of sensation. It is clearly impossible." Quoted in Jan Ehrenwald, *Telepathy and Medical Psychology* 1947, 23–24.

16. Carlos Alvarado, in a tribute to parapsychologist William Roll, notes that Roll looked into cases dating back to the 19th century." In this he was following the long-established tradition in science for researchers to use references about past developments to establish continuity and discontinuity in arguments, and to seek support to present new ideas and hypotheses. But not all of Roll's contemporaries were as interested in the old literature as he was ... Roll's attention to the old literature while he was helping us craft the modern canon should be remembered with appreciation, particularly in these days of myopic citation practices." (Alvarado, "Roll")

17. http://www.definitions.net

PART ONE: *Separation*

1 Saltmarsh, *Evidence of Personal Survival*, 31

Chapter One: Separation from the Body

1. Brown, *Mediumistic Experiences*, 87–91

2. Weiss, *The Vestibule*, 128; quoting McMillan and Brown, *Canadian Medical Association Journal* May 1971, 104:889
3. Thomas, *From Life to Life*, 121–122
4. Crookall, *More Astral Projections*, cases 328, 327, & 324
5. Moody, *Life After Life*, 35–38
6. Ibid., 38
7. Snell, *Ministry of Angels*, 40–47
8. DeSalvo, *Andrew Jackson*, 63–64
9. Tymn, "Opera Composer"
10. Ring, *Life at Death*, 231–232, citing Charles Hampton, *The Transition Called Death*, Theosophical Publishing House 1972 (1943)
11. Crookall, *Out of the Body*, 155–156
12. Ibid., 153ff
13. Ecclesiastes 12:6–7 (King James Version): "Or ever the silver cord be loosed, or the golden bowl be broken, or the pitcher be broken at the fountain, or the wheel broken at the cistern. Then shall the dust return to the earth as it was: and the spirit shall return unto God who gave it."
14. Crookall, *Out of the Body*, 12
15. Fenwick & Fenwick, *Truth in the Light*, 37
16. Gurney et al., *Phantasms of the Living*, case 26, 149–151
17. Crookall, *What Happens*
18. Ring, *Life at Death*; the Wiltse case is presented in detail in my book *The Far Horizon*
19. Gurney et al., *Phantasms of the Living*, case 28, 152–154
20. Ibid., case 25, 146-149
21. Weiss, *Many Lives, Many Masters*, 140–141; ellipses in original
22. Gurney et al., *Phantasms of the Living*, case 29, 155–156
23. Fenwick & Fenwick, *The Art of Dying*, Continuum 2008, p. 63, quoted in Pearson et al., "Crisis Impressions"
24. Barrett, *Death-bed Visions*, 85–86
25. Ibid., 82–84
26. Taylor, *Stop Worrying*, 139–140, citing Samuel H. Paist, *A Narrative of the Experience of Horace Abraham Ackley, M.D., Late of Cleveland, Ohio, Since His Entrance Into Spirit-life Received Through the Mediumship of Samuel H. Paist, of Philadelphia* 1861
27. Chism, *Afterlife of Leslie Stringfellow*, 68–69
28. Fenwick & Fenwick, *Past Lives*
29. Ring, *Life at Death*, 229

Chapter Two: Separation in OBEs

1. Buhlman, *Adventures Beyond the Body*, 5
2. Ibid., 11–13
3. Ibid., 29
4. Buhlman, *Secret of the Soul*, 18

5. Samantha Treasure, "Out-of-Body," in Hunter, *Deep*
6. Ibid., citing Green 1968 p. 79
7. Bach, *The Bridge Across Forever*, quoted in Buhlman, *Secret of the Soul*
8. Fenwick, *Truth in the Light*, 171–172
9. Rogo, *Leaving the Body*, 3
10. Samantha Lee Treasure, "Out-of-Body Experiences in the Screen Age," in *Deep Weird*, ed. Hunter
11. Quoted in Crookall, *What Happens*, case 774
12. Monroe, *Journeys out of the Body*, 122–123
13. Tom McNear, "Analytical Overlay"
14. Rogo, *Leaving the Body*, 29–30
15. Crookall, *What Happens*, 54
16. In his writeup of the case, Tart conceded the remote possibility that Miss Z could have seen the hidden number reflected in the black plastic facing of a clock, though the light in the room was much too faint to make this scenario at all likely. Tart later explained, "I thought I was just making a standard statement of caution, because no one experiment is ever absolutely conclusive about anything, but overzealous pseudoskeptics have pounced on this statement as saying that I didn't think there were any parapsychological effects in this study." Tart, *End of Materialism*
17. Tart, *End of Materialism*, 199–206
18. Ibid., 205–6
19. Alvaredo, "Out of Body," citing K. Osis & D. McCormick, "Kinetic Effects at the Ostensible Location of an Out-of-Body Projection during Perceptual Testing," *Journal of the American Society for Psychical Research* 1980 no. 74, pp. 319–29.

Chapter Three: Patterns and Exceptions

1. Ring, *Omega Project*, 99–100
2. Fenwick & Fenwick, *Truth in the Light*, 26
3. *Awaken*, "Hemingway's Near Death Experience"
4. Fenwick & Fenwick, *Truth in the Light*, 26
5. Sabom, *Light and Death*, 122–123
6. Crookall, *Out of the Body*, 13–14

Chapter Four: Perception outside the Body

1. Thomas, *From Life to Life*, 79
2. Ring, *Lessons from the Light*, 35
3. Ibid., 57
4. Ibid., 62–63
5. Atwater, *We Live Forever*, 27, 30
6. Moorjani, *Dying to Be Me*
7. Crookall, *What Happens*

8. Ring, *Lessons from the Light*, 58
9. Ring, *Omega Project* 1992 pp 99–100
10. Ring, *Heading Toward Omega*, 42–43
11. Ring & Cooper, *Mindsight*
12. Weiss, *The Vestibule*, 82, quoting Helen Keller, *My Religion* (1927)
13. Moody, *The Light Beyond*, 172
14. Ibid., 170–171
15. Clark, K. (1984), "Clinical Interventions with Near-Death Experiencers," in *The Near-Death Experience: Problems, Prospects, Perspectives*, eds. B. Greyson & C. P. Flynn, 242–255; quoted in Ring & Lawrence, "Further Evidence," 225–226
16. Ring and Lawrence, "Further Evidence," 226–227
17. Ibid., 227
18. Ibid.
19. Laurin Bellg, *Near Death in the ICU*, quoted in Rivas et al, *The Self Does Not Die*
20. Sabom, *Light and Death*, 12
21. Greyson, *After*, 132–3
22. Weiss, *The Vestibule*, 111–112, quoting EL Huffine, "I Watched Myself Die" (1964)
23. Sabom, *Light and Death*, 41
24. Morse, *Closer to the Light*, 6

Chapter Five: Deathbed Visions

1. Dostoevsky, *Crime and Punishment* Part IV chap. 1, trans. C. Garnett
2. Haraldsson, "Survey of Claimed Encounters"
3. Stevenson, "Contribution of Apparitions", 345
4. Wedgwood, *The Thirty Years War*, 20–21
5. Barrett, *Death-Bed Visions*, 42–43
6. Ibid., 54–55
7. Ibid., 56–59, quoting Vale Owen & H. A. Dallas, *The Nurseries of Heaven*, 1920,, 117ff; Daisy's extended monologues seem overly elaborate to me, but enough witnesses are cited to indicate a core of truth to the account
8. Janssen, "Near the End"; thanks to Roger Knights
9. Hoffman, "New Vision"
10. Barrett, *Death-Bed Visions*, 67–69, quoting E.H. Pratt, *American SPR Journal* 1918, vol. 12 p 623; originally all one paragraph, which I've broken up for easier reading
11. Meredith, "Going into the Light"; thanks to Chris Carter
12. Hoffman, "New Vision"
13. Nahm & Greyson, "Terminal Lucidity in Patients"
14. Nahm, "Terminal Lucidity in People," citing du Prel, 1888/1971
15. The term "peak in Darien," referring to deathbed visons, was coined by Frances Power Cobbe in her book of the same name; it is taken from a line in John Keats's poem "On First Looking into Chapman's Homer"
16. Barrett, *Death-Bed Visions*, 10–14

17. Callanan & Kelley, *Final Gifts*, 92
18. Ibid., 93–94
19. Greyson, "Seeing Dead People"; thanks to Vitor Moura
20. Moody, *The Light Beyond*, 173
21. Barrett, *Death-Bed Visions*, 33–34
22. Ibid., 74, quoting *Proceedings of the Society for Psychical Research* vol. 6 p 293
23. Ibid., 76-80, quoting W.C. Crosby, *Proceedings of the Society for Psychical Research* vol. 8 pp 229–231
24. Everitt, *Augustus*, 314

Chapter Six: NDEs throughout History

1. Ring, *Life at Death*, 225–226
2. Erman, *Life in Ancient Egypt*, 306-308
3. Finkel, *First Ghosts*, 18, 1
4. Fenwick & Fenwick, *Truth in the Light*, 165–166, summarizing Sogyal Rinpoche's analysis in *The Tibetan Book of Living and Dying,* Rider 1992
5. Shushan, *The Next World*, 13
6. Ibid., 72–73
7. Ibid., 79 (Nga's account),, 133 (Buddhist monk's account)
8. Shushan, *The Next World*, 71, 77, 33
9. Neihardt, *Black Elk Speaks* chap. 3; questions have been raised about the reliability of Neihardt's account, but as far as I know, the claim that Black Elk had a powerful vision while deathly ill has not been challenged.
10. Playfair, *If This Be Magic*, 18

Chapter Seven: How Is It Possible?

1. Greyson et al., "Surge of Neurophysiological Activity"
2. LaMotte, "Near-Death Experiences Tied"; see also Sam Parnia et al., "AWAreness during REsuscitation—II: A Multi-Center Study of Consciousness and Awareness in Cardiac Arrest," *Resuscitation*, July 07, 2023; https://doi.org/10.1016/j.resuscitation.2023.109903
3. The birth canal hypothesis, proposed by Carl Sagan, was rebutted when NDEs were reported by patients born via cesarean section. There's also no evidence that newborns can form long-term memories. Moreover, a baby in the birth canal would not perceive an approaching light, as its face would be pressed against the passageway.
4. Cassol, "Near-Death Experience Memories"
5. Lopez, "Near-Death Experience in a Boy"; thanks to Markus Hesse
6. Woerlee, "Review of 'Evidence of the Afterlife'"
7. Texas State University Department of Philosophy; https://www.txst.edu/philosophy/resources/fallacy-definitions/Begging-the-Question
8. Woerlee, "Review of 'Evidence of the Afterlife,'"

9. Radin, *Supernormal*, 185
10. Ibid., 189–196
11. Broughton, "An Attempted Replication"; the experimenters note, however, that "all sessions combined ... resulted in a nonsignificant hit rate of 25.8%."
12. Quoted in Penman, "Could There Be"
13. Quoted in Dean Radin, "Skeptic agrees ..." See Radin's comment (in thread) dated Nov 7 2009
14. Schwartz, *Secret Vaults of Time*
15. Schwartz, "Finding Saddam Hussein"
16. Wetenhall, "Lucky Four-Time Lottery Winner"
17. Graveland, "Five-Time Lotto Winner"
18. CBS News, "3-Time Lottery Winner"
19. Huddleston, "These People Won the Lottery"

Chapter Eight: The Double

1. Cummins, *Beyond Human Personality*
2. Ibid. chap. 3
3. Ring, *Life at Death*, 231–232, citing Charles Hampton, *The Transition Called Death*, Theosophical Publishing House 1972 (1943)
4. 1 Corinthians 15:42–49 New International Version
5. Buhlman, *Adventures Beyond the Body*, 29
6. Crookall, *Out of the Body*, 33–34; also note Crookall's discussion in *What Happens When You Die*, 139ff: "The fact that some astral projectors reported a 'silver cord' which was attached to the solar plexus while others reported one that was attached to the head caused some to doubt their testimonies, but five different groups of people have observed both conditions in a single person ... Mrs. Gladys Osborn Leonard ... noted that many projectors saw their 'cord' attached at the head but added, 'I believe there is also a connection ... with the solar plexus' ... French sensitives who were in mesmeric trance told their mesmerizer, Dr. H. Durville, that they saw 'a wave-motion that comes from two centers,' i.e., the solar plexus and the head ... Major W.T. Pole observed both cords when a relative was dying ... The Soul Body [leaves] the physical chiefly via the head (whereas the vehicle of vitality [leaves] chiefly via the solar plexus)."

PART TWO: *The Dark Side*

1 Wickland, *Thirty Years Among the Dead*, 138

Chapter Nine: Death by Violence or Suicide

1. Sherwood, *The Country Beyond*, 61
2. Crookall, *The Supreme Adventure*, 21–22

3. Ibid., 22–23 citing Edward C. Randall, *Frontiers of the After Life*, Alfred A Knopf, 1922
4. Ibid., 23 citing Florence Barrett, *Personality Survives Death*, Longmans, Green & Co 1937
5. Ibid., 25 citing Mrs. L. Kelway Bamber, *Claude's Book*, Psychic Book Club 1918
6. Crookall, *The Supreme Adventure*, 31
7. Ibid., 31 citing Oliver Lodge, *Raymond*, Methuen & Co Ltd 1916
8. Heath & Klimo, *Suicide*, 112
9. Ibid., 112
10. Ibid., 113
11. Ibid., 133
12. Ibid., 145, citing Geraldine Cummins, *Swan on a Black Sea*, 31
13. Ibid., 141, citing Carl Wickland, *The Gateway of Understanding*, 30–31
14. Ibid., 109
15. Ibid., 178, citing Michael Newton, *Destiny of Souls*, 153
16. Ibid., 170 citing Michael Newton, *Destiny of Souls*, 162
17. Ibid., 176, citing Bill Guggenheim & Judy Guggenheim, *Hello from Heaven*, 236
18. Ibid. chap. 8
19. Ibid., 151. Citing Moody, *Life after Life*, 143
20. Ibid., 166, citing an interview with the authors
21. Ibid., 124
22. Ibid., 124
23. Ibid., 127
24. Ibid., 182 citing Whitton and Fisher, *Life Between Life*, 46–47
25. Ibid., 130
26. Ibid., 162
27. Ibid., 170

Chapter Ten: Negative Experiences

1. Fitzgerald, "As I Lay"
2. Crookall, *The Supreme Adventure*, 70–71
3. Sherwood, *The Country Beyond*, 58–59
4. Rommer, *Blessing in Disguise*, 73
5. Ibid., 80–81
6. Sherwood, *The Country Beyond*, 58–59
7. Samantha Lee Treasure, "Out-of-Body Experiences in the Screen Age," in *Deep Weird*, ed. Hunter
8. Chism, *Afterlife of Leslie Stringfellow*, 105–106
9. Strassman, *DMT*, 189
10. Ibid., 206–207
11. Though I'm not persuaded by the "alternate history" theories Hancock presents in his other writings, *Supernatural* strikes me as more credible.
12. Sabom, "Response to Gracia Fay Ellwood"

13. Fisher, *Siren Call of Hungry Ghosts*
14. John Hopkins Medicine, "Hopkins Scientists Show Hallucinogen"
15. James, *Varieties of Religious Experience*

Chapter Eleven: Lost Souls

1. Finkel, *First Ghosts*, 31
2. Contenau, *Everyday Life in Babylon*, 254–255
3. Finkel, *First Ghosts*, 77
4. Ibid., 36
5. Contenau, *Everyday Life in Babylon*, 255–256
6. Finkel, *First Ghosts*, 56
7. Ibid., 72
8. Haraldsson & Stevenson, "Communicator of the 'Drop In' Type"
9. Crookall, *What Happens* case 777, quoting Dr. Karl Novotny, *Mediale Schriften* ("Communications through a Medium"), Therese Krauss Publishing House, 1968
10. Alan Murdie, "Poltergeists and High Strangeness" in *Deep Weird*, ed. Hunter
11. McLuhan, *Randi's Prize*, 36–37
12. Ibid., 32
13. McLuhan, "Miami Poltergeist"
14. McLuhan, *Randi's Prize*, 53, 16
15. Ibid., 27
16. Alan Murdie, "Poltergeists and High Strangeness" in *Deep Weird*, ed. Hunter
17. Ibid.
18. Rubenstein, *Consulting Spirit*

Chapter Twelve: Possession

1. Finkel Ghosts, *First*, 58
2. Ibid., 125
3. Ibid., 60
4. Ibid., 111–112
5. Tymn, "Lurancy Vennum"
6. Wickland, *Thirty Years Among the Dead*
7. Ibid.
8. Heath & Klimo, *Suicide*, 141, citing Wickland, *The Gateway of Understanding*, 30–31
9. Wickland, *Thirty Years Among the Dead*
10. Heath & Klimo, *Suicide*, 142 citing Wickland, *The Gateway of Understanding* 1934
11. Wickland, *Thirty Years Among the Dead*
12. Ibid.
13. Sanderson "Spirit Releasement"
14. Sanderson, "Spirit Release"

15. Fiore, *The Unquiet Dead*; in this excerpt the narrative has been converted to the style of a transcript for easier reading.
16. Ibid., 138–40, 116
17. Ibid., 3
18. Crookall, *What Happens*, 149

PART THREE: *Transition*

1 Whitton & Fisher, *Life Between Life*, 115–116; Irving was regressed to a lifetime in Spain, which ended when she threw herself from a window; excerpt at https://allabouteaven.org/observations/whitton-dr-joel-case-history-linda-irving-extract-from-full-case-history-026317/221

Chapter Thirteen: Beginning the Transition

1. Similarly, one advantage of reading books like this one, even if you don't entirely believe them, is that you may find yourself better equipped to understand what's happened after you pass over.
2. Ring, *Heading Toward Omega*, 38–40
3. Sabom, *Light and Death*, 63–64
4. Ibid., 63–64
5. Ibid., 65ff
6. Ring, *Heading Toward Omega*, 54–55
7. Fenwick & Fenwick, *Truth in the Light*, 3–4
8. Ibid., 47–48
9. Ibid., 50
10. Ibid., 52–53
11. Ibid., 55
12. Ibid., 264–265
13. Ibid., 56
14. Ibid., 59
15. Ibid., 59–60
16. Ring & Cooper, "Near-Death and Out-of-Body", 113
17. Moody, *The Light Beyond*, 69, quoting Morse, "A Near-Death Experience in a Seven-Year-Old Child," *The American Journal of the Disabled Child* vol. 137 pp 939–961
18. Ibid., 61–62
19. Ibid., 62–65
20. Ring, *Lessons from the Light*, 112
21. Crookall, *The Supreme Adventure*
22. Ibid., quoting Plutarch, "On the Delay of Divine Justice"
23. Leland, *The Unanswered Question*, 36ff
24. Crookall, *The Supreme Adventure*; to protect the family's privacy, communicator George Pellew was known as "George Pelham" in published accounts.

25. Ring, *Lessons from the Light*
26. Fenwick & Fenwick, *Truth in the Light*, 251–252
27. Ibid., 254–255

Chapter Fourteen: Encounter

1. Shushan, *The Next World*, 40
2. Fenwick & Fenwick, *Truth in the Light*, 72–73
3. Ring, *Heading Toward Omega*, 61–62
4. Hodgson "Further Record"
5. Weiss, *Many Lives, Many Masters*, 46–47
6. Fenwick & Fenwick, *Truth in the Light*, 264–265
7. Kardec, *Heaven and Hell*, 227–228
8. Ibid., 259–260
9. Dostoevsky et al., *Petersburg Visions in Verse and Prose* (1861), quoted by Richard Pevear in his Introduction to *Crime and Punishment*. A character in Dostoevsky's *Demons* (trans. R. Pevear & L. Volokhonsky) recounts similar experiences: "There are seconds, they come only five or six at a time, and you suddenly feel the presence of eternal harmony, fully achieved … The feeling is clear and indisputable. As if you suddenly sense the whole of nature and suddenly say: yes, this is true … You don't forgive anything, because there's no longer anything to forgive. You don't really love—oh, what is here is higher than love! What's most frightening is that it's so terribly clear, and there's such joy. If it were longer than five seconds—the soul couldn't endure it and would vanish. In those five seconds I live my life through, and for them I would give my whole life, because it's worth it."
10. Bucke, *Cosmic Consciousness*
11. Roberts, *The Seth Material*
12. Alexander & Tompkins, *Map of Heaven*
13. Ibid.
14. Ibid.
15. Jansen, "Ketamine and Quantum Psychiatry," 19–21
16. Michael Grosso, "Superhumanity" in *Deep Weird*, ed. Hunter
17. Jones, "Oral Histories of 2013"
18. Fenwick & Fenwick, *Truth in the Light*, 74
19. Potter, "Proof of Heaven"; my book *The Far Horizon* considers the notion of an information-based reality in some detail; see also Whitworth, "Quantum Realism"
20. James W, "James W NDE"
21. Cicoria, "Getting Comfortable"; thanks to Carol Lorraine
22. Sacks, *Musicophilia*
23. Peter N, "Peter N NDE"
24. Moorjani, *Dying to Be Me*
25 Wade, *Changes of Mind*, chap. 11; Wade says that the level of development seen in most NDEs is dramatically lower than Unity consciousness: "Consciousness after

death is somewhat anticlimactic after the exalted ordinariness of enlightenment. It does not represent a more complex stage, but one akin to the Transcendent level ... The near-death survivor records do not appear to include people who were operating at the Transcendent or Unity levels during life (an extremely rare group in any population); in fact, those records seem to describe mainstream populations, whose demographics are largely Conformists and Achievers (in US studies)." (p. 223) She goes on to note, however, that immersion in the light—not reported in all or even most NDEs—elevates consciousness to a higher level: "A complete merger with the Light is reported by some people ... From the accounts, it is impossible to tell whether the merger is a dualistic at-oneness (like Transcendent consciousness) or a direct apprehension of reality (Unity consciousness)." (p. 229)

26. Fenwick & Fenwick, *Truth in the Light*, 74
27. Farr, *What Tom Sawyer Learned*, 165
28. Fenwick & Fenwick, *Truth in the Light*, 167
29. Khanna & Greyson, "Near-Death Experiences and Posttraumatic Growth"
30. Ibid.
31. Greyson, *After*, 186–187
32. Ibid., 187
33. Ibid., 188
34. Ibid., 191–192
35. Ibid., 194–195
36. Ibid., 195–196
37. Ibid., 199–200
38. Piippo, "A.J. Ayer Was Nicer." The complete quote from Wells is: "He became so much nicer after he died. He was not nearly so boastful. He took an interest in other people."

Chapter Fifteen: A Presence in the Light

1. Fenwick & Fenwick, *Truth in the Light* 59-60
2. Peter N, "Peter N NDE"
3. Sabom, *Light and Death*, 116
4. Ring, *Heading Toward Omega*, 56–59
5. Sabom, *Recollections of Death*, 48
6. Ring, *Life at Death*
7. Benedict, "The Light Kept Changing"; as noted in the Introduction, I find Benedict's account suspiciously elaborate and don't give it total credence.
8. Shushan, *The Next World*, 22
9. Sabom, *Light and Death*, 222–223
10. Ibid., 134–141
11. Myers, *Human Personality* passim
12. Prescott, "The Diamond"

13. Buhlman, *Secret of the Soul*

Chapter Sixteen: Beings of Light

1. Ring, *Heading Toward Omega*, 64–66
2. Sabom, *Light and Death*, 91–92
3. Ibid., 68
4. Bonenfant, "Visitation of an 'Angel-Like' Being"; thanks to Markus Hesse
5. Weiss, *Many Lives, Many Masters*, 82–83
6. Fenwick & Fenwick, *Truth in the Light*, 81–82; the Year of the Horse is the seventh year in the 12-year cycle of the Chinese zodiac. "Year of the Seventh Horse" doesn't make sense; presumably something was lost in translation.
7. Ibid., 83
8. Weiss, *Many Lives, Many Masters*, 70–71
9. Sabom, *Recollections of Death*, 48
10. Carter, *Science and the Near-Death Experience*, 118
11. Carter, Ibid., 119–120
12. Sabom, *Recollections of Death*, 53–54

Chapter Seventeen: The Life Review

1. Zaleski, *World to Come*
2. Crookall, *More Astral Projections*, 86, citing J.W. Haddock, *Somnolence and Psycheism*, 1851
3. Zaleski, *World to Come*, citing William Munk, *Euthanasia or Medical Treatment in the Aid of Easy Dying* (1887)
4. Taylor, *Stop Worrying*, 96
5. Ring *Lessons from the Light*, 145; originally in Ring, *Life at Death*, 117
6. Heim, "Dying from Falls"
7. Ibid.
8. Project, "I Noted the Situation"
9. Ring *Lessons from the Light*, 146, originally in Ring, *Life at Death*, 116
10. Ibid., 148–149
11. Tolstoy, *Hadji Murad*, 284
12. Ring *Lessons from the Light*, 154–155
13. Ibid., 155
14. Farr, *What Tom Sawyer Learned*, 32–33
15. Ring *Lessons from the Light*, 159, citing Moody, *Reflections on Life after Life,*, 35
16. Ring *Lessons from the Light*, 159, citing Moody, *The Light Beyond,*, 37–38
17. Ibid., 158–159; source is the Seattle IANDS newsletter
18. Ibid., 172
19. Taylor, *Stop Worrying*, 94–95, citing Sam Parnia, *Erasing Death*

20. Finkel, *First Ghosts*, 33
21. Ibid.
22. Cummins, *Road to Immortality*
23. Sherwood, *The Country Beyond*, 135–136
24. Roberts, *Seth Speaks* chap. 6
25. Ring *Lessons from the Light*, 167
26. Fenwick & Fenwick, *Truth in the Light*, 114–115
27. Sherwood, *The Country Beyond*, 61
28. The discarded energy body may linger for a while as a mindless automaton, responsible for reports of hauntings in which the ghost performs the same pointless, repetitive actions over and over.

Chapter Eighteen: Mediumship

1. For a famous example, see "Chaffin Will Case," *Occult World* (blog); https://occult-world.com/chaffin-will-case/ ; or "Where There's a Will, There's a Ghost," *Strange Company* (blog), August 15, 2016; http://strangeco.blogspot.com/2016/08/where-theres-will-theres-ghost-or-guide.html
2. Holt, *Cosmic Relations and Immortality*
3. Prescott, *The Far Horizon*, 19–24
4. Barrett, *Personality Survives Death*, 138–139
5. Ibid., 154–155
6. Ibid., 37–38. When the transcript is quoted, here and elsewhere, the names William and Florence are substituted for "W.F.B." and "F.E.B."
7. Ibid., 70–71
8. Ibid., 41–45
9. Ibid., 79–80
10. Ibid., 154
11. Ibid., 99–100
12. Keene & Spraggett, *The Psychic Mafia*, 39–41; this book is recommended for a wealth of details about fake mediumship of both the physical and mental varieties.
13. Prescott, "Under the Table"; a Google Image search for "Daniel Dunglas Home" will bring up photos showing his less-than-formidable 'stache.
14. Prescott, "Palladino"; see also "Arthur Conan Doyle, Sherlock Holmes & the Medium of Naples," *Naples Life, Death & Miracles* (blog), July 2009; http://www.naplesldm.com/Doyle.php
15. Barrett, *Personality Survives Death*, 99
16. Ibid., 128
17. Ibid., 121
18. Ibid., 133
19. Barrett, *Personality Survives Death*, 171
20. Ibid., 48–49

21. Alice Johnson, "On the Automatic Writing," 230
22. Barrett, *Personality Survives Death*, 93
23. Ibid., 85–86
24. With regard to spirits who communicate through a Ouija board or similar apparatus, Robert Crookall took the view that most of them are earthbound and have not yet shed the intermediate body, thus allowing them to influence physical objects as poltergeists do. Since the enveloping "vehicle of vitality" (as he calls it) engenders confusion, many of these communications are unclear, even nonsensical, and can take the form of unconvincing role-playing—hence the many would-be Shakespeares whose doggerel would embarrass the real Bard.
25. Moody, *Life after Life*, 26, quoted in James Beichler, *To Die For*, chap. 11 (2017 rev. ed.)
26. Edwin A. Abbott, *Flatland*

PART FOUR: *Arrival*

1 Heath & Klimo, *Suicide*, 114, quoting J.-B. Delacour, *Glimpses of the Beyond* 1974

Chapter Nineteen: Otherwhere

1. Alexander & Tompkins, *Map of Heaven*
2. Riggs, *Ancient Egyptian Magic*
3. Mark, "Egyptian Afterlife"
4. Bunson, *Encyclopedia of Ancient Egypt*, Gramercy 1991. Gibson, *The Hidden Life of Ancient Egypt*, Saraband 2009; both quoted in Mark, "Egyptian Afterlife"
5. Mark, "Egyptian Afterlife"
6. Swedenborg, *Heaven and Hell*, 10
7. Swedenborg Foundation, "Swedenborg's Life"
8. Swedenborg, *Heaven and Hell*, 261
9. Ibid., 322, quoting his pamphlet "Other Planets"
10. Ibid., 256–344, 345
11. Ibid., 180–182
12. Ibid., 180
13. Ibid., 176–177
14. Ibid., 185
15. Ibid., 180
16. Ibid., 175
17. Ibid., 172
18. Ibid., 329
19. Ibid., 351–353
20. Ibid., 416
21. Ibid., 153–154
22. Lodge, *Raymond*, 197–198
23. Stead, *Life Eternal*, 170-171

24. Shushan, *The Next World*, 166; the consciousness-based nature of the afterlife explains why it's pointless to ask for its physical location, which is like asking for the physical location of a dreamscape. Although mediums talk about the "higher vibrations" of certain planes, in my view they're referring to a spectrum of frequencies of consciousness, rather than of matter. *The Betty Book*, by Stewart Edward White (1937), makes this point explicitly.
25. Shushan, *The Next World*, 170-171
26. Thomas, *From Life to Life*, 63

Chapter Twenty: Life on the Other Side

1. Robbins, *Both Sides of the Veil*, 116
2. Ibid., 1183. Thomas, *From Life to Life*, 90; the quote is from Shelley's poem "Adonais": "Peace, peace! he is not dead, he doth not sleep!/ He hath awakened from the dream of life."
4. Robbins, *Both Sides of the Veil*, 137–140
5. Ibid., 142–144
6. Ibid., 140
7. Thomas, *From Life to Life*, 23
8. Fenwick & Fenwick, *Truth in the Light*, 25–26
9. Ibid., 30–31
10. Ibid., 206
11. Ibid., 75–76
12. Ring & Cooper, *Mindsight*, 22–26
13. Ibid., 22–23
14. Ring, *Lessons from the Light*, 75–78
15. Ring & Cooper, *Mindsight*, 28–33
16. Fenwick & Fenwick, *Truth in the Light*, 76–77, 166
17. Greyson, *After*, 132–133
18. Crookall, *More Astral Projections*
19. Fenwick & Fenwick, *Truth in the Light*, 78
20. Ibid., 251–252
21. Ibid., 252–253
22. Botkin & Hogan, *Induced After Death Communication*, 104
23. Moody, *Reunions*, 99–100
24. Fenwick & Fenwick, *Truth in the Light*, 80, 101
25. Ibid., 108–109
26. Ring *Heading Toward Omega*, 91
27. Ibid.
28. Ibid., 21
29. Emmons, *Guided by Spirit*, 219, citing Allen Putnam, *Biography of Mrs. J. H. Conant, the World's Medium of the Nineteenth Century*, 1873
30. Fenwick & Fenwick, *Truth in the Light*, 118–119

31. Wells, *Door in the Wall*
32. Doyle, *History of Spiritualism*, vol. 2, chap. 25

Chapter Twenty-One: Higher Planes

1. Alvarado, "Skepticism about Reincarnation"
2. Cummins, *Road to Immortality*, 67
3. Cummins, *Beyond Human Personality* chap. 10
4. Taylor, "The Dude's Mind Abides," quoting from *Mind That Abides: Panpsychism in the New Millennium*, ed. David Skrbina, chap. 5
5. Cummins, *Road to Immortality*, 72
6. Stead, *Life Eternal*, 4–5
7. The term "intermission" was coined by Ian Stevenson in 1974.
8. Newton, *Journey of Souls*, 73–78
9. Ibid., 79–83
10. Matlock, "Reincarnation Intermission Memories"
11. Interestingly, this color scheme corresponds to the ancient system of chakras, which associates the red end of the spectrum with the lower (and baser) parts of the body and the blue-to-white end with the higher faculties. Cornillier gives no indication of any knowledge of chakras.
12. Cornillier, *Survival of the Soul*, 461
13. Cummins, *Road to Immortality*, 57–58, 63–64
14. Quoted in Betty, *The Afterlife Unveiled*, 43–44
15. Greaves, *Testimony of Light*, 34
16. Ibid., 141
17. I talk much more about this in my book *The Far Horizon*, where I suggest some ways of looking at it, but this material would take us well beyond the scope of the present book.

Chapter Twenty-Two: Reincarnation

1. Cornillier, *Survival of the Soul*, 461
2. See "Bridey Murphy (reincarnation case)," by K.M. Wehrstein, *Psi Encyclopedia*, especially the section titled "Controversy"; https://psi-encyclopedia.spr.ac.uk/articles/bridey-murphy-reincarnation-case.
3. Bowman, *Children's Past Lives*, 8–10
4. Ibid., 21–24
5. Whitton & Fisher, *Life Between Life*, 154
6. Ibid., 154–156
7. Bobrow, *Witch in the Waiting Room*, 159
8. Ibid., 161
9. Ibid., 161–162
10. It's rare, though not unheard of, for a child to remember living to old age and dying peacefully. On the occasions when this does happen, the previous

personality is often a family member who reincarnated in order to remain close to his or her loved ones.

11. Stevenson, *Twenty Cases*, 67–68
12. Ibid., 81
13. Ibid., 71, 80
14. Ibid., 82, 85
15. Ibid., 101–102
16. Ibid., 102
17. See Stevenson, "Birthmarks and Birth Defects"
18. Kardec, *The Spirits Book*, 120–121
19. Carrington, *The Story of Psychic Science*, quoted in Cox, "Science of Mediumship", 91
20. Alvarado, "Skepticism about Reincarnation"
21. The Coleman quote is from Alvarado, "Skepticism about Reincarnation"; the Howitt quote is from Doyle, *History of Spiritualism*, chap. 21
22. Doyle, *History of Spiritualism* chap. 21
23. Wambach, *Reliving Past Lives*, 116–118
24. Ibid., 118–125
25. See Chapter 20
26. Roberts, *The Seth Material*, 147–148
27. Ibid., 149
28. Ibid., 136
29. Cummins, *Road to Immortality*, 62–63

Postscript

1. Tolstoy, *Death of Ivan Ilych*, chaps. 9 & 12

Printed in Great Britain
by Amazon